£4

St Michael

THE
IMPRESSIONISTS

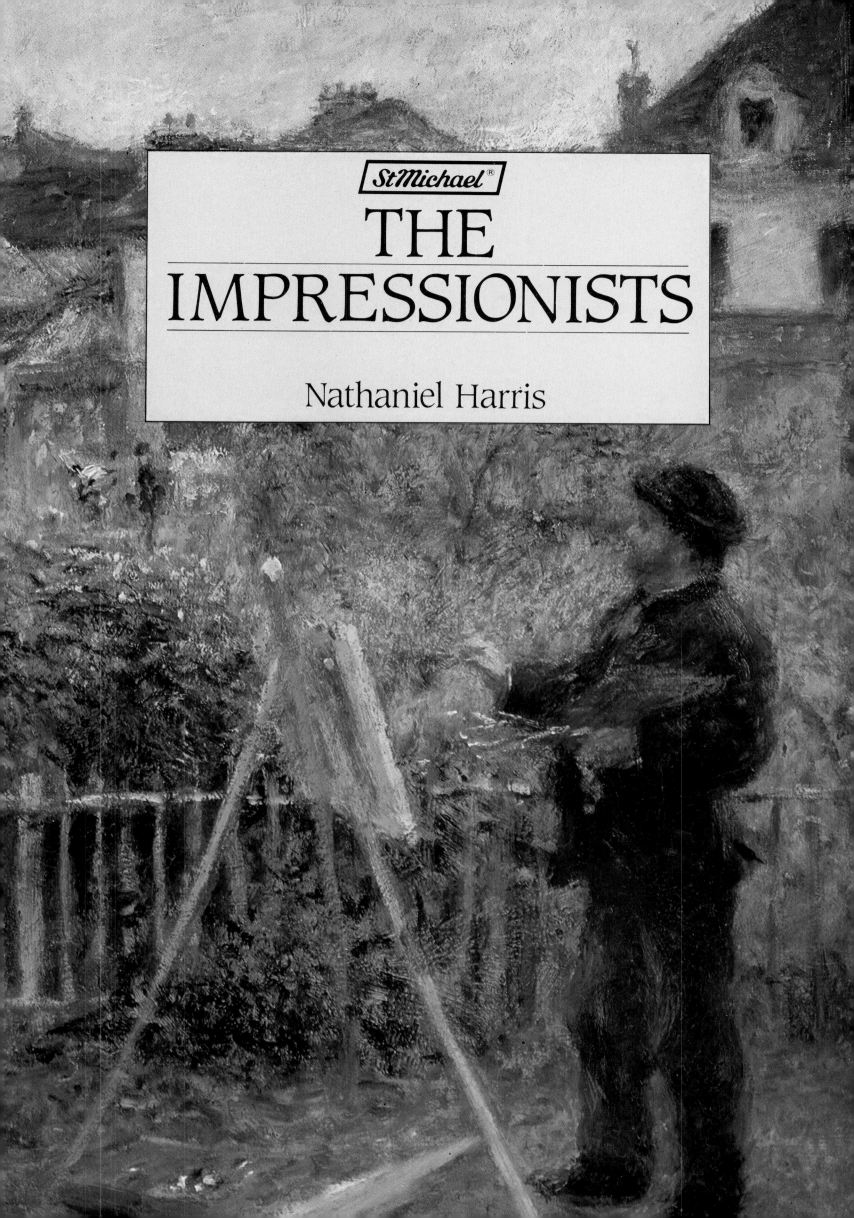

THE IMPRESSIONISTS

Nathaniel Harris

First published in 1984 exclusively for
Marks and Spencer p.l.c., Baker Street, London
by Newnes Books
a division of The Hamlyn Publishing Group Limited
84-88 The Centre, Feltham, Middlesex, TW13 4BH
Copyright © Newnes Books 1984
ISBN: 0 600 35847 X

Originally published as *A Treasury of Impressionism*
Copyright © The Hamlyn Publishing Group Limited 1979.

Contents

The Social and Artistic Background 6

Forerunners and Influences 17

The Older Masters 24

Manet 24
Degas 42

Early Lives 53

Pissarro 53
Monet 57
Renoir 70
Bazille 79
Sisley 85
Morisot 88
Cézanne 91

The Impressionist Years 97

The Impressionists Before 1869 97
Summer 1869: Breakthrough 100
The Franco-Prussian War and the Commune 106
The First Impressionist Show 114
The Years of Struggle 129
The Break-up 138

Later Lives 142

Manet 142
Degas 149
Pissarro 160
Monet 170
Renoir 178
Sisley 196
Morisot 202
Some Minor Impressionists 205

Beyond Impressionism 210

Cézanne 210
Gauguin 222
Van Gogh 233
Impressionism After 1886 246

Conclusion 253

Index 254

The Social and Artistic Background

The extent to which people enjoy Impressionist paintings can be gathered from museum sales of cards, slides and posters: unless the museum has a Leonardo, its biggest sellers will almost certainly be works by the Impressionists or members of their circle. This represents the opinion not of the experts but of the man in the street – or at least the man in the gallery. Yet at the first Impressionist exhibition, little more than a hundred years ago, the spectators came for a good laugh, convinced that the whole display was a grotesque bohemian joke; and the critics backed them up.

What makes this all the more peculiar is that Impressionist paintings seem, more than any others, designed for immediate popularity: for the most part they are colourful, cheerful in mood, easy to understand, and utterly uncontroversial in intention – without, for example, any political, social or moral undertones that might offend spectators with strong views of their own.

The reaction against the Impressionists – and, for that matter, the nature of their achievement – becomes clearer when looked at against the larger background of French art and life. The rest of this introduction is therefore given over to a description of that background. The personalities and movements of 19th-century French painting are also sketched in, providing a framework for the more detailed information given in later chapters.

Late 19th-century France is the setting for most of the people and events described in this book. In political terms this means it was the France of the Second Empire under Napoleon III (1852-70), and of the Third Republic (1870-1940). France was a society deeply divided between Royalists, Republicans and Bonapartists – divisions that went back to the Revolution of 1789, which had overthrown the old Bourbon monarchy and was followed by the (First) Empire established by the military dictator Napoleon Bonaparte. The first half of the 19th century witnessed the restoration of the Bourbon monarchy, its replacement by the more liberal Orléans line in the person of Louis Philippe, and the short-lived Second Republic. Napoleon's nephew, Prince Louis Napoleon, then took control of the Republic and transformed it into the Second Empire, with himself, re-named Napoleon III, as Emperor. On the whole, Napoleon III was successful in papering over the cracks in French society by a mixture of autocracy, concessions to public opinion, and limited wars waged in the Crimea and Italy. But when Napoleon led France to disaster in the war of 1870–1 against Prussia, the Empire disappeared almost overnight. The Third Republic, born of defeat, seemed likely to break down under Monarchist pressure in the early years; but it survived, if only for the negative reason proposed by the politician Louis Thiers – that the Republic was the form of government that divided Frenchmen least. In the long run the Republic even emerged the stronger for the Dreyfus case; this scandal, which dominated the 1890s, united the army, the Church, Monarchists and antisemites – forces generally hostile to the Republic – in an effort to defend the wrongful conviction of a Jewish officer on a charge of spying for Germany; in time the anti-Republicans and anti-Dreyfusards were discredited by the accumulating evidence of prejudice and perjury.

Away from the political dramatics, France was going through an economic and social transformation: her version of the Industrial Revolution, with its accompanying factories and workshops, booms and slumps, railways and steamships. The middle class, or *bourgeoisie*, grew rich and powerful from the proceeds of expanding industry and trade. A new industrial working class began to resent the appalling conditions in which it lived and laboured. The spectres of socialism and communism began to haunt France; and indeed the radical workers of Paris took the opportunity provided by the defeat of 1870 to organise a revolutionary government, the Commune, that was bloodily suppressed by the regular army. Bourgeois distaste for *exposés* of economic realities, and a deep fear of revolution in any form, were two shaping factors in contemporary attitudes to art. Another factor, as we shall see, was prudery. The later

Self-crowned victors in the Franco-Prussian War: Prussian soldiers in the Tuileries Gardens. One of the terms of the armistice granted to the French by the Prussians was that the Prussian army should be allowed to march in a victory parade through Paris – an event that helped to disillusion Parisians with their new Republican government. On 28 March 1871 a popular-revolutionary government, the Commune, was set up in Paris in opposition to the national government which established itself at Versailles. There were shorter-lived Communes at Marseilles and Lyons.

Right:
Thomas Couture. *Romans of the Decadence*. 1847. One of the most-praised paintings of the 19th century, by an artist who believed himself greater than Ingres. The pseudo-accuracy of academic history painting could hardly find a better illustration than this combination of feverish eroticism and sentimentality (notice the disapproving statues). Musée du Louvre, Paris.

6

Pierre-August Renoir, *Couple Lisant*, oil on canvas, signed and dated 1877, 32·4 by 24·8 cm., £400,000–500,000.

From the Collection of Henry Ford II.

Maurice de Vlaminck, *La Perissoire à Chatou*, oil on canvas, signed, *c*. 1906, 49 by 65 cm., £225,000–275,000.

From the Collection of Henry Ford II.

Léon Gambetta proclaiming the Republic in 1870. A series of French disasters in the war against Prussia brought down the Second Empire. It was succeeded by the Third Republic which, though rocked by scandals and politically fragmented, survived until 1940. Gambetta, a fiery Republican, had been one of Napoleon III's most unrelenting opponents.

Left:
Prince Louis Bonaparte, later Napoleon III.

Honoré Daumier. *The Last Meeting of the Ex-Ministers*. Daumier (1808-79) was both a left-wing cartoonist and a major artist in a distinctive, powerfully expressive vein. In this cartoon, the Liberty-figure of the Commune puts to flight the 'bourgeois' government of Louis Adolphe Thiers.

19th century was the Victorian age in Britain, and bourgeois attitudes in France were not essentially different despite the French reputation for 'gallantry'. Open secrets were a little more open, crimes of passion were a little more common, and literary censorship was a little less heavy-handed; but ordinary bourgeois life was, on the surface, as intolerantly chaste, monogamous and censorious as any Victorian might wish; and, beneath the surface, just as adept at manipulating hypocritical double standards.

This was the atmosphere in which the official and semi-official artistic establishments functioned, whether in France, Germany, Austria, Britain, or the United States. But in France, art was institutionalised to a far greater extent than in other countries, and all who hoped for success were compelled to pursue their careers with a kind of bureaucratic tenacity. Cultural life was governed by an organisation called the Institut de France, in which the Academy of Fine Arts was the subordinate body responsible for painting and sculpture. The Academy was a self-perpetuating élite of artists who elected their own new members and kept a tight hold on the two key institutions that determined the fate of aspiring painters: the École des Beaux-Arts and the Salon. As well as inculcating a strict orthodoxy in its teaching, the Beaux-Arts awarded markings, distinctions and prizes that constituted the earliest honours to which ambitious painters aspired. Later, these artists would hope to have their works shown at the Salon, a great exhibition held once every two years until 1863, and annually after that. Regular showings at the Salon were necessary if a painter was to become well-known enough to make a good living by selling his works; and the jury of the Salon, which selected the pictures to be hung, consisted of – Academicians. In this closed system there was no room for dissent, except on the part of painters who had become established – by which time they had a vested interest in maintaining the 'academic' style which had become second nature and had been the medium of their eminence. In retrospect, the surprising fact is that there were so many dissenting groups, among them the Impressionists, prepared to suffer for years outside the system.

The academic art of the 19th century saw itself as celebrating the 'noble' and the 'ideal' in 'classical' style. What this meant in practice emerges in a revealing anecdote put on record by Claude Monet, one of the leading figures of Impressionism. As a young man, Monet came to study at the studio of Marc Gabriel Gleyre, one of the Beaux-Arts teachers. During the first week he applied himself conscientiously to painting the nude male model. On the following Monday, when making his rounds,

Gleyre sat down in front of Monet's effort and said 'That's not bad at all! But it's too much like the model. The man you can see is short and broad, so you paint him as short and broad; he has big feet, so you show them as they are. That sort of thing's terribly ugly. Remember that when you draw a figure you should always bear in mind the example of Antiquity [ancient Greece and Rome]. Nature is all very well as an element of study, but it offers no interest. Style, you see, is everything'. And the same teacher told Auguste Renoir that the painter should render the big toe of the hero Germanicus more majestically than the big toe of a coalman.

Such instruction was not of much value to young men who wanted to confront the realities of their time, or to capture the sensations received from living nature. Academic dictatorship and academic dogma – like all dictatorships and dogmas – stifled creativity. But despite the hilarities associated with Germanicus' big toe, academic art had a certain validity for those who practised it from choice: Gleyre's attitude was less ridiculous than it sounds, however wrong it may have been for him to impose it on another artist. The 19th-century academic tradition still finds few critics prepared to defend it, and it can hardly be denied that its creative harvest was scanty. But it is worth remarking that, as theories go, it was no stupider than most others. The classical sculpture of Greece is precisely an idealised account of humanity, which clothes divinities in the human form and equates the human form with divinity. And there is nothing inherently more absurd in transforming the real for the sake of the ideal, than in transforming it for the sake of expressing the artist's emotions or sensations, as artists such as Gauguin and Van Gogh were to do. The faults of academicism lay not in the taste for 'nobility' and 'ideals' as such, but in the way it had hardened into a set of formulas that ensured artistic, social and political acceptability. This approach to art guaranteed success and respectability for a host of technically accomplished conformists who were able to group themselves into a self-perpetuating establishment; and they, even more than most establishments, persecuted all those who took other paths with the spiteful outrage of threatened mediocrity.

They were able to do so because they exercised an unusually great influence over public opinion. In previous centuries, artistic patronage had mainly been wielded by the cultivated sections of the aristocracy – men certain of their own taste and standards, which they unhesitatingly imposed upon society as a whole. By the middle of the 19th century, economic power had largely passed to the industrial and commercial classes, who now became the main 'public' for art. Lacking a traditional culture – and, it should be said, living in a difficult period of change and confusion – they were uncertain in their judgements and inclined to trust 'experts' who pandered to their prejudices and emotional preferences. In art as in literature, they enjoyed anodyne fantasies, moral stories, 'jolly' humour, pathos and sentiment; and they shied away from sexuality and anything connected with the less glamorous realities of life.

These factors in combination gave rise to the characteristic subject matter and style of academic art. The most common of all subjects was 'classical' – that is, derived from the history or myths of ancient Greece and Rome. Hallowed by the prestige of antiquity, the 'classical' picture or statue was by definition serious and respectable, provided it was rendered in a vapidly graceful-sentimental vein. It was the only context in which the nude was acceptable – which made it all the more popular with artists, for whom the unclothed body had been a challenge and preoccupation for centuries. This nakedness also provided an outlet for stifled eroticism; indeed Victorian art, with revealingly titled popular successes such as *The Birth of Venus* and *The Greek Slave*, is a-tremble with erotic feeling, though hardly anyone at the time admitted or appeared to notice the fact. It actually was concealed, in the sense that very strict rules were observed: nude women, for example, did without body hair, had nothing much in the way of nipples (let alone aureoles), and tended to display pale or rosy skin tones that concealed surface detail. Yet the outlines of female figures are unmistakably voluptuous, and beneath the sentimentality their attitudes frequently convey a dissolving, even masochistic surrender. These points are worth making because one of the sins of the anti-academic painters was, as we shall see, to violate the sexual conventions despite being less sexually saturated than the show-pieces in the Salon.

Other favoured subjects of academic art included roses, pets, elegant ladies, and children, in various permutations and even in classically draped semi-undress; story pictures of all kinds, but especially those drawn from history (*When Did You Last See Your Father?*); the picturesque rural poor, cheerful inns, the thrills of the chase and the cavalry charge, and so on. The academic style, with its high finish and firm outlines, was derived from a theory that made drawing the basis of all artistic practice and might be summed up as Sentimental Realism.

The leader of the academic school of painters from the 1820s to his death was Jean Auguste Dominique Ingres (1780-1867). Being a genius as well as an ideologue, Ingres escaped many of the limitations of his own theories when he came to put paint on canvas; but as an oracle and as a Salon juryman he threw the weight of his authority behind academic art at its most sterile. His attitudes hardened with age, possibly accentuated by the emergence of a younger rival in Eugène Delacroix (1798-1863). Delacroix represented in painting the Romantic movement that was challenging 'classical' notions of correctness in all the arts. For the Romantics, spontaneity, passion and love of nature were the supreme attributes of the artist. Delacroix, like many French painters and writers of this school, was particularly attracted towards the exotic, often with a pungent admixture of erotic violence, as in the famous *Death of Sardanapalus*. Of greater importance for the history of Impressionism was Delacroix's liberation of colour from the formulas of academic painting: the brightness of his palette, and the naturalism with which his colours were applied, acted as an inspiration to young painters who were dissatisfied with the orthodox teachings. For years the cafés and studios buzzed with heated discussions in which Delacroix and colour were pitted against Ingres and drawing. But whereas Victor Hugo and the Romantic writers won their battle against Classicism, Delacroix and his followers failed to capture the Academy; Delacroix himself was not elected to membership until he was an old man close to death. Some academic painters incorporated elements of Romantic warmth and exotica in their more sentimentally-slanted works, but (on the level of official art) that was all.

During the 1850s a new movement of dissent appeared in the attractively noisy, bull-like person of Gustave Courbet (1819-77). At the International Exhibition of 1855 in Paris, Courbet's great pictures *The Funeral at Ornans* and *The Painter's Studio* were rejected by the jury. He responded by setting up his own pavilion, showing a wide selection of his works under a single heading-cum-battle-cry: Realism. Courbet's socialist ideas no doubt reinforced his interest in the ordinary and everyday, but ideas are largely excluded from the pictures themselves. Courbet condemned historical painting, and for that matter all art involved with abstract ideas: painting, he insisted, was concerned solely with the concrete and visible. His realism was not 'proletarian', or even 'modern' in either sense of the word: he drew on the life of the countryside rather than that of big cities, and his style is firmly in the tradition of the 17th-century Dutch and Spanish masters. But in the context of the 19th century it was undeniably subversive: nothing could be further from the majesty of Germanicus' big toe than *The Funeral at Ornans*, with its perfunctory celebrants and Sunday-best-dressed peasants, torn between grief, self-importance and whatever is going on outside the picture frame. The paintings into which Courbet puts himself – exuberant narcissistic masterworks such as *Bonjour, Monsieur Courbet!* and *The Ocean* – were equally offensive to academic notions of distance and dignity.

Despite Courbet, despite Delacroix, the school of Ingres took all the prizes and medals at the 1855 Exhibition. Courbet none the less became a rallying-point for many students in the '50s, and for a time he even ran his own teaching studio in opposition to the officially-backed ateliers. The growing dissatisfaction came to a head in 1863, when an unusually ruthless Salon jury rejected some 3,000 paintings out of the 5,000 submitted. The resulting uproar was so great that the Emperor himself asked to see some of the rejects. Later he announced that the public would be given the chance to decide for itself: any of the rejected artists who cared to do so could exhibit at a separate show – the Salon des Refusés – opening a fortnight later than the official Salon and in another part of the building (the Palais d'Industrie). On the face of it this was a reasonable decision; it was also a characteristic action by Napoleon III which indicates why he has been called the first demagogic dictator. His intervention did not discredit the artistic establishment or diminish its real power; yet it made the Emperor appear to be above and outside that establishment – a well-intentioned Olympian who was not responsible for the mistakes made by bureaucrats, and who would put things right if he knew the real state of affairs. The Emperor's 'democratic' gesture cost him nothing, and left the artistic establishment free to sabotage the Refusés if it could. A good many

Jean Auguste Dominique Ingres. *Count Emilien de Nieuwerkerke*. 1856. A pencil drawing heightened with white. Nieuwerkerke, a sculptor and sleek adventurer notorious as the lover of Princess Mathilde Bonaparte, became the Imperial Superintendent of Fine Arts. He was a thorough reactionary who opposed even the quiet art of Corot; and of the Barbizon painters he said, 'This is the painting of democrats, of people who don't change their linen and want to put themselves above men of the world. This art displeases and disquiets me.' Inevitably, his influence was thrown against the Impressionists. Fogg Art Museum, Harvard University, Cambridge, Massachusetts (G. L. Winthrop Bequest).

Right:
Jean Auguste Dominique Ingres. *The Bather of Valpinçon*. 1808. A superb example of Ingres' clear-cut yet delicate art. He represented a strong tendency in French painting – evident since at least the 17th century – to emphasise drawing at the expense of colour. This painting illustrates the virtues of the linear style; but when hardened into a dogma, it produced a sterility from which it took the Impressionists to liberate French art. Musée du Louvre, Paris.

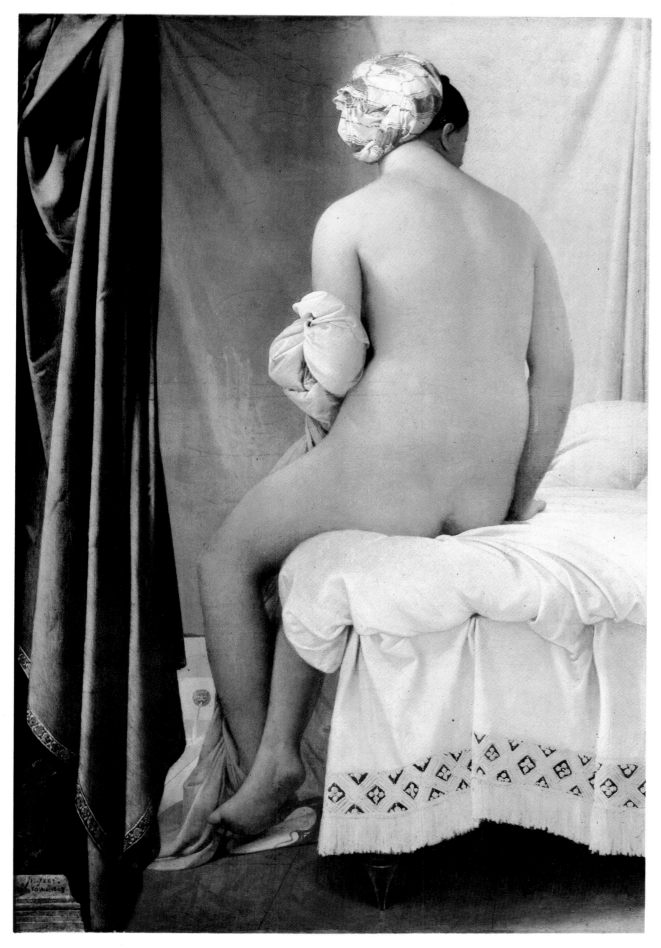

rejected painters shrewdly chose to withdraw their works without showing them at all;
if they still hoped to make a successful career along conventional lines, it would have
been unwise to exhibit with the 'opposition' and so become marked men. There may
even – who knows? – have been souls modest enough to believe the jury knew best.

The overwhelming majority of such losses must have been orthodox academic
pictures – not much of a loss in retrospect, though their presence might have made the
exhibition look more 'normal' and acceptable to the average spectator. As it was,
people came to the Refusés predisposed to laugh since the press had told them the show
was laughable; and when, among the confusion of thousands of paintings, they saw
what seemed to be ridiculous and extravagant daubs, thoughtfully hung for them in

prominent places by the official Salon jury, many of them did – laugh. In fact, these ridiculous and extravagant daubs were not incompetent paintings (perhaps there were not enough of them), but works such as Whistler's *White Girl* and Manet's *Déjeuner sur l'Herbe*, which have become universally admired.

The Salon des Refusés was a fiasco which was generally held to have exonerated the official jury. Some of the jury's decisions had admittedly been mistakes, even by academic standards, and there were paintings at the Refusés that did succeed with the public. But though some modifications had to be made to the system, they only benefited those academic painters who had previously been badly treated; the dissidents, rejected by the public as well as the establishment, seemed more isolated than ever. And, having made their point, the artistic authorities staged a diminished Refusés the following year, and then discontinued the 'experiment' which was deemed to have failed.

But the Refusés did have one positive result: all those who were working outside the establishment became aware of one another, and gained something of the confidence that comes from knowing one is not alone against the whole world in seeking new paths. Some of the younger generation of painters found a man they looked on as their leader: Édouard Manet, whose *Déjeuner sur l'Herbe* had shocked the Emperor and outraged the public by showing a distinctly unclassical nude relaxing at a picnic with two men in contemporary dress. As so often happens, both friends and enemies of Manet were mistaken about him, seeing radical inclinations and realistic intentions in an artistic development that was concerned with neither for its own sake. Still, Manet was, among other things, a painter of modern life in an important sense that Courbet was not – a painter of town life and café society, of men sporting top hats and of naked ladies who wore high heels. Such an approach, uncluttered with moralising or story-telling, was deeply alien to the classicising ideals of academic art – and wonderfully refreshing. Understandably, the young Impressionists began to think of Manet as their chief.

Left:
Marc Gabriel Charles Gleyre. *La Charmeuse*. 1868. Academic art in its sentimental-erotic vein, by the teacher of Monet, Renoir, Sisley and Bazille. In Gleyre, the sentimental was uppermost; his best-known painting is the gently nostalgic *Lost Illusions*. But all the same Renoir told his son a number of entertaining anecdotes about Gleyre that hinged on the Swiss painter's bashfulness and prudery. Kunstmuseum, Basel.

Above right:
Eugène Delacroix. *Women of Algiers*. 1834. Delacroix was the greatest French Romantic painter, notable for violent erotic-exotic works such as *The Massacre at Chios* and *The Death of Sardanapalus*. Here he enters the enclosed existence of Moslem women. Musée du Louvre, Paris.

Right:
Daguerrotype portrait of Eugène Delacroix, taken in 1832. An astonishingly early and appropriately romantic photograph of the leader of French Romantic painting.

The Impressionists-to-be came together in the period after the Salon des Refusés in 1863. The leading figures were Claude Monet, Auguste Renoir, Alfred Sisley and Frédéric Bazille, who had met one another not long before at Gleyre's studio; and an older man, Camille Pissarro, with his friend Paul Cézanne. Their chief interest in the years ahead was landscape painting, executed on the spot, out of doors, and rendered with the greatest possible fidelity to the light, colour and atmosphere prevailing at the moment of painting. This was very much against the academic tradition, with its dark colours, meticulous rendering of details the eye never takes in, carefully drawn and finished studio (that is, indoor) working methods, and preference for the 'timeless' over the particular. Landscape itself was discounted by the strict academic painters unless it was employed simply as background; but it was tolerated as a minor art. Among the most important influences on the Impressionists were such landscapists as the Barbizon school and Camille Corot, who anticipated Impressionism in doing much of their work in the open air. By the 1850s these artists exhibited regularly at the official Salons, and most of the Impressionists hoped for a similar degree of acceptance; militant temperaments (Monet, Cézanne) were at first in a minority among them.

If the Impressionists were at first little more than a group of friends with interests in common, working together (in various permutations) gave them a certain cohesion that was reinforced by lack of success. From the late 1860s they also met of an evening in Paris at the Café Guerbois, along with Manet and another older artist, Edgar Degas. The role of the café in French art is so well known, albeit in Hollywood terms (bearded artists in berets shouting one another down), that it hardly needs stating. But the function of the café went (and goes) beyond the picturesque and social: by bringing together gifted people, known and unknown, in informal, inexpensive surroundings, it helped to make French painters and writers more conscious and finished artists than most of their equivalents elsewhere; it helped to give them an ésprit de corps that raised the prestige of the arts in France; and the mutual stimulation and support resulting from all this meant that French artists are perhaps less than usually liable to flag through discouragement, or to become creatively exhausted. (There is a less admirable

Édouard Manet. *Monet and his Wife in his Floating Studio*. 1874. Monet was devoted to painting *sur le motif* (directly from the subject), which normally meant working in the open air. When he lived on the river at Argenteuil, he even fixed up a boat as a floating studio. This painting is a fascinating example of reciprocal influence: Manet, the older master, influenced Monet and his friends to break with conventional techniques; in turn, Monet influenced Manet to try painting in the open air, as he has here. Neue Pinakothek, Munich.

Above left:
Gustave Courbet. *The Funeral at Ornans*. 1850. Painted quite early in Courbet's career, but one of his strongest works. Comparisons with Corot on the one hand, and with Couture on the other, indicate the particular qualities of Courbet's realism. For all its power, this is an ordinary, unidealised scene; the inattentive participants emphasise the fact without the intrusion of satire. Musée du Louvre, Paris.

Left:
Gustave Courbet. *Bonjour, Monsieur Courbet*. 1854. Courbet's exuberant self-regard comes through in this painting, which celebrates his visit to Alfred Bruyas, a distinguished collector resident at Montpelier. In a 19th-century context Courbet's pack, stick and carelessly discarded coat amount to an anti-bourgeois gesture. Musée Fabre, Montpellier.

side to this artistic sociability, naturally: French writers and artists have tended to be exceptionally jealous of and spiteful about their colleagues, and inclined to group themselves in violently hostile and doctrinaire cliques.)

These close relationships also involved shared technical experiments and advances. By about 1870 the Impressionists had developed the painting method that distinguished them from other schools. This was to use small brush-strokes of pure colour, where previous artists had used colours mixed to give smooth tonal shadings. In Impressionist paintings the eye does the mixing, working on the skilfully juxtaposed blobs of pure colour; but it simultaneously remains aware of the individual colours, and the oscillation between the two modes of vision creates an intense vibrancy. This method (chromatic division, or, in painting terms, broken brush-work) is superbly adapted to rapid execution on the spot, and gives the finest Impressionist landscapes their wonderful freshness and immediacy – the sensations of moving skies, rippling waters, and stirring grasses and trees, with the whole view dancing and dappled with light. Light, finally, is what makes the 'purest' Impressionist paintings so brilliantly alive and so different from everything that had been produced before them.

Only a handful of people in the 1860s and '70s saw any of this. Most spectators took their standards from academic art and the Old Masters: one may have been no more than a debased version of the other, but generally speaking they had in common a high finish, a solidity of forms, a definiteness of outline, a precision of detail and a restraint of colouring that seemed to fix the boundaries of 'great art'. According to these definitions it was impossible to take seriously the Impressionists' daubs, with their sketchy, unfinished look, child-bright colours, and forms which dissolved into splashes of paint when you got up close to them.

In 1874, believing they might succeed with the public where they had failed with the academicians, the Impressionists took the audacious step of holding their own independent exhibition. Instead of the hoped-for success, they suffered public ridicule and the witlessly witty insults of journalists. But, largely thanks to the dogged efforts of Pissarro, the group exhibitions went on. Seven more were held between 1875 and 1886, and in spite of itself the public gradually became used to the new style. A sign of the times – of the greater acceptance of artistic diversity – was the establishment in 1884 of a Salon des Indépendants, affiliated to neither the Impressionists nor the Salon.

Ironically, the Impressionists had begun to go separate ways in the very years when

15

Pierre Auguste Renoir. *Woman of Algiers*. 1870. A tribute to Delacroix's *Women of Algiers*. The Impressionists generally preferred 'modern' and everyday subjects, but Renoir did share the Romantics' taste for the exotic; characteristically, however, his work is colourful and opulent, but lacking in the intensity and mystery beloved of Delacroix and his fellow-Romantics. National Gallery of Art, Washington, DC (Chester Dale Collection, 1962).

Left:
The most famous places associated with the Impressionists.

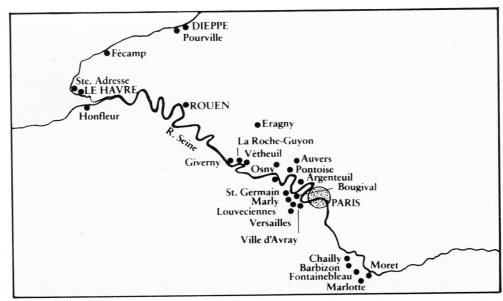

Impressionism was gaining public tolerance. This was not really surprising, since there had always been a variety of aims and personalities within the movement. The account given above, along with its description of a quintessential Impressionist landscape, is a simplified one, made for the purposes of summary. At this point it is perhaps enough to say that Impressionism as a *movement* was a considerably more mixed affair; like other movements – especially movements in opposition to a ruling system – it represented a spectrum of types and opinions, including some which might have been considered incompatible.

In the 1880s, while the original Impressionists were going their own ways, other artists appeared who had passed through Impressionism and found it insufficient in some respect or other. Cézanne, a minor and uncertain figure in the history of Impressionism proper, went on in middle life to create an art with the kind of constructive strength absent from paintings dissolved in light; he became the major pioneer of Cubism and other 20th-century movements. A younger man, Paul Gauguin, passed through Impressionism to forge a more simplified decorative style which also restored a sense of the mysteriousness of existence. And the Dutch painter Vincent Van Gogh adapted the Impressionist brush-stroke to a thickly, wildly applied painting style that charged everything – landscapes, people, flowers, furniture – with a frenzied, visionary emotion.

By 1900 Impressionism was internationally known, and had its disciples in many countries. It also formed an element in the early styles of major modern artists who developed beyond it. This, the first movement in modern art, conceived in the 1860s, can only really be said to have ended with the death of its last great exponent, Claude Monet, in 1926.

Forerunners
and Influences

Something of the influence of Courbet and Manet on the Impressionists has already been indicated. Courbet brought a sense of excitement and actuality to an art that seemed to have become over-conventionalised; and he encouraged young artists to believe that humdrum subjects and unusual modes of approach offered fresh possibilities to those with the courage to explore them. The very finish of his pictures was often rougher than that of the Old (and also the academic) Masters, thanks to his use of a palette knife instead of brushes to apply paint to the canvas. This roughness became one of the trademarks of the advanced artist; most of the future Impressionists used both the manner and the instrument in imitation of Courbet at some point in the 1860s, before they became converted to the rapid application of pure colour patches, which gives a similarly rough finish in pursuit of a different effect. Courbet's 'rough' manner, evolved to heighten his characteristically monumental forms, therefore proved, almost by accident, more widely fruitful than might have been expected.

Édouard Manet also abandoned the high finish and meticulous detail of academic art, though for rather different reasons from Courbet. His involvement with Impressionism was so considerable that he rates separate treatment (in Chapter 3). Depending on definitions, he can be regarded as a forerunner of Impressionism, a mere friend and good example, or as the half-reluctant leader of the movement.

Courbet and Manet inspired the young Impressionists with an interest in the ordinary, the contemporary, the 'roughly' executed. Another important element in Impressionism – many would say its central feature – was the practice of working directly from nature in the open air, often called *plein-air* painting after the French term. This was developed from the example of a number of important landscapists who were older contemporaries of the Impressionists-to-be. These men, notably Camille Corot (1796-1875) and Charles François Daubigny (1817-78), had acquired a certain authority by the 1860s, when most of the Impressionists began working; and, as we have seen, the Academy of Fine Arts was not unrelievedly hostile to them, though few of its members would have put landscape on a par with painting in the 'Grand Style'.

Camille Corot devoted almost the whole of his long life to painting nature; in his very large output there are only a handful of portraits and nudes. Corot's landscapes are inhabited – often, in line with the Salon tradition, by more or less conspicuous classical or literary figures. Generally speaking, however, it is the landscape that gives the painting its mood – the gentle, still silvery-toned mood of slightly overcast days, often with twilight approaching. This is in sharp contrast with the bright colours and all-suffusing light of the Impressionist palette, and is the result of temperamental as well as technical differences. Corot is a transitional figure in that he painted outdoors but finished the work in the studio; that he constantly praised nature, told his disciples to hold fast to the first impression they received from a scene – even told them to look to nature rather than Corot himself or the Old Masters – and yet added trees and similar features to 'improve' his paintings, put nymphs into landscapes to please the Salon, and ultimately condemned the Impressionists. But if there were limits to Corot's sympathies, he was a helpful influence on Pissarro, Berthe Morisot and other younger painters, and his own works have a fresh, country-air feeling unmatched by any French painter of his generation.

Corot painted from time to time near Barbizon, a village on the edge of the forest of Fontainebleau. This spot had become the headquarters of a whole school of landscapists, for whom the peasants' houses, the forests and the plain became an endless source of inspiration. The first painter to work regularly at Barbizon was Théodore Rousseau (1812-67), whose retirement to the country was partly caused by repeated rejections at the Salon. He was followed by Jean François Millet (1814-75), who was also notable for somewhat idealised peasant studies; by Narcisse Virgile Diaz

(1808-76); and by Jules Dupré (1811-89). Daubigny was also associated with the Barbizon school; he was a member of the Salon jury in the later 1860s and struggled manfully to gain acceptance for Monet, Renoir and other young painters at odds with academic standards.

A painter's choice of a place to work tells us a good deal about his intentions. The strength and density of the forest of Fontainebleau invited a romantic response; and though the Barbizon painters intended to record nature without literary, historical or mythical trappings, there is still a touch of romantic feeling – gloom or grandeur or melancholy – in their works. It is still visible in the early paintings of the next, Impressionist generation, done in the same forest setting at nearby Chailly. In the case of the Barbizon painters a 'literary' tendency was probably encouraged by the practice of working in the open air only for sketches and studies; the final painting was done in the studio, where – consciously or unconsciously – the painter tended to add 'meaning' or 'emotion' to what he had seen. By contrast, the kind of open-air painting evolved by the Impressionists in the 1870s was essentially a direct, on-the-spot record of the then-and-there, with ideas and feelings given little opportunity to intrude. From that point of view – immediacy, the primacy of the impression – the name of the movement was well chosen.

At this point a disclaimer has to be made. A book about one particular school of painting tends to sound disparaging in its treatment of all artists outside the school. Here, for example, it may seem that Corot and the Barbizon painters were *nothing more* than forerunners of Impressionism – artists who 'failed' to go the whole distance. Not so, of course; but in the present context we are interested in them only in so far as they pioneered Impressionist techniques and subjects, just as we are interested in Delacroix and Courbet as liberators rather than major artists who can bear comparison with any of the Impressionists. In the same way, Impressionism is an 'advance' in that it gave the world a new vision achieved with new techniques; it is not an 'improvement' that makes the authentic works of the past obsolete. Widening a vocabulary does not mean that the older words become somehow inferior or are superseded: if it did, we should not be studying Impressionism but the movements that 'superseded' it, or the movements that 'superseded' them . . .

To pursue the 'pre-history' of Impressionism back beyond the 19th century is outside the scope of this book, though it would of course be feasible to construct lines of development (from the Danube school through the 17th-century Dutch landscapists; from the 'rough' manner in the later works of masters such as Titian; and so on). But one group of painters outside the 19th-century French school does regularly come up in discussions of Impressionist origins.

The influence of the English landscapists on Impressionism became a controversial subject even before the Impressionist movement had come to an end; inevitably, the issue has been confused by trivial national prejudices. Most of the arguments centred on the fact that Pissarro and Monet spent part of the Franco-Prussian war period in London, where they evidently saw paintings by John Constable (1776-1837) and J. M. W. Turner (1775-1851). Later in life Pissarro expressed conflicting opinions about the impact of the paintings on himself and his friend; but the evidence of his work would seem to indicate that by 1870 Monet, at least, had little to learn from the English on the technical level.

On the other hand, there can be no doubt about Constable's influence on French painting many years before 1870. In 1824 *The Hay Wain* won a gold medal at the Paris

Charles Daubigny. *The Great Vale of Optevoz.* 1857. Daubigny was one of the leaders of the Barbizon school of painters, who did much of their work in or near the forest of Fontainebleau; though more 'finished' and also more romantic in feeling, their paintings deeply influenced the Impressionists. Daubigny's art became sufficiently accepted for him to be chosen as a member of the Salon jury on a number of occasions; and unlike Corot he used his position to help his younger contemporaries. Musée du Louvre, Paris.

Right:
Camille Corot. *The Banks of the Cousin.* About 1840–50. One of Corot's most informal paintings. Its unexpected 'close-up' quality, and its mood of quiet pleasure in the natural scene, make it clear why Corot is considered a forerunner of the Impressionists. Musée du Louvre, Paris (Personnaz Bequest).

Salon, and some years later Rousseau and the Barbizon painters explicitly acknowledged their debt to Constable. Some French critics were hostile, and applied to Constable terms of abuse such as 'sketchy' that were later to be applied freely to the Impressionists. And in fact passages in the English painter's life actually read like an Impressionist's biography. Dissatisfied with the conventional landscapes admired in London, Constable eventually returned to his native Suffolk; there, working on the banks of the River Stour, he strove to capture the appearance of the skies and the changing effects of light on the meadows and water; and these were for years the least regarded of his works. He also, incidentally, painted seascapes that immediately bring to mind Eugène Boudin (see below) and may well have influenced him.

   In France itself, other English masters such as John Sell Cotman and the East Anglian school had some influence, but Turner's most relevant work seems not to have been known until quite late in the 19th century. This is ironical, since Turner was the

supreme English painter of light and like Claude Monet ended by verging on abstraction in his renderings of swirling, brilliant mists and storms.

Finally, two painters whose influence on Impressionism was so direct and personal that they might almost be called its earliest practitioners: Eugène Boudin (1824-98) and Johan Barthold Jongkind (1819-91). The life of Boudin provides one of the nicer examples of the Apostolic Succession at work in the world of art: he was 'called' by the Barbizon painter Millet, and in turn 'called' the great Monet – thereby making a contribution to the history of painting that has tended to overshadow Boudin's own achievement.

He was born into a seafaring family at Honfleur and spent most of his life at various places on the Normandy coast, where the beaches, sea swells, clouds and holiday atmosphere inspired his most characteristic work. As a young man he opened an art materials and picture-framing shop in Le Havre, taking advantage of the resort's popularity with both amateur and professional painters. He also began to paint on his own account, and eventually showed his work to a customer, Jean François Millet, who recognised his talent and helped him to improve. Thus encouraged, Boudin sold his shop and became a full-time painter.

In 1850 two of his pictures were bought by the Le Havre Friends of Art, and the municipality gave him a three-year grant to study in Paris. But instead of making a successful career as an academic painter, Boudin neglected the École des Beaux-Arts in favour of painting direct from nature. He returned to Le Havre, if not an outright failure, then at least a disappointment: a sometime artist of promise who had persisted in 'sketches' instead of progressing to serious work, carried out on a large scale in the studio. Still, one of his paintings was accepted by the Salon in 1859, and he had other successes from time to time.

In the 1850s Boudin met and was largely instrumental in forming the young Monet; the story is told later on as part of Monet's life. Boudin had already formulated the conviction central to Impressionism, that 'Everything painted on the spot has a strength, a power, a vividness that can't be recaptured in the studio'. Indeed his notebooks are a virtual exposition of Impressionism, though he himself admitted that his practice could be a good deal more timid. He seems to have been a particularly gentle, self-effacing soul, content to remain in provincial obscurity despite the rousing

Jean François Millet. *The Angelus*. 1859. As well as being a landscapist of the Barbizon school, Millet painted a number of studies of peasant life. This, the most famous, is also characteristically sentimental; but Millet's rendering of the peasant's simplicity and life of devoted toil was of considerable social importance. He influenced Pissarro, and had an even greater impact on Van Gogh, who always regarded him as a great artist. Musée du Louvre, Paris.

summonses to conquer Paris issued by friends like Monet and the academic painter Troyon. He never quite freed himself – in theory, at least – from the idea that moral and social elements were important in painting; for example, influenced by Courbet, he even worried about the legitimacy of painting middle-class pleasure seekers – that is, idlers and parasites – on the promenades. When it came to the point, he always managed to square it with his conscience, for strolling gentlemen and ladies with crinolines and parasols give a charming social slant to the beach and sky-scenes in Boudin's paintings down to the 1870s. Still, this kind of dilemma must have made plein-air paintings of pure land- and seascapes all the more attractive to him. These became the bulk of his works only after his stay in Belgium during the Franco-Prussian War; perhaps the disruption caused by the war had the effect of breaking his habit patterns.

For Boudin, accuracy became a kind of moral imperative: the poet Baudelaire remarked that you could always guess the season, time of day and direction of the wind in his paintings. The speed with which he worked to catch transient effects astonished sympathetic observers, and his renderings of the sky in all its moods came to be admired by masters as dissimilar in temperament as Corot and Courbet; even when he was portraying fashionable folk at Deauville or Trouville, Boudin put in tremendous skies that dominated the picture. He continued to develop as a painter until the very last years of his life, shunning the artistic politics of the capital: as a gesture of solidarity he exhibited with the Impressionists at their first show (1874), but never again. Full recognition and with it the Légion d'Honneur – came only in the last ten years of his life, with the public triumph of the Impressionist art Boudin had done so much to promote.

His contemporary, Johan Barthold Jongkind, had a more turbulent life and met a less happy end. Jongkind was a Dutchman, but did most of his important work in France after 1846. His character was unstable, and at one time Monet wrote a letter to his friend Boudin reporting that Jongkind was 'completely crazy' and so 'dead to art' that his friends were taking up a subscription to support him. The main form that Jongkind's 'madness' took at this time was destructively heavy drinking, but before he died he did literally go mad. Between times he recovered, met and influenced Monet and Boudin, and took part in the Salon des Refusés of 1863. Jongkind's watercolours,

Eugène Boudin. *The Jetty at Deauville*. 1869. A characteristic example of Boudin's modest but considerable art; it captures wonderfully the salt freshness of a fine day on the Normandy coast. Musée du Louvre, Paris.

Right:
Johan Barthold Jongkind. *Notre Dame from the Quai des Tournelles, Paris*. Musée du Petit Palais, Paris.

Above left:
John Constable. *The Hay Wain*. 1824. Shown at the Paris Salon of 1824, where it won a gold medal. Delacroix is supposed to have repainted parts of his *Massacre of Chios* in brighter colours after seeing Constable's painting. A mass of even more 'Impressionistic' works by Constable remained virtually unknown until 1885, when his daughter donated a large collection to the nation. National Gallery, London.

Below left:
Joseph Mallord William Turner. *Rain, Steam and Speed, Great Western Railway*. Early 1840s. A superb example of the English master (1775–1851) exploiting much the same effects as those achieved by Monet (1840–1926) in his Gare St Lazare paintings. National Gallery, London.

and even his studio-executed oil paintings (built up from on-the-spot watercolour 'notes'), can easily pass for full Impressionist works, though neither he nor Boudin consistently replaced tonal painting by chromatic division (small brush-strokes of pure colour), which constituted the 'breakthrough' for Monet and Renoir after years of study and intermittent working side by side. However, Jongkind did anticipate Monet in making several paintings of the same scene under different light conditions; he even did much of his best work on the Seine, like the Impressionists. After Jongkind there were no more steps to be taken towards Impressionism: the next step *was* Impressionism.

The Older Masters
Manet

Some men are born rebels; others, like Édouard Manet, have rebellion thrust upon
them. Courbet, the rumbustious hero of the young in the 1850s, was a fighter who
chose to be provocative in both his art and his politics. Manet, the central figure of the
1860s, was a well-off, upper-middle-class gentleman who looked for an equivalently
conventional recognition, respect and security in his career as a painter. Year after year
he pinned his hopes for success on the Salon and the bourgeois public that attended it.
Even abuse and rejection did not shake his conviction that 'the Salon is the real field of
battle', though his young friends urged him to break with the system and exhibit with
them. Manet's only acts of rebellion were the pictures he painted, not in any spirit of
defiance but because the study and practice of his art took him in the direction it did.

Manet was born on 23 January 1832 in Paris, where his father held a senior position
in the Ministry of Justice. Down to the Revolution there had been a judicial nobility
(*noblesse de la robe*), and the prestige associated with judicial functions remained

particularly high in France. If not quite aristocratic, Manet's family was not far from it; and they were wealthy too – not, on the face of it, a promising environment for a painter who aspired to be anything more than a talented amateur. Manet showed promise at school, where he was allowed to take drawing lessons, but a couple of years later the elder Manet appears to have scented danger and hurried to settle his son in a useful career before he became too difficult to control.

Offered a choice between the civil service and the navy, Manet chose the navy. But either through lack of ability or as a form of passive resistance, he failed the entrance examination that had to be taken by would-be officers. Before re-taking the

examination he was sent off to gain some experience, sailing as a cadet on the *Guadeloupe*, which took him into the South Atlantic and over to Rio de Janeiro, giving him his first experience of southern colour and exoticism. Then, back in France, he re-sat his examination in July 1849 and failed again. With a naval career now out of the question, Manet's father reluctantly agreed that Édouard should study painting.

Manet was enrolled in orthodox fashion at the École des Beaux-Arts. His teacher there was Thomas Couture, whose technical accomplishment and sterility are revealed in paintings such as *The Romans of the Decadence*. Couture was famous as a teacher as well as a painter, so Manet may well have learned a good deal from him; but it remains surprising that he stayed on as long as six years, even to please his parents. The only plausible explanation is that he was, as ever, reluctant to do anything but 'the done thing'. Couture's vanity and reactionary arrogance must have been difficult to put up with. His critical views are adequately summed up by a caricature he created for the benefit of his students: *The Realist* shows an artist blasphemously seated on an idealised classical stone head while he calmly sketches the fatty features of a pig. That was all Couture could see in the new movements of his own time. Clearly there were severe limits to what Manet could learn from such a dogmatist. There are various accounts of their disagreements, but when Manet finally broke with Couture – on or after leaving Couture's studio – there was evidently bad feeling between them. After his first acceptance at the Salon, Manet refrained from calling himself 'pupil of Couture', which was the customary courtesy newcomers paid to their old teachers.

Immediately after leaving Couture, in 1856, Manet travelled for much of the next two years through Belgium, Holland, Germany and Italy, carefully studying the Old Masters and making copies of their works. In the 19th century this activity had a double function. When faithfully done, it created the closest equivalent to the modern colour-reproduction photograph, which is still the only form in which many paintings can be seen at all, let alone re-experienced, by large numbers of people; painters who were short of money often worked full-time as copyists, like Manet's friend and contemporary Henri Fantin-Latour, who was later to win fame as a portraitist and flower painter. The other function of copying was to learn by re-living the experience

Above:
Sources for Manet's *Déjeuner sur l'Herbe*:
Giorgione, *Concert Champêtre*. Manet is known
to have copied Giorgione's work in the Louvre
when he was a young man. Paintings of upper-
class men and women relaxing in the
countryside are known as *fêtes champêtres*;
Manet's scandalous painting was a re-
interpretation of the genre in 'bourgeois' terms.
Musée du Louvre, Paris.

Left:
Sources for Manet's *Déjeuner sur l'Herbe*:
Marcantonio Raimondi, *Engraving after
Raphael's Judgement of Paris: detail of River
Gods*. This is evidently the source for the main
grouping in the *Déjeuner*, though the subject is
a modern variation on Giogione's *Concert
Champêtre*. Metropolitan Museum of Art, New
York (Rogers Fund 1919).

Above right:
Édouard Manet. *Le Déjeuner sur l'Herbe*
(Luncheon on the Grass). 1862–63. A study for
the big *Déjeuner*, or perhaps a copy of it; it is
very roughly a quarter the size of the finished
work. Courtauld Institute Galleries, London.

Below right:
Édouard Manet. *Le Déjeuner sur l'Herbe*
(Luncheon on the Grass). 1862–63. The
scandal of the 1863 Salon des Refusés. The
nude is Victorine Meurent, who posed for
several of Manet's pictures, including *Olympia*.
The men are Ferdinand Leenhoff, who was to
become Manet's brother-in-law, and the
painter's brother Eugène. Musée du Louvre,
Paris.

of the painter – solving problems of composition, perspective, colour mixing, and so on. In Manet's case this meant learning a good many things ignored by the academy classes, which taught only those aspects of the Old Masters that fitted in with contemporary practice. Copying helped Manet acquire a veneration for tradition that was to express itself in terms of reworking rather than tamely producing variations on it.

On his return to Paris, Manet painted *The Absinthe Drinker* and submitted it to the Salon jury for 1859, who rejected it. This is already a characteristic Manet in its simplifications – in the elimination of detail that the eye does not see, and in the relative absence of the halftones that made for smooth transitions from one subject to the next. Both of these were heretical omissions; but Manet may have been correct in believing that it was the contemporary quality of *The Absinthe Drinker* that most repelled the jury. Couture is said to have remarked that only another absinthe drinker could have perpetrated such a painting, which no doubt ended any vestigial contact he may have had with Manet.

The Absinthe Drinker is actually as close to moralising as Manet ever came, though the jurymen either failed to notice or were shocked by the absence of more overtly uplifting sentiments. The drinker is a dimmed, rag-shrouded figure – one whose light has gone out; by contrast, the glass is sharply rendered, hovering like an unholy grail rather than sitting on the wall as a 'technically accomplished' academic artist would have shown it. It was this kind of daring – though he was hardly aware of it as daring – that was to give Manet his ongoing unpopularity.

This must have seemed unlikely in 1861, when the next Salon came round: Manet had two pictures accepted, and one of these, *The Spanish Guitarist,* was a distinct success. This may have owed something to the vogue for all things Spanish, which was of long standing in France (Victor Hugo's *Ruy Blas,* Mérimée's *Carmen*), and had no doubt been reinforced by Napoleon III's marriage to the Spanish princess Eugénie de Montijo. Manet shared this taste, being attracted by the exotic and passionate elements that were supposed to characterise Spanish life, and (in the long run more to the point) by the work of Velázquez and other Spanish masters. *The Spanish Guitarist* was a tribute to Spanish painting in style (particularly the dramatic lighting) as well as subject. Presumably it was acceptable to the Salon jury just because, as Manet had predicted, its subject matter was picturesque, which is to say uncontaminated by the squalid city-street realities implied by the *Absinthe Drinker.* For the first and virtually the last time Manet pleased everybody: *The Spanish Guitarist* won an Honourable Mention at the Salon, and at the same time impressed a group of younger painters and writers so forcibly that they made up a deputation to visit Manet in his studio. It is difficult now to see what the fuss was about – or rather, difficult to conceive of the banality that must have reigned where the *Guitarist* seemed the most avant-garde picture in an exhibition running to thousands of items.

His success brought Manet into contact – direct or indirect – with some of the famous men of his time. Courbet, perhaps sensing the emergence of a rival, was tepid in his reactions, and kept his distance. But the writer Théophile Gautier, one of the major pioneers of literary Romanticism – and with it the Spanish-exotic – was enthusiastic about *The Spanish Guitarist,* though he proved unable to understand Manet's subsequent work. A profounder critic was the poet Charles Baudelaire (1821-67), whose sensibility – urban, dandified, sensual, guilt-stricken – had already found its most enduring expression in *Les Fleurs du Mal* (1857). Baudelaire had already written perceptively about Delacroix, the great Romantic of French painting, and he now became Manet's staunchest supporter, as both a friend and a writer. He quickly diagnosed Manet's weakness – his utter unpreparedness for struggle, for coping with hostility – and encouraged the side of Manet's sensibility that was drawn to the portrayal of contemporary life.

One result of this interest was *Concert in the Tuileries Gardens,* which was much more firmly of its time and place than a rather generalised 'contemporary' painting such as *The Absinthe Drinker.* The location was a real park, and many of the people were Manet's friends, including Baudelaire, Gautier and Fantin-Latour. He himself appears in the scene, and most of the other people were originally sketched on the spot; but the painting itself was done in the studio. The composition has often been criticised as inept, yet everything works to make the eye scurry about over the canvas in much the same fashion as it would over a real crowd. Despite the posed figures in the foreground there is a feeling of slight perturbation – of shifting about rather than directed movement – that owes a good deal to the bold colour contrasts and variations in the detail with which members of the audience are rendered. And the flattening-out of the picture, violating orthodox perspective and bringing everything to the front, works here to emphasise the crowding; it was to become one of the hallmarks of Manet's style, contradicting notions of him as a 'photographic' realist – and, of course, outraging the academic critics.

The *Concert* was one of 14 of Manet's works shown in the gallery of Louis Martinet in March 1863. Martinet was a dealer who had been handling Manet's paintings for the previous two years, and a group of the sort he now displayed was as near as anybody

Édouard Manet. *Portrait of Zacharie Astruc.* 1864. Astruc was a writer and amateur artist; he was a close friend and admirer of Manet, wrote a notice explaining the painter's intentions when Manet exhibited in his own pavilion at the 1867 International Exhibition, and is the sitter in Fantin-Latour's painting-of-painting *A Studio in the Batignolles Quarter.* Kunsthalle, Bremen.

at the time came to the modern 'one-man show'. That was why the Salon made or broke painters' reputations: it had a near-monopolistic control over whether or not a painter was shown, and, if he was shown, whether his picture was well or badly hung. In a room lined with canvases – lined vertically as well as horizontally – being hung high-up in the dark top corner of a room was not much better than being rejected outright. With the Salon coming up, Manet may have hoped to win some flattering newspaper notices with his exhibition, and perhaps to influence the jury in his favour. But the enthusiasm of 1861 had begun to evaporate. The paintings at Martinet's included a number featuring the Spanish entertainers who had appeared in Paris the previous year, but even this safely exotic material did not completely disarm criticism of Manet's bold colouring. On the other hand, young men such as Monet admired the pictures, and Bazille wrote that 'An experience like this is worth a whole month's work'.

All three of Manet's submissions to the Salon were rejected: they were two paintings on Spanish themes which were unconventionally handled although the subject matter was acceptable enough; and the *Déjeuner sur l'Herbe.* But this was the year Napoleon III intervened to decree an exhibition of rejected paintings, the Salon des Refusés, as described in the Introduction. Manet decided to show along with the majority; but if he hoped to appeal to the public over the heads of the jury, he was bitterly disappointed. Thousands of people came to the exhibition, primed by the newspapers to jeer; and the pictures they jeered at most relentlessly were *The White Girl*, by the American painter

James McNeill Whistler, and Manet's *Déjeuner sur l'Herbe.* According to some accounts, the Emperor himself gave the public its lead, announcing loudly that 'This picture is an offence against modesty', while the Empress turned away, pretending not to have noticed it; another version even has Louis Napoleon striking the picture with his cane. It seems almost needless to add that the Emperor's chamberlain regularly provided actresses for him and sent them into the imperial bedroom with the admonition that they might kiss any part of the Emperor's person except his face. In France, as elsewhere, this was the great Age of Hypocrisy.

What made the *Déjeuner* so outrageous was the grouping of a nude with two fully-dressed young men – and, worse, two unmistakably modern young men at that, wearing conventional jackets, trousers and boots. There were no classical trappings to distance the spectator from the scene; and at the same time there was no easily comprehended erotic appeal in the picture. The girl on the grass looks out at the spectator with an expression of no more than faint interest, causing one critic to complain that she was a commonplace woman of dubious morals; he would obviously have thought more highly of a Helen of Troy, or a Venus caught in the act by her husband Vulcan. What people expected in a painting of the nude is indicated by the most successful picture of the official Salon: Alexandre Cabanel's *Birth of Venus*, which was bought by the Emperor himself and gained the artist the Légion d'Honneur – the 'little bit of ribbon' every Frenchman has coveted since the days of the First Empire. Cabanel's *Venus*, done in deathless chocolate-box style, was a voluptuously rounded young woman reclining on the waves in what looks like a state of dreamy erotic abandon rather than post-natal bemusement; a cluster of conch-blowing cupids hover overhead to provide the necessary illusion of festive innocence. True, the painting was considered rather daring, but the general opinion was that its tastefulness saved it from being offensive.

The contemporary aspect and lack of coyness in Manet's *Déjeuner* were just what made it tasteless and offensive to the 19th-century public. Manet might have pointed out that the subject was partly suggested by a famous Renaissance painting in the Louvre, Giorgione's *Concert Champêtre,* in which the gentlemen are dressed in what was then contemporary clothing. The point is one that always embarrasses puritans,

Above right:
Sources for Manet's *Olympia*: Giorgione, *The Sleeping Venus*. Manet was not the first painter to rework the masterpieces of the past, though he was the first serious artist to do so in modern times. Titian's *Venus of Urbino* itself derives from this painting by Giorgione, a fellow-Venetian who died young (c. 1477–1510). Titian is said to have put the finishing touches to Giorgione's work. Gemäldegalerie, Dresden.

Right:
Sources for Manet's *Olympia*: Titian, *Venus of Urbino*. This was Manet's chief source, and an item-by-item comparison between the two paintings reveals an unexpectedly mischievous element in Manet's transposition. Galleria degli Uffizi, Florence.

Below:
Édouard Manet. *Olympia*. 1863. Held back until the 1865 Salon, where it was accepted but universally abused. The model, Victorine Meurent, also posed for Manet as a bullfighter and in several other figure paintings as well as the famous *Déjeuner sur l'Herbe*. Musée du Louvre, Paris.

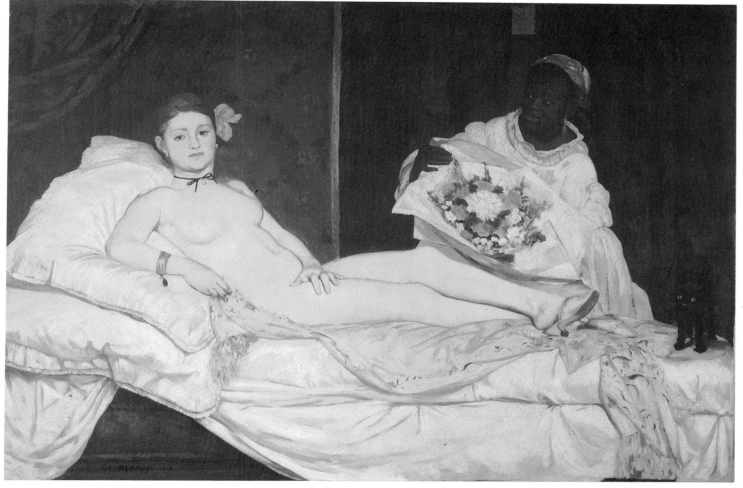

whether they are trying to repress undesirable forms of sexuality or politics or art: why should nudity or trade unionism or fantasy have been praiseworthy in the past but immoral now? (Only a few puritans have been logical enough to condemn most of the past and try to abolish it: the Chinese, that nation of traditionalists, have done so twice, in the second century BC and again rather more recently.) Discussing the *Déjeuner*, one English art critic did try to grapple with the difficulty:

'I ought not to omit a remarkable picture of the realist school, a translation of the thought of Giorgione into modern French. Giorgione had conceived the happy idea of a *fête champétre* in which, although the gentlemen were dressed, the ladies were not, but the doubtful morality of the picture is pardoned for the sake of its fine colour ... Now some wretched Frenchman has translated this into modern French realism, on a much larger scale, and with the horrible modern French costume instead of the graceful Venetian one ... There are other pictures of the same class, which lead to the inference that the nude, when painted by vulgar men, is inevitably indecent.'

Thus P.G. Hamerton in the *Fine Arts Quarterly Review*; readers may find it entertaining to analyse the various evasions and examples of double-think that infest this short piece of writing. The emotion behind the writing is surely clear in his description elsewhere in the piece of 'two Frenchmen ... sitting on the very green grass with a stupid look of bliss'. Hamerton assumes they are French, presumably because they are being immoral. And the 'look of bliss', stupid or otherwise, is quite invisible, and can only be put down to envious imaginings.

Although the hostile reception given to his work was upsetting, Manet was luckier than many of his fellow-pioneers in his freedom from money worries: his father had died in 1862, and Manet's share of the inheritance was a substantial one. In October 1863 Manet established himself still more firmly as a respectable bourgeois by marrying. His wife, Suzanne Leenhoff, was a Dutch piano teacher; according to one of his friends, Antonin Proust – writing many years after Manet's death – she had had a child by Manet as early as 1852.

Manet's submissions to the next Salon must also have been inspired by hopes of recognition and respectability. His *Dead Christ with Angels* and *The Bullfight* were accepted by the jury but unfavourably received: Jesus was wounded on the wrong side of his body, and the bullfight was, according to critics, a mere imitation of the Spanish masters.

Manet had painted *Olympia* in plenty of time for the 1864 Salon, but had cautiously refrained from submitting it. He sent it in the following year, however, perhaps on the nothing-to-lose principle: if a religious painting and a bullfight scene by him could be savaged, he could hardly do any worse with a modern subject. If this is what he thought, he was proved disastrously wrong. The jury, which had tended to be more lenient since the scandal of the Salon des Refusés, accepted both *Olympia* and *Christ Insulted by Soldiers*. But both the public and the reviewers hurled abuse at the paintings. The religious picture was dismissed as a joke, but *Olympia* evoked real hatred: she was an 'odalisque with a yellow belly, a degraded model picked up I don't

know where', a 'female gorilla', rendered with 'an almost childish ignorance of
drawing'. Even critics such as Jules Castagnary and Théophile Gautier, who passed as
friends to the modern and realistic, were harsh in their condemnation. The jury ordered
Olympia to be moved up into 'the sky' – the top of a room, where it would be less
conspicuous; and Manet, bewildered and hurt, fled to Spain.

Like the *Déjeuner, Olympia* was an erotic shock. Instead of a dewy classical nude
absorbed in the picture-reality, Manet presented a young woman with erotic modern
trappings – the neck-ribbon, bracelet, slipper – that served to emphasise her nakedness,
while she gazed directly out of the picture at the spectator. To add to the puzzlement of
the ordinary man, Olympia's gaze was not in the least inviting, or provocative, or even
enigmatic in the sexual-riddle connotation of the word: it was simply neutral. Perhaps
it is not too fanciful to see that neutrality as one more affront to the 19th-century male,
whose picture-women were supposed to yield, to comply, to demand nothing for
themselves. Here the girl is cool and confident, and it is the setting and properties that
suggest sexuality – perhaps a commercialised sexuality that is none too reassuring to
the male ego. In fairness to the critics, they did at least make some points relevant to
painting rather than morals. The innovations in the *Déjeuner* – the mixture of studio-
lighted figures and open-air-style landscape, for example – went virtually unnoticed. In
reviewing *Olympia* Gautier complained that the model was puny, the bed covered with
the cat's footprints, the general effect ugly; but then he made the point that 'we would
forgive the ugliness, were it only truthful ... The least beautiful woman has bones,
muscles, skin, and some sort of colour', whereas on this woman the flesh colour was
dirty and the modelling non-existent.

While we may not sympathise with Gautier's preference for 'beautiful' subjects and a
kind of photographic realism, we can see that he did succeed in identifying some
genuinely radical features of Manet's art. Over the years, several people – Courbet,
Castagnary, Degas – were to describe Manet's paintings in almost the same words: they
looked like playing cards – arrangements of forms with little or no depth, which
ignored the time-honoured conventions of modelling, detail and illusionistic
perspective. What most critics failed to see was the positive achievements that
motivated and justified these grand simplifications: the splendidly harmonious interplay
of masses and colours and tones – pictures that were 'poor likenesses' just because they
were not representations so much as new realities. The modern idea of a work of art –
that it is not a mirror of the world but an independent entity, a *new thing* in the world
– makes its first appearance in painting in the works of Manet.

Because of this it has sometimes been argued that Manet was not interested in

35

Left:
Édouard Manet. *The Engagement of the Kearsarge and the Alabama.* 1864. This was a duel between cruisers in the American Civil War. It took place on 19 June 1864 just outside Cherbourg, where the Confederate *Alabama* had been taking on supplies. The sinking of the *Alabama* ended the career of the South's most formidable commerce raider. Manet is said to have sailed out of Cherbourg harbour to watch the engagement. John G. Johnson Collection, Philadelphia, Pennsylvania.

Right:
Édouard Manet. *The Fifer.* 1865–66. Rejected by the jury of the 1866 Salon. The boy was a real cadet musician from a military barracks, an example of Monet's preference for working from authentic models. Musée du Louvre, Paris.

Below:
Édouard Manet. *Portrait of Théodore Duret.* 1868. Duret was a critic who met Manet in Spain, where the painter had fled after the *Olympia* fiasco (1865). Duret praised Manet's work and became a regular at the Café Guerbois. Manet is said to have put his signature upside down on this picture so that Duret would show up the prejudices of the anti-Manet school by letting them praise the work of this 'unknown' painter. Musée du Petit Palais, Paris.

subject matter. It tends to be argued most forcibly by apostles of abstract painting, who view abstraction – the arrangement of forms, colours, brush-strokes etc., without reference to any external reality – as the 'purest' form of painting. But, as far as Manet is concerned, most of the evidence runs the other way. He detested the theatrically elevated postures adopted by models trained in the academic tradition: as a student in Couture's class he told one bluntly that she wouldn't strike such a pose if she was buying radishes. He laboured for authenticity, employing a real absinthe-swilling rag-and-bone-man to model *The Absinthe Drinker,* and having himself rowed out of Cherbourg harbour to see the *Kearsarge* sink the *Alabama* in an American Civil War sea duel of which he later made a painting. And, as we shall see, he approached the *Execution of Maximilian* with documentary zeal.

On the other hand, the resulting paintings are not accurate documents, let alone convincing 'photographs'. One of Manet's staunchest defenders, the novelist Émile Zola, was close to the heart of the matter when he wrote that a work of art was 'a bit of creation seen through the medium of a powerful temperament'. Manet wanted to come face to face with reality, not the academic cliché representing it in the person of a well-rehearsed model; but the experience of reality was then filtered through his own temperament. And through more than temperament: through his painter's sensibility, which responded to the requirements of the medium even more than to reality or temperament. However much hard work Manet put into the 'documentary' preparation of a picture, the act of painting was largely concerned with a continuous adjustment of forms and colour harmonies, made solely for aesthetic reasons and, if need be, in violation of 'reality'.

In discussing a painter like Manet it is difficult to maintain a balanced view that excludes neither the importance of what was being painted nor the transforming function of temperamental-painterly factors. After looking at more conventional portraits, a picture like *The Fifer,* for example, is striking as well as enchanting in its simplifications and harmonies; but though the rendering cannot be called emotional, it would obviously be absurd to argue that the chosen subject – a small solemn boy in uniform, playing his instrument – has nothing to do with the spectator's response to the picture.

Another aspect of Manet's work that has been much debated is its relationship to the art of the past. The *Déjeuner* was partly inspired by Giorgione, and, as somebody noticed after the fuss had died down, the actual composition of the picture was derived from a 16th-century engraving by Marcantonio Raimondi. *Olympia* is clearly a variation on Titian's *Venus of Urbino,* even down to the servant, the animal on the bed, and the vertical division of the background. And Manet's admiration for

36

Velázquez and other Spanish painters involved borrowing pictorial devices as well as the subjects, which actually led to accusations of plagiarism.

None of this nowadays causes much surprise. We are used to this kind of referencing: it is seen, for instance, in James Joyce's *Ulysses,* where every episode is related to Homer's *Odyssey*; in Picasso's variations on Velázquez; and in modern French films which reinterpret American B pictures in terms of *cinéma vérité.* It is possible to argue, of course, that this merely convicts modern artists and writers of a lack of originality, a tamely derivative spirit such as 19th-century (and later) commentators saw in Manet. A more plausible explanation is that Manet's 'borrowing', like the later examples, also reflects his view of art as an autonomous field of activity in which such cross-referencing might be a legitimate device if it served to

Édouard Manet. *The Execution of the Emperor Maximilian.* About 1868. Maximilian is being executed along with two of his generals. This is the last of five versions done by Manet. He borrowed a group of soldiers from a military friend to act as models for the firing squad, but the composition owes a good deal to Goya's *The 3rd of May 1808.* Städtische Kunsthalle, Mannheim.

Left:
Édouard Manet. *Le Déjeuner à l'Atelier* (Lunch in the Studio). 1868. Shown at the Salon of 1869. The boy is Léon Leenhoff, who may have been Manet's son. Neue Pinakothek, Munich.

Édouard Manet. *Portrait of Émile Zola.*
1867–68. Shown at the 1868 Salon. Zola was
Manet's literary champion, and the various
properties around the writer form a kind of
summary of Manet's sources and career;
Olympia, a Japanese screen and Japanese print,
and above it a Goya print representing the
'Espagnolisme' of Manet's work. Musée du
Louvre, Paris.

produce new effects. The academic artist tried to paint just like the Old Masters while
varying their subjects; Manet seized directly on Old Master subjects and compositional
elements, and then developed and commented on them freely. Since Manet rarely
explained his art, it is easy to miss some effects that must be deliberate – for example,
the sheer cheekiness of the *Olympia* in relation to Titian's *Venus*: the substitution of a
knowing negress for the discreet servants; the changed position of the girl's hand; and,
above all, the inclusion of the spectator in the picture: where Venus is clearly alone,
looking out dreamily over the voyeur's shoulder while her little dog lies curled up at
her feet, Olympia's gaze takes in the spectator, and her cat (even the pet is colder, less
soft) stands and stares malevolently with a high, question-mark tail.

If they noticed any of these things, the Parisian critics saw no virtue in them. Manet was condemned as incompetent and/or subversive, and his work received short shrift over the next few years. Both his submissions to the 1866 Salon, including *The Fifer*, were rejected, and he fared no better at the 1867 Paris International Exhibition. As a result, he decided to follow the example set by Courbet in 1855 and erect his own pavilion, where some 50 of his paintings were put on show. Courbet, who had carried on the struggle even longer, did the same. Among the canvases Manet had intended to show was *The Execution of the Emperor Maximilian*. Maximilian was an Austrian

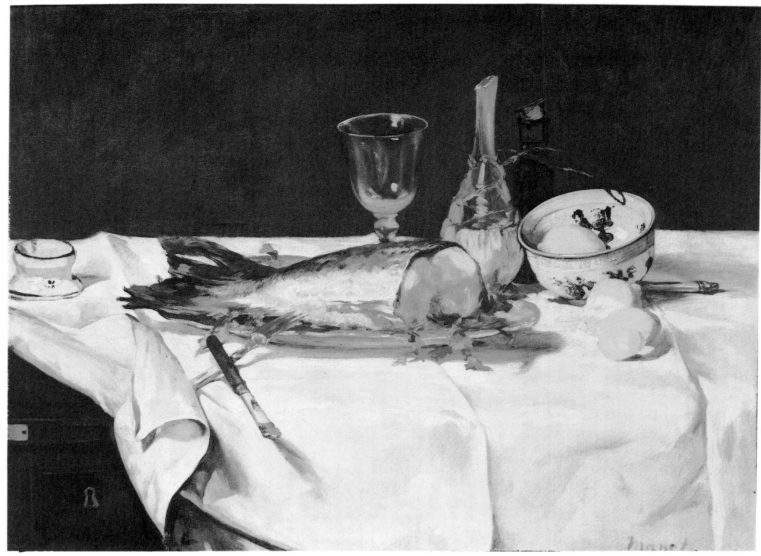

Édouard Manet. *Still Life with Salmon.* About 1869. Manet's still-life paintings are relatively little known, though he in fact worked quite often in the genre. Shelburne Museum, Shelburne, Vermont. On loan from the Electra Havermeyer Webb Fund Inc.

Left:
Édouard Manet. *The Balcony.* 1868–69. Shown at the 1869 Salon. The figures on the balcony are the painters Berthe Morisot and Antoine Guillemet, and the violinist Jenny Claus. The picture may have been suggested by a not dissimilar balcony scene by Goya. Musée du Louvre, Paris.

archduke who had become Emperor of Mexico with French help in 1864, only to be overthrown and shot three years later after a rebellion led by Benito Juárez. The French abandonment of Maximilian made the incident a politically sensitive one, and it is possible that Manet was deliberately making anti-Bonapartist propaganda with the painting. But though he was a liberal republican by conviction, Manet was scarcely politically active, and it seems more likely that the incident fascinated him simply because it was contemporary and dramatic. His approach to the subject was exactly what we have come to expect: he carefully collected photographs and descriptions of the execution, and employed real soldiers as models; yet he based the composition on Goya's *The 3rd of May 1808* and, as he went on, made numerous modifications to the picture on purely painterly grounds. In the event the government became nervous and forbade the showing of the picture.

Manet was psychologically unprepared for all these reverses, since he appears to have had no conception of the artist as a lonely pioneer or superior spirit. After the *Olympia* scandal he wrote to Baudelaire lamenting the insults that poured down on him like hail and saying vaguely that 'it is evident someone or other is at fault'. Baudelaire, a bolder spirit who had been prosecuted for *Les Fleurs du Mal*, wrote a scoffing but encouraging letter in reply: 'Are you a greater genius than Chateaubriand or Wagner? Yet they were certainly made fun of, and they didn't die of it.' But Manet never got used to the antagonism his paintings aroused. In 1869 the painter Berthe Morisot, who had become a close friend and had posed for *The Balcony,* wrote that Manet seemed perpetually surprised by his failures with the Salon and the public.

Perhaps it was this naiveté that saved him from capitulating and painting in conventional style, as one might have expected from an artist who set such store on approval: he never realised how slim his chances were of being even tolerated.

All the same, by the late 1860s Manet had built up a circle of admirers, literary friends and sympathetic younger artists. Baudelaire died in 1867, but Manet found another literary champion in Émile Zola, not yet the famous novelist but already an aggressive critic who combined genuine perceptiveness with a publicity-seeker's taste for provocation and battle. Manet enjoyed spending evenings at cafés with his friends, and by the late 1860s his table at the Café Guerbois had become the place where Zola, Degas, Monet, Renoir, Bazille, Sisley, Pissarro, Cézanne, Fantin-Latour and others met to argue about art and agree on the need to stand firm against the mediocre majority. Even Manet was known to say as much! If not the chief of a party, he had at least become its revered elder; at the same time his commitment remained in question.

41

Degas

It has often been said that Degas was not an Impressionist at all; and he himself repudiated the term, though on occasion he alluded to himself and painters like him as 'realists'. He was a solitary, a dandy, and a snob: at the Café Guerbois he delighted in provoking the company, defending unpopular notions such as that 'art should be kept from the working classes'; when he was on the point of being argued down, he would take refuge in an irony intended to undermine the seriousness of the whole discussion. And eventually, being the difficult man he was, Degas quarrelled with all his associates in the Impressionist movement.

As an artist he was equally out of step with the Impressionists. He was first and foremost a draughtsman, an admirer of Ingres with only a limited interest in colour experiments and none at all in plein-air painting; he was preoccupied with the human figure to the exclusion of almost everything else. And, though quarrelsome, and certainly an innovator, he was accepted at the Salon. Yet the misanthropic, classically inclined, socially acceptable Degas was to be one of the most vigorous organisers of the Impressionist group shows of the 1870s – an Impressionist by party, if nothing else. And, it should be said, as great an artist as any in the group.

Despite his aristocratic airs, Degas was actually of wealthy *bourgeois* origin. His father, Auguste de Gas, was the founder of the Banque de Naples; his mother, Céléstine

Musson, came from a wealthy Creole family with interests in cotton, sugar and rum. Edgar de Gas (later contracted to Degas) was born on the actual premises of his father's bank in Paris on 19 July 1834. He received an excellent classical education at the Lycée Louis le Grand, and went on to study law; but his vocation for art soon made itself felt. Although he was the eldest of the five de Gas children, Edgar seems to have changed direction without serious opposition from his father, who was himself a man of some cultivation. Degas was allowed to turn a room in the family house into a studio, and in 1853 went to study under a minor master called Félix Joseph Barrias. Unlike Manet he entered his profession without a struggle; like Manet, and unlike most of the younger generation of Impressionists, he was financially secure and never needed to fear poverty or the slow arrival of public recognition. Whereas Manet none the less craved success, Degas was uncompromising in his independence and was perhaps even by temperament an oppositionist – an attitude not all his younger, poorer colleagues proved capable of sustaining.

Degas's leaning towards draughtsmanship soon revealed itself. He started making etchings at home, and began studying the engravings in the print room at the Louvre, to which his family connections were useful in gaining him admittance. He also enrolled at the École des Beaux-Arts under a new teacher, Louis Lamothe, who reinforced his young pupil's admiration for Ingres.

In the same year, 1855, Degas met the great master himself; Degas loved to tell the story ever afterwards, and particularly to use it against his young painter friends, to whom the magisterial, austere outlines of Ingres were anathema. With the Paris Exhibition about to be held, plans were made for a special gallery devoted entirely to the works of Ingres, by that time the 75-year-old Grand Old Man of French art. Ingres asked for the inclusion of a *Bathers* he had painted years before, but the owner, a well-known collector called Valpinçon, refused to lend it. As it happened, Valpinçon was a close friend of the Degas family, and Edgar was able to visit him and argue the issue so vehemently that Valpinçon changed his mind. He was sufficiently entertained by the incident to introduce Degas to Ingres himself with an account of the young man's enthusiasm. The master was pleased, and lived up to expectations by delivering some weighty advice: 'Draw lines, young man, many lines, from memory or from nature; it is in this way that you will become a good artist'. Since the advice was congenial to Degas, he never forgot it; and he never lost his admiration for Ingres and the tradition he represented. Degas's devotion to the draughtsman's technique, to 'many lines' which he made and corrected and varied endlessly, was the permanent and traditional element underpinning his astonishingly original composition and subject matter.

Little of this appears in his early work. His self-portrait is an extremely accomplished work for a man of 20, and even has a touch of quiet poetry; but it is conventional in its dark tones, dignity and centralised composition – three academic characteristics that Degas was eventually to dispense with.

Degas's affiliation to the École des Beaux-Arts seems to have been purely formal: he despised the studio teaching method and preferred private study. And travel: in the mid-to-late '50s he spent a good deal of time in Italy. Degas's grandfather had fled from revolutionary France, made his fortune in Naples, and married an Italian girl; so Degas had Italian blood and Italian relatives. One result of his stay was *The Bellelli Family*, a painting of Degas's uncle and aunt and their children. This looks conventional enough now, but was relatively casual for its time; for example, Signor Bellelli is shown sitting in his armchair with his back virtually turned to the spectator. Degas also made some friends in Italy, and especially in Rome, among French artists at the French School set up by the Academy. One of these was Gustave Moreau, whose developed style – a bejewelled mysticism translated into paint – was to be the antithesis of everything Degas stood for.

Degas's character seems to have been formed remarkably early. He was already dedicated to art and was apparently uninterested in women, at least on an emotional level: 'There is love and there is work, and we have only one heart'. But physical movement – above all, the bodies and movements of women – fascinated him; and in this sense he was passionately interested in humanity. Nature had little attraction for him. Even Italy, which has been a revelation of light, colour and freedom for generations of Northern writers and artists, had quite another meaning for Degas: he 'soon got bored looking at nature', but revelled in the gestural variety of the cities and immersed himself in the art treasures of the peninsula.

However, even Degas was not immune to conventional expectations in his youth. His more ambitious paintings in the early 1860s were the historical set-pieces beloved of the academicians. The most interesting is the *Young Spartans Exercising* of 1861, which has a certain rough energy; earlier studies show that Degas removed some 'classical' trappings in the final version and made the boys and girls less idealised and more urchin-like. This characteristic gesture is not repeated in *Semiramis Building a City*, which is very static for a Degas, and has a dreamy, hieratic quality. Degas's first submission to the Salon was – wisely, no doubt – an even more conventional picture called *Scenes of War in the Middle Ages* (1865). This has just the combination of sex and violence that contemporaries enjoyed: while deploring rapine and murder, the solid citizen could feast his eyes on a collection of magazine nudes that seemed to be either in an orgiastic frenzy or else laid out in attitudes of sexual exhaustion.

But in these years Degas was working hard on other subjects too. He was painting portraits of increasing excellence, including the mysterious, exquisite little study of a young woman which has often been compared with the works of Clouet, the master of the French Renaissance portrait. Degas's friend Manet also sat for him. The two men met in 1862 and were drawn together by social and artistic sympathies that at first concealed their temperamental differences. They were of much the same age (Manet was the older by two years), both upper-middle-class, and both interested in painting modern-life subjects. Manet had been painting such subjects for a number of years, whereas in Degas this taste had only just become unmistakable in 1862; he had become interested in horses while staying with the Valpinçons in Normandy, and in 1862 had gone to Longchamp to sketch the racecourse, animals and jockeys. These were to become one of his favourite – and most famous – subjects, alongside dancers and domestically engaged nudes.

Degas's relationship with Manet seems to have been close down to about 1865; after about this time they were somewhat cooler towards each other, tending to meet within the context of larger gatherings. Degas was never an easy man to get on with, and it is possible that he resented Manet's notoriety as the painter of the *Déjeuner* and *Olympia*: 'You're more famous than Garibaldi!' he told his friend, who at the time was smarting from the critics' violent attacks. Degas affected an attitude of superior independence, and despised Manet's aspirations to rewards and decorations: when Manet enthusiastically congratulated a painter friend on being awarded the Légion d'Honneur, Degas snapped 'I'd already realised before this what a bourgeois you are, Manet!' Manet seems to have been at fault too: in 1865, when Degas painted him sitting on a sofa while his wife played the piano, Manet disliked the portrayal of his wife so intensely that he cut off the right-hand side of the picture in which she appeared. Degas was naturally furious and took back the painting, though he never got round to restoring it as he had intended. The oddity of the story lies not in Manet's dislike of the painting or even in his mutilation of it, though that was a pretty savage reaction to a fellow-artist's work. The oddity is that he allowed Degas to find out what he had done; probably they were already on bad terms about something else. This incident belongs to the eternal conflict between artist and sitter, which now affects photography just as

Top:
Edgar Degas. *Young Spartans Exercising*. 1860.
The girls are challenging the boys to some kind
of athletic contest, in true Spartan style, yet
somehow the military-muscular atmosphere
appropriate to its supposed subject is missing.
Degas must have been fond of this picture since
he exhibited it 20 years after it was painted, at
the fifth Impressionist show in 1880. National
Gallery, London.

Above:
Edgar Degas. *Semiramis Building a City*. 1861.
One of several conventional history paintings by
Degas at this stage in his career. The hieratic
figures and mural-like arrangement perhaps
reflect the influence of Italy and Puvis de
Chavannes, Semiramis was a mythical queen
said to have founded many cities including
Babylon and its hanging gardens. Musée du
Louvre, Paris.

Right:
Edgar Degas. *Scenes of War in the Middle
Ages*. 1865. Also called *Malheurs de la Ville
d'Orléans*. Shown at the Salon of 1865. A
curiously overripe history painting by the artist
who was to become, beyond all others, the
master of the modern. Musée du Louvre, Paris.

much as painting and sculpture: the artist strives primarily for an effect, whereas the sitter's hope is to end up looking nice – and not unreasonably so if he is paying rather than being paid. Generally speaking, neither side is candid about the situation: artists defend the accuracy of an 'expressive' portrayal, while sitters claim to be outraged by the purely aesthetic demerits of the work in question. Manet's reaction simply proves that there is a furious sitter inside every high priest of art.

In the later 1860s Degas concentrated mainly on portraits, the sitters for which were always taken from his immediate circle of family or artistic friends. Though he had already discovered a passion for the stage, his only significant rendering of it was the fairly conventional *Mlle Fiocre in the Ballet 'La Source',* which he showed at the 1868 Salon. But he did a whole series of paintings of musicians, most of whom he knew well through his father's Monday-night musical evenings; at least one, the bassoonist Désiré Dihau, became a close friend. Most of the paintings were portraits, but the series culminates in *Musicians in the Orchestra,* which is a kind of group portrait of his friends at work. It is also the first of Degas's paintings in which the composition is distinctively his.

Two things strike most spectators about the *Musicians* straight away: the bunching of the figures in the centre-front of the picture and the headless dancers at the top. The effect resembles a photograph: there is the same apparent finality about the edge of the picture, which cuts off heads, shoulders or part of a sheet of music. But in the painting, of course, there is no such finality: the effect is not accidental or imposed, but chosen. It was in fact suggested to Degas by photography, which interested him deeply; but he adapted it to his own purposes. He was convinced that the centrally-posed painting which gave a dignified, best-behaviour, as-if-eternal view of the subject had outlived its usefulness. That approach was adopted in the traditional painting which Degas venerated; but he saw no virtue in merely copying it.

His feelings were reinforced by the conviction that the 19th century was profoundly different from every other period in history: without fully articulating the fact, he evidently realised that the great rural-based societies of the past, with their hierarchies and values hardly changing over the generations, had given way to a new sort of society – urban, mobile, competitive, fluid, often vulgar; *bourgeois,* as its detractors liked to call it. On one level of his mind Degas was such a detractor: he compared 19th-century France unfavourably with the France of Louis XIV, commenting that 'They

Left:
Edgar Degas. *Portrait of a Young Woman*. 1867.
A beautiful portrait, reminiscent of French
Renaissance masters such as Clouet even in its
small size (27 × 22 cm). The sitter's identity is
unknown. She is sometimes named as Rosa
Adélaïde de Gas, the painter's aunt; but she
would have been an old woman in 1867, and
age-manipulating fantasy seems out of
character for Degas. Musée du Louvre, Paris.

Below:
Edgar Degas. *The Meet*. About 1864–68.
Private Collection.

Right:
Edgar Degas. *Mlle Fiocre in the Ballet 'La
Source'*. 1866–68. Shown at the Salon of 1868.
Here, interest is concentrated on the scene
being performed; in later and more characteristic
ballet studies Degas ignores or deliberately
violates the stage illusion. Brooklyn Museum,
New York. Gift of James H. Post, John T.
Underwood and A. Augustus Healy.

were dirty but distinguished; we are clean but common'. But his very contempt helped him to take a fresh look at the 19th century: unlike Ingres – and despite his admiration for the older painter – Degas felt committed to his own 'clean but common' century. In this he was encouraged by the mood of the 1850s, which picked up the controversial side of Courbet, and by writings such as Baudelaire's *Painter of Modern Life* and the de Goncourt brothers' *Manette Salomon*, published in 1859, which Degas is known to have read with particular attention.

Neither Baudelaire nor the de Goncourts advocated realism in the 'grim realities' sense, concerned with industrial conditions or peasant customs; but both saw 'modern life' – the age of the top hat and lace-up boots – as a subject from which a distinctive poetry could be extracted. Manet certainly did so, and indeed liked to tell Degas that 'I was painting modern life while you were still painting Semiramis building Babylon'. But it was Degas who was to become 'the painter of modern life' par excellence, giving his theatre and horse-racing scenes – even his nudes – a quality that is at once timeless and an epitome of its particular time. He did so by surprising his contemporaries while they were in movement, and by emphasising the casual and discrete nature of their activities. The scenes are apparently arbitrary, like snapshots taken at random. The result is that the event is deprived of any 'historic' look; it is appreciated as part – and not the most important part – of reality, which is understood to extend beyond the 'arbitrary' picture frame. The casual quality is strengthened by the absence of a central subject or focal point: several things are often going on at the same time in Degas's paintings, with none being given primacy by the design. In *Musicians in the Orchestra* these effects are restrained by the group-portrait aspect of the painting, which gives it a certain unity of the traditional type. But in a picture like the *Racecourse Scene* Degas has taken his method a stage further. Here there is no unifying design or, for that matter, drama: we are not shown the race but the preliminaries, with the horses all facing in different directions and apparently moving about aimlessly, while one rider in the distance struggles to control his mount. Instead of drama or the Grand Manner, this is an apparently uncomposed, desultory scene, as is, for example, the later *Cotton Market, New Orleans*.

So far from being uncomposed, Degas's paintings originated in a multitude of sketches and studies, and were endlessly worked over, sometimes for years. 'Nothing is less spontaneous than my art', he declared. His is, above all, the art that conceals art. Without superb draughtsmanship and relentless work, his paintings would have been no more than the snapshots they superficially resemble; and, above all, without a subtle, original compositional sense he could not have created the feeling of strength and durability so often lent to a painting by a 'dignified' subject. In view of these facts, it is easy to understand why Degas thought of himself as a painstaking traditionalist, for all his originality. The way in which the two are integrated can be seen in a detail of the *Musicians*. The curving neck of the double-bass is viewed from an angle that makes it appear to rise above the level of the stage – a characteristically casual touch that also cheekily serves to bring the headless dancers to the spectator's notice. But the

Left:
Edgar Degas. *Musicians in the Orchestra*. About 1868–69. Painted for Degas's friend, the bassoonist Dihau, who is shown right at the front. The other players are also members of the Degas circle, including the cellist Pillet on the left, the flautist Altès, and, seen from the back, the double-bass Gouffé. The head just visible in the box next to the stage is that of the composer Emmanuel Chabrier. Musée du Louvre, Paris.

Below left:
Edgar Degas. *Mlle Marie Dihau*. 1869–72. Marie Dihau was the sister of Degas's friend Desiré Dihau, the bassoonist who appears in *Musicians in the Orchestra* and other paintings. It has been suggested that Degas was in love with Marie Dihau – but mainly on the dubious grounds that he never showed much interest in any other women. Musée du Louvre, Paris.

Below right:
Edgar Degas. *The Artist's Father Listening to Pagans*. 1869–72. Auguste Degas was a man of wide culture whose musical evenings led to several important friendships for Edgar Degas. The artist's evident affection for his father is confirmed by the place of honour assigned to this painting in his living room, just to one side of the fireplace. Musée du Louvre, Paris.

Right:
Edgar Degas. *Madame Camus at the Piano*. 1869. Bührle Collection, Zurich.

neck is also part of the overall design, which derives much of its strength from the linear pattern made by the harp, cello, bassoon and double-bass. The device is used in *Café-Concert at the 'Ambassadeurs'* and elsewhere.

Degas's aims, and his laborious methods, were not compatible with plein-air working. He was temperamentally averse to it, in any case: uninterested in nature for her own sake, and with an enclosed, secretive personality for which his studio served as a carapace; it is impossible to imagine him painting by a roadside and submitting to the stares and comments of passers-by. At the Café Guerbois he would, characteristically, give his preferences a social rather than aesthetic expression: 'If I were the government, I'd have a detachment of gendarmes keep an eye on people who paint landscapes from nature' – an attitude which was not, as it happened, far removed from that actually held by the Imperial Superintendent of Arts. This sort of outburst reflects Degas's difficult temper, probably inflamed in this case by jealousy of Manet, who was widely regarded as the presiding genius at the Guerbois; Degas can hardly have relished the description of its habitués as 'Manet's gang'. But however much he delighted in overstating them, the differences between Degas and the younger men were in truth significant ones. Their point of sympathy was opposition to the posed, the grand, the dignified, the historical – to everything that stood in the way of contact with contemporary reality.

As far as his own art was concerned, Degas had set his course by 1870, and his later work represents a steady development without dramatic turns or reversals. He made increasingly daring use of certain techniques (notably the unusual viewpoint, as in *Miss Lala at the Cirque Fernando*) and widened his repertoire of subjects; but above all he worked, worked, worked to refine and improve. His biography is sparse, since his art absorbed his life. Even during the Franco-Prussian War, when he was called to serve in the National Guard, he seems to have spent more time painting than drilling; and the blood-bath of the Commune was merely the occasion of a painting holiday at the Normandy home of the Valpinçons. The '70s too brought no involvement for Degas – except involvement with his own art and the fate of the Impressionist movement.

Below:
Edgar Degas. *Racecourse Scene, with Jockeys in front of the Stands*. 1869–72. Characteristic of Degas in its casual, undramatic quality in marked contrast to Manet's *Races at Longchamp*. Manet discovered the racecourse as a subject after Degas and probably through Degas's work – as Degas liked to remind him. Musée du Louvre, Paris.

Bottom:
Edgar Degas. *Carriage at the Races*. About 1870. Museum of Fine Arts, Boston, Massachusetts.

Early Lives
Pissarro

Camille Pissarro. *La Roche-Guyon*. 1866-67.
An example of Pissarro's work from the period
when he was most influenced by the rugged,
massy manner of Courbet. Nationalgalerie,
Berlin.

Camille Pissarro was about ten years older than the other pioneers of Impressionist landscape painting. In the 1860s, when the movement was taking shape, he was a man in the prime of life – in his thirties – while the rest were still very young men; and this, together with a taste for theorising, gave him a certain authority over them. He was an idealist too: his socialist-anarchist opinions are well known, though he seems never to have become seriously involved in politics – unlike Courbet, for example, who suffered imprisonment and exile for his part in the Commune. All in all, Pissarro embodied a kind of high seriousness that attracts respect and attention within a new movement. At the same time he was personally mild and unassuming, so that he made an ideal mentor for younger men of genius; he was still acting the part in the early 1870s with the moody, unsociable Paul Cézanne, and as late as 1880 with the arrogant and unsociable new-comer Paul Gauguin.

Born on 10 July 1830, Jacob Camille Pissarro was actually older than the 'older masters' we have just been looking at; he was Manet's senior by two years, and Degas's by four. His slow development was partly a matter of temperament and partly the

53

result of circumstances. He was born far away from the cultural and artistic heartland of France, in the West Indies: on St Thomas, a small island which was part of the then Danish West Indies (now the Virgin Islands of the United States). This environment was not quite as daunting as it sounds: Pissarro's father, a French shopkeeper of Spanish-Jewish descent, made enough money to send Camille to school in Paris when he was 12; and there, inevitably, he discovered the fascinations of art. But if he felt any vocation in his teens, its call was not strong enough to resist a parental summons, and Pissarro returned to St Thomas when he was 17, dutifully taking up the family business. By his own account Pissarro hated commerce and longed to paint; but he put up with St Thomas for over five years before taking action. In November 1852, having failed to convince his father that he was destined to be an artist, Pissarro left for Venezuela with Fritz Melbye, a Danish painter he had met while sketching around the island's harbour. By comparison with St Thomas, Caracas was a sophisticated cultural centre. Pissarro's two years there confirmed his vocation, while his prolonged absence weakened his father's will to resist; Frédéric Pissarro probably agreed in principle to his son's choice of career even before Camille returned to St Thomas. After this Camille stayed on in the West Indies for about a year before taking ship for France in the autumn of 1855. Doubtless Frédéric Pissarro, like other middle-class parents of future Impressionists, hoped and believed his son would study under accepted masters, exhibit through recognised institutions, and adapt himself to the public's taste; and, like the other parents, he was to be deeply disappointed.

Pissarro's early career was unspectacular enough. When he reached Paris, the International Exhibition – the French answer to London's Great Exhibition of 1851 – was taking place. Out of the vast array of canvases on show, Pissarro was attracted not by the sublimities of Ingres or the Romantic violence of Delacroix, but by the silvery landscapes of Corot, whose genius was only just beginning to be recognised. Pissarro sought out Corot and became his follower; Corot refused to teach on a regular basis, but enjoyed being surrounded by disciples to whom he gave friendly advice.

On the more formal level, Pissarro entered the École des Beaux-Arts, but soon abandoned it for the Académie Suisse. This was the first indication that his career might not follow the prescribed course, since it was through the Beaux-Arts that painters acquired fame and fortune. The Académie Suisse was something else again: a 'free' studio in a dingy building on the Quai des Orfèvres, which lay on the southern edge of the Cité, the island in the Seine on which Paris originated and Notre-Dame stands. The Académie Suisse has a modest place in history, since not only Pissarro but Manet, Courbet and other famous painters worked there. It was 'free' in the sense that there were no formal classes or examinations: on payment of a small sum, any painter could work there from the model. From what we have already seen of the rigid, hectoring teaching style of the Beaux-Arts, it is hardly surprising that the creative and the unorthodox preferred freedom to experiment at the Académie Suisse.

Still Pissarro had by no means abandoned hope of conventional success. His earliest

Above:
Camille Pissarro. *View of Pontoise, Quai de Pothuis*. 1868. Pontoise was exactly what the name suggests: the place where a bridge (*pont*) crossed the River Oise. The bridge figures prominently in Pissarro's occasional paintings of the village, about 25 kilometres from Paris. He lived there from 1866 to 1869, and again from 1872 to 1884. Städtische Kunsthalle, Mannheim.

Above right:
Camille Pissarro. *The Diligence at Louveciennes*. 1870. Probably Pissarro's finest work in the period before his residence in London. His use of broken brush-work is astonishingly effective in this (for Pissarro) unusually watery scene, with its rippling reflected lights and shadows. Musée du Louvre, Paris.

Below right:
Camille Pissarro. *A Road in Louveciennes*. 1870. Mr and Mrs Paul Mellon.

Below:
Photograph of Camille Pissarro in old age.

surviving pictures are exotic views of his native St Thomas; as these paintings were done in Paris as well as on the spot in the Virgin Islands, they may represent a beginner's effort to achieve both originality and conventional acceptance through unusual subject matter. And while working at the Académie Suisse, Pissarro also studied under an established painter, Antoine Melbye, who was the brother of Pissarro's old friend Fritz. Pissarro also submitted works to the Salon. He sent in his first painting, *Landscape at Montmorency*, in 1859, and exhibited at the Salon quite frequently in the 1860s; however, he also showed three pictures at the Salon des Refusés. If he attracted little positive attention, he did secure a degree of acceptance, at first as a follower of Corot and later as a young man approved of by Daubigny, who was now a recognised master. In spite of this limited success, Pissarro put his signature to a petition for the re-establishment of the Salon des Refusés in 1867. He was certainly not making an adequate living by his work: at various times he was forced to decorate screens and blinds, and do similar odd jobs in order to support his growing family by Julie Vellay, who had been his mother's maid after the rest of the family had returned to France.

There was already a certain typical restraint in Pissarro's treatment of landscape that delayed general recognition of its avant-garde qualities. The restraint was partly inspired by Corot, and partly by the 'peasant realism' of Millet, whom Pissarro admired on both artistic and social grounds; many of his village scenes owe something to the earthy-idealistic manner of this Barbizon painter, who influence was reinforced later in the 1860s by the more massy forms of Pissarro's fellow-socialist, Gustave Courbet. This new influence so incensed Corot that he and Pissarro quarrelled, and after 1865 Pissarro no longer sent paintings to the Salon as 'pupil of Corot'.

Yet, quiet though his art seemed, Pissarro was moving towards an innovative style. He was never a 'painter of modern life' like Manet; and least of all a painter of urban life. At a very early date he followed the example of his master Corot and painted landscapes on the spot. The woods around Pontoise, a little town on the River Oise, about 25 kilometres north-west of Paris, became his favourite place for working, and he eventually settled there. Almost from the first his colours were lighter than those of Corot, who is said to have told him 'We don't see things the same way. You see green where I see grey', while encouraging him to go on cultivating his own sensations. Two of the cardinal features of Impressionism – open-air painting and a lighter palette – can, therefore, be found in the relatively small number of Pissarro's early works that have survived. By the later 1860s he was turning his personal practice into an artistic doctrine, and trying to convert his friends.

No doubt his ideas became clearer as the circle of Impressionists-to-be came together. For a long time Claude Monet was the only major figure Pissarro knew: they met around 1859, while Monet was briefly affiliated to the Académie Suisse. A little later, Pissarro became friendly with Armand Guillaumin, afterwards a minor Impressionist, and with Paul Cézanne, who was not to reach full stature for a good many years. At some time after the Salon des Refusés scandal of 1863, Monet introduced Pissarro to Renoir, Sisley and Bazille; and the Impressionist nucleus was formed. Though these painters were not yet a group – still less a 'movement' – their discussions and mutual criticisms were evidently effective.

Pissarro no doubt influenced these younger men, but he was probably also influenced by them; at any rate his colours grew notably brighter as the '60s went on, and his work became sufficiently distinctive to attract a certain amount of hostility. In a review of the 1866 Salon, the critic Jean Rousseau attacked Pissarro for his ugly and vulgar subjects – by which he meant subjects lacking in picturesqueness or grandeur. Pissarro had already arrived at the opinion he was to express many years later to his son Lucien: that beautiful scenes end up by looking merely theatrical, whereas less striking views give more scope to what matters – the artist's ability to interpret what he sees.

The complaints were caused not only by the choice of subject but also by its treatment: the ostensible subject was often seen at a distance, diminished by contrast with the extent of earth and sky. Such a treatment emphasised atmosphere – the veil of light – at the expense of the subject in the traditional sense. This was to be a quintessentially Impressionist outlook, carried to its furthest extent by Pissarro's friend Monet. Incidentally, it is only in fiction that critics are wrong-headed from beginning to end: Rousseau, despite his fixed ideas about subject matter, praised Pissarro's 'abrupt energy of execution' – the very 'sketchiness' that other critics found so objectionable about Impressionist paintings, done rapidly and on the spot in order to capture a particular place, time and atmosphere.

In 1869 Pissarro moved from Pontoise to Louveciennes, also on the outskirts of Paris. After the outbreak of war in 1870, as the victorious Prussians advanced, he removed his family from danger, first to Brittany and later to London. While he was away, the Prussians took over his house and, rather than splash their uniforms with French country mud, put down Pissarro's stored paintings as duckboards and tramped over them. According to Pissarro's own estimate, no more than 40 paintings survived out of 1,500. In this respect, at least, Pissarro would have suffered less if his paintings had sold more readily and been dispersed. As it is, he is known primarily for his work after 1869. Fortunately he had not yet reached his most creative period.

Monet

Claude Monet. *The Pointe de la Hève, Honfleur.*
1864.

Below:
Photograph of Claude Monet.

In point of technique, Monet was the most thoroughgoing of all the Impressionists, travelling fastest and also furthest along the line of march opened up by plein-air painting and the use of pure colour. But Monet's development was less a matter of technique than of attitude – of an unceasing obsession with the unique moment as created by light and atmosphere. Other Impressionists pulled up short or changed direction at various times, feeling that the actual subjects of their paintings required more attention, or that the firm structures and solid forms of the Old Masters should not be abandoned completely; Monet carried on steadily in pursuit of the moment and the sensation given by the moment. Eventually this was to lead him to the verge of abstraction, as the subjects of his paintings dissolved in a swirling mass of light-drenched colours. In the 1860s it made him the most resolutely independent of the young painters he met in Paris.

Claude Oscar Monet was born in the French capital on 14 November 1840, but he was brought up in the coastal town of Le Havre, at the mouth of the Seine; his father settled there in 1845 to set up in business as a wholesale grocer and ships' chandler. Monet's school career was undistinguished, and by his own account he played truant a good deal. He preferred to be out and about, tramping along the cliffs or splashing through the shallows on the beach. In these years he acquired a passion for the sea and a permanent affection for the coasts of Normandy, which he returned to again and again in adult life. But his first artistic efforts were not land- or seascapes but portraits – mainly caricatures of relatives, friends and the notables of Le Havre. Though very much in the comic style of the time, with rather solemn enlarged heads and set poses, the best of these caricatures are remarkable for a boy of 15. Ironically, the future Impressionist, who was later to be told that he could not draw, shows himself as being already a bold, accomplished draughtsman; the future landscapist, never much interested in the human figure, manages to deftly characterise his monocled, dandyish art teacher, the long-nosed notary Machon, the melancholy flâneur with his cigar, and

similar types. Some of these drawings are signed 'O. Monet' – his parents preferred 'Oscar' to his first name – but others have 'Claude Monet', which appears on most of his paintings.

His caricatures gave Monet a certain local celebrity, and he even received commissions to do more for quite generous payments – a lavishness of appreciation that was not to be repeated for more than 30 years. His works became well-known enough to hang up in the window of Le Havre's one picture framer, where they often appeared next to seascapes that won less public approval. These turned out to be by Eugène Boudin, who still exhibited in his old shop, though he had sold it several years before. Monet shared the general opinion of Boudin's work, presumably finding it too sketchy, and with none of the high artistic seriousness (that is, pretentious subject matter) expected from an easel painter. He actually avoided meeting Boudin until they were introduced by the picture framer when they happened to be in the shop at the same time. And even after this, though he took to Boudin at once as a man, Monet excused himself from working with the older artist for as long as he could. It is a measure of Boudin's zeal – and perhaps of his sense of isolation – that he persisted in telling his teenage friend that there was more to art than caricatures, however well received by the good people of Le Havre. Running out of excuses, Monet worked alongside Boudin in the summer of 1858. As a result, Monet admitted, 'My eyes were opened at last, and I really understood nature'.

Boudin, as we have seen, was a painter of advanced ideas; he must have been one of the best possible models on which Monet could form himself. But, even more than the joys of open-air painting and nature, it was the dedication of Boudin that impressed Monet. 'The mere example of this artist, devoted to his art and his independent way of life, made me realise what painting could mean'. After a few months of working with Boudin, Monet had become certain of his own vocation, and informed his parents that he proposed to become a painter.

They seem to have taken the idea quite calmly; after their son's success as a caricaturist – which probably embarrassed and gratified them in about equal parts – they may have been relieved that he was opting for a more dignified career than that of newspaper cartoonist or commercial artist. They may also have been influenced by Monet's aunt, Madame Lecadre, who was the elder Monet's sister and the wife of his business partner; she was herself an amateur painter and allowed her nephew to use the attic of her house as a studio. At any rate, Monet's father applied for a study fellowship for his son from the Le Havre authorities, and meanwhile agreed to let Claude – still called Oscar Monet in the fellowship application – pay an artistic-educational visit to Paris.

Since Monet's parents seem to have been quite prosperous at this time, their grant application may indicate that they were unwilling to finance their son in an artistic career, or merely that they felt they might as well get what they could out of the municipality. In view of subsequent events it is impossible to be certain. Incidentally, since Boudin was named in the application as one of Claude Monet's teachers, his reputation in Le Havre cannot have been quite so low as Monet and later writers were inclined to claim.

The Le Havre council rejected Monsieur Monet's request on the curious grounds that his son's talents as a caricaturist would probably lead him astray. They seem to have been impressed by young Monet's past earnings – presumably common knowledge

Claude Monet. *Bazille and Camille*. 1865-66.
National Gallery of Art, Washington, DC (Ailsa
Mellon Bruce Collection 1970).

in a small town – and to have believed that no well-brought up young man could abandon such a lucrative practice for 'the more serious but less rewarding' career of a painter, which it was alone proper for the municipality to subsidise. This may have been no more than a pretext for refusing, but it is given some credibility by the fact that Monet paid for the trip to Paris out of his own savings.

Presumably Monet's parents had to contribute once they had been persuaded to let him stay on in the capital for a few months. He had been sent to Paris in order to consult recognised masters, and had no doubt anticipated that they would advise him to remain in the capital. When he visited Troyon, one of Boudin's sponsors among the Barbizon painters, the master gave a conventional appraisal of the young man's work: his talent as a colourist was evident, but he needed to study drawing; he should enter a studio where nothing was done but figure drawing from a model. As far as it went, Troyon's appraisal was a shrewd one: Monet was indeed a colourist, and remained a colourist before all else; his 'deficiency' in drawing, as the academic artists saw it, was never to be cured. However, Monet used Troyon's counsel to persuade his father that he should study in Paris for a time, so it was by no means wasted.

Monet himself was later to admit that, overwhelmed by the glamour of Paris and the *vie de bohème*, he wasted a lot of time. Much of the 'wasted' time was probably spent in passionate discussions of art, an activity which the mature artist is generally inclined to undervalue when he considers it in retrospect. Monet became a regular at the Brasserie des Martyrs, a bar that was rather aptly named in view of the struggling young writers and artists who frequented it. The great Courbet was also an habitué, but Monet missed seeing him; ironically, the Paris-based Courbet was on a painting trip in Normandy at this very time, and made the acquaintance of Eugène Boudin in his shop at Le Havre. Monet, meanwhile, remained convinced that he was living at the centre of things, and wrote urging Boudin to leave Le Havre for Paris. He also found time to make several visits to the Salon, where he admired Troyon's work and raved over Corot and Daubigny: his affinities were already becoming clear.

Troyon had recommended that Monet should enrol with Thomas Couture, one of the leading academic painters of the day. Monet was already independent-minded enough to trust his own judgement, and perhaps also unwilling to commit himself to regular hours on his first trip to the big city: he ignored Troyon's advice. Instead, when he did study, it was in the free-and-easy atmosphere of the Académie Suisse, where he worked from a model, learning what he could of figure drawing, much as Troyon had suggested, but also collecting a circle of like-minded friends who were interested above all in landscape painting. One of these was Camille Pissarro, whose influence deepened Monet's appreciation of Corot; both men admired anti-academic masters such as Delacroix and Courbet, but rightly saw that Corot was the artist most relevant to their own development as painters. Both, too, were trying to move beyond Corot without recognised guides, relying on unsystematic study and expeditions to paint in the

Left:
Claude Monet. Study for *Le Déjeuner sur l'Herbe* (Luncheon on the Grass). Dated 1866. The nearest thing in existence to the complete, huge *Déjeuner*, which now survives only in two large fragments. The study is itself a large (130 × 181cm) painting. Monet probably touched it up and dated it in 1866, but most of the work must have been done the year before, since the style of the women's dresses was in fashion earlier than the style shown in the fragments. Pushkin Fine Arts Museum, Moscow.

Right:
Claude Monet. *Le Déjeuner sur l'Herbe* (Luncheon on the Grass): fragment from the left-hand side of a much larger painting, of which the central portion also survives, 1865-66. The existence of this fragment was unknown until the 1950s, when George Wildenstein discovered it rolled up in Monet's Giverny studio. Wildenstein donated it to the Louvre in 1957. Musée du Louvre, Paris.

Below:
Claude Monet. *Le Déjeuner sur l'Herbe* (Luncheon on the Grass): fragment from the centre.

country; they may actually have worked together on occasion even at this early date, though if so it did not prevent them from losing contact for several years after Monet had been whisked away from Paris.

Monet's father disapproved deeply of his son's way of life. The errant Oscar had outstayed the month or two projected for his Paris trip, had failed to start work under an established teacher, and had defiantly survived the cutting-off of his allowance; apparently his aunt, Madame Lecadre, loyal to a fellow-artist, sent on his savings (and perhaps supplemented them, which would go some way to account for their seeming inexhaustibility). To a solid middle-class citizen of Le Havre, Monet Junior must have looked like a lost soul, sliding into bohemian anarchism – a downward path that led

through free love and hashish to the fiery pit of radicalism and realism. To save his son
from this living death, Monsieur Monet adopted the only course open to him: he let the
army take Claude.

In principle, universal conscription reigned in France; but as it would have been too
expensive to call up every 19-year-old male, the recruits were chosen by lottery. The
system favoured the propertied classes, since they were allowed to buy their sons out if
they wished to do so; and despite the glories of the Napoleonic past – and the
somewhat shakier victories of the Louis-Napoleonic present – most middle-class people
agreed with the Duke of Wellington that soldiers were 'the scum of the earth', and they
gladly paid to keep their sons out. One good reason was that the middle-class recruit
thought himself too good to be a common soldier like a working man, but was rarely
considered good enough by his superiors to join the officer caste, which was mainly
staffed by scions of the aristocracy. And since the unlucky conscript had to serve for no
less than seven years, any civil career he had in mind was likely to suffer. None the less,
when Claude Monet's number came up in the military lottery, his father refused to buy
him out.

If Monsieur Monet offered his son any kind of deal – respectability in return for
exemption – Claude must have refused it. It seems unlikely that he went into the army
for seven years willingly, though later in his career he insisted he had fallen under the
spell of military life, which he apparently believed to consist of sabre thrusts and nights
spent out under desert skies.

This is hard to reconcile with his behaviour before and after military service, which
suggests Monet was already an exceptionally determined and dedicated young painter.
He certainly dressed the part. Photographs of him in the late 1850s show a handsome
young man with a thick mass of hair swept back from a high forehead; everything
bespeaks the artist – the luminous eyes, the poetic smudge of hair under the lower lip of
an unobtrusively bearded face, the taste for flowing cravats and waistcoats and capes,
the casual hand-in-pocket stance. But in assuming the role of the artist, Monet rejected
the weak and ineffectual aspects that formed part of the popular image: he was to show
again and again that he remained determined as well as dedicated, with something of
the tough, pushy provincial about him – no bad thing in a world unfriendly to
originality.

He seems to have exercised this quality to get himself accepted in the Chasseurs
d'Afrique serving in Algeria. This, if anywhere under the French flag, was the place in

which romance could be found. Algeria, though so near to France, was still an exotic, half-known land which had only been conquered by the French as recently as the 1840s. Since then, painters like Delacroix had been dazzled by the splendid oriental subjects and rich colours offered by the Algerian scene; for Romantics in particular, it represented a heady, over-ripe experience of Casbah fantasies – of passion, danger, sexual release and drugged dreaming. Monet had as little taste for all this as any painter who ever lived: there is no equivalent in the whole range of his work to the Algerian women of Delacroix and Renoir, or for that matter to the fantasies that surface from time to time among the monumentalities of Cézanne. Monet 'paints what he sees', at least in the sense that he excludes ideas, associations and all non-visual emotions from the achieved picture; that is what Cézanne meant by his famous remark that 'Monet is only an eye. But, my God, what an eye!' And so, whatever his romantic notions about army life in the desert, Monet received from Algeria not some exotic emotion but 'impressions of light and colour' that he was later to say 'carried the germ of my future researches'.

Which may or may not be so: it looks as though Monet romanticised his Algerian experience, perhaps because it proved to be his last fling before he began his lifetime's joyful servitude to art. And he seems to have found an easy berth, well away from flashing sabres, as a result of painting the wife of one of his officers. Still, if he had served out the full seven years with the Chasseurs his memories might have been less bright. After less than two years Monet became seriously ill with anaemia and was invalided home to Le Havre. Since the climate was blamed for Claude's malady, his father probably felt guilt-stricken about letting him go to Algeria; at any rate he accepted the family doctor's opinion that Claude could not go back to Africa without endangering his life, and bought his son out. It would be interesting to find out whether Claude and the family doctor were good friends: could the doctor have been a devotee of landscape painting?

Meanwhile, Monet spent six months convalescing pleasantly at Le Havre. This soon came to include painting and sketching from nature again, often in the company of his old friend Boudin. But the next stage in his development began with one of those fortunate encounters that seem to haunt the history of Impressionism: he was introduced to Johan Barthold Jongkind, who had come to work in the area, and he soon realised that the older artist – Jongkind was 42 – had a great deal to teach him. This was the man whose alcoholic 'madness' in 1860 had been dispassionately recorded by Monet in his letters to Boudin. At the time Monet had suggested that Boudin might take the place left vacant by Jongkind, but the Dutchman had proved not to be 'dead

Above:
Claude Monet. *The Quai du Louvre, Paris*. 1866-67. One of several city views done by Monet in this period (compare *St Germain l'Auxerrois*). They still have a somewhat 'set-piece' quality by contrast with later works such as *The Rue Montorgeuil Decked out with Flags* (1878), though both exhibit Monet's fondness for plunging views painted from balconies. Haags Gemeentemuseum, The Hague.

Above left:
Claude Monet. *St Germain l'Auxerrois, Paris*. 1866. The Impressionists were effectively the first painters to approach 'cityscapes' in the same spirit as landscapes, seeking to register light and life rather than to make a documentary record. This picture was painted from the balcony of the Louvre. Nationalgalerie, Berlin.

to art' after all; so Monet now found himself introducing the two men to each other. All three became firm friends; they worked together in that summer of 1862, and again two years later. However erratic Jongkind may have been in his personal life, he was just the sort of teacher Monet required – one who, like Boudin, explained his methods rather than lecturing in dogmatic terms; Boudin too, though only five years younger, recognised Jongkind as a master and admitted that he learned much from him. For Monet, Jongkind 'completed the teaching I had already received from Boudin. From that time he was my real master' and responsible for 'the final education of my eye'.

Monet's parents and relations were less pleased. He had persisted for so long that they realised he was in deadly earnest; but they saw no future in his wandering about in the open air with two rather cranky older men; that was not how real artists behaved. Even his aunt was no longer an ally: Monet had passed beyond her conventional amateur's notions, and she resented the fact. In a letter to a painter friend, she complained that his sketches were no more than rough drafts, and his finished pictures 'frightful daubs which he swanks in front of and finds idiots to congratulate him on'. The idiots, presumably, were Jongkind and Boudin. Then in the unmistakable, self-contradictory language of hurt pride, she adds 'He pays no attention to my remarks. I am not on his level, so I remain completely silent'.

Monsieur Monet felt the same way, and resolved to send Claude to Paris again; but this time his son must work regularly under a proper teacher or find his allowance cut off once and for all. Claude accepted his father's terms and set off for the capital in November 1862. He sought out a cousin by marriage, Auguste Toulmouche, who was a successful painter of sugar-sweet young ladies, and showed him a still life he had done. Toulmouche liked it well enough to recommend Monet to his own teacher, the Swiss painter Marc Gabriel Gleyre; and Monet duly entered Gleyre's studio.

Monet's version of his first week at Gleyre's has already been told in the Introduction: he found himself instructed that 'Nature is all very well as an element of study, but it offers no interest' – a point of view singularly difficult to accept for a man who had just spent months working on beaches and in the countryside with Jongkind and Boudin. With this experience behind him, and a natively stubborn temperament, Monet was unhappy at Gleyre's from the first. Actually Gleyre seems to have been less of a martinet than most academic teachers: if nothing else, he left his pupils alone a good deal of the time, perhaps because he was suffering from failing health. It seems likely that Monet would have found it impossible to fit into any kind of institution, whatever its artistic complexion, for any great length of time.

The most important thing that happened to Monet at Gleyre's was that he found a group of gifted and like-minded friends. Serendipity – the art of making happy chance discoveries – reaches its climax in Monet's life with his meeting Renoir, Sisley and Bazille at Gleyre's. Bazille was to die young, before his strengths and limitations had fully revealed themselves, but the other two were to become giants of Impressionism. Even allowing for the narrowness of the academic teaching system, the odds must have been very large against four young men of such powerful talent and mutual sympathy finding one another under the same institutional roof.

Monet seems to have infected the others with his discontent; until his arrival they are said to have been working conscientiously to win the master's approval, though Renoir in particular was not very successful in hiding his talent as a colourist from the orthodoxy of Gleyre. In later life Monet claimed to have spent no more than two weeks in Gleyre's studio before leaving in disgust, but this story was a piece of self-dramatisation: in fact he worked at Gleyre's for over a year, whether through timidity or the need to satisfy his parents that he was observing conventions. Timidity seems out of the question: at this period of his life Monet was by all accounts a very self-assertive young man; Renoir never forgot his 'lordly' ways both in- and outside the studio. Though about the same age as his new friends, Monet was much the most experienced painter, with an air of authority gained from working on equal terms with Boudin and Jongkind. He became, if not the leader, then the inspirer of the chosen few at Gleyre's. But whether Monet and his friends would actually have abandoned the studio must remain an open question, since Gleyre abandoned them instead: failing eyesight and financial difficulties caused him to shut the studio in January 1864.

Once liberated, however, Monet revelled in his independence. He persuaded his friends to come with him to Chailly, where he and Bazille had spent some time painting during their Easter holiday the previous year. Chailly was a little village on the edge of the forest of Fontainebleau – hallowed ground for those who admired the pioneers of outdoor landscape painting; Barbizon itself was little more than two kilometres away, and revered masters such as Corot, Millet and Diaz were to be seen and even encountered at work in the area. Monet, like his friends, painted his forest scenes in a style that owed much to the older masters; yet even at this stage of his career there is a more noticeable play of light upon people and objects than the Barbizon painters tried to achieve.

In the summer of 1864 Monet returned to the Normandy coast with Bazille. Their headquarters was the Saint Siméon farm, just outside Honfleur, where they could paint both landscapes and the mouth of the Seine. This farm-inn was another well-known painters' haunt: several Barbizon masters had visited it, and Boudin had taken Courbet there after their chance meeting at Le Havre. After Bazille left to resume his medical studies, Monet stayed on, enthusiastically working beside his old friends Boudin and Jongkind. His relationship with his family was deteriorating, despite the good impression made on them by his wealthy, well-bred friend Bazille; but though he stayed away from home, Monet remained at Honfleur until January 1865, when he joined Bazille in his Paris studio.

The hard work of the previous months was rewarded materially as well as artistically: two of Monet's sea-and-shore paintings were accepted by the Salon jury, shown, and favourably reviewed. Readers of this book who have ever mixed up Monet and Manet can take comfort from the fact that some critics and spectators did the same at the Salon – to Manet's annoyance, since he was congratulated on 'his' seascapes while being flayed for perpetrating the *Olympia*.

Monet himself was not present to see his works shown. The Salon was held in May 1865; by early April he had gone back to Chailly, where he was planning to execute an ambitious new work. This was nothing less than a new *Déjeuner sur l'Herbe*: an enormous landscape with figures that must have been intended to establish Monet at a single blow as the leading painter of his generation. Unlike its scandalous predecessor by Manet, this *Déjeuner* was not to feature any nude women. This may have been a concession to puritanism, since Monet certainly hoped to score a success with the picture at the Salon. Alternatively, it may simply indicate Monet's determination to outdo Manet in modernity; after all, Manet's nude, like his composition, was inspired by respect for the past, even if it had been interpreted as a gesture of erotic radicalism. Monet had less sympathy for tradition than any of his contemporaries: he had even boasted of never having visited the Louvre until his friend Renoir dragged him there. On the other hand, his revolutionary approach was expressed technically rather than in terms of subject matter; only in this period does he even show much interest in the human figure. Monet's *Déjeuner* seems to represent an effort of synthesis: to depict his contemporaries, to convey something of the modern spirit, while remaining an exponent of open-air painting and light effects.

For a poor young painter, such a project required tremendous self-confidence and a willingness to put his immediate future at risk: the picture was to measure about six by five metres, and Monet was occupied with it almost exclusively for a year. He painted several landscapes of the district (in part, at least, as preliminary studies), but otherwise his six months at Chailly (April-October 1865) were devoted to sketches and studies for the *Déjeuner*.

66

Some of the time was taken up by infuriating delays, such as waiting for Bazille to turn up. Bazille had agreed to model the male figures, while the females were to be variations on Camille Doncieux, a young woman Monet had recently met, and who had become his mistress. Monet's use of variations on the same model may, as has sometimes been suggested, indicate a certain indifference to human individuality on the part of a master of landscape, colour and light; but it seems simpler to accept the obvious explanation – that Monet could not afford the services of professional models for weeks at a time, and accepted the services of those who would pose without being paid.

When Bazille did arrive, there was a further delay: Monet injured his leg and had to stay in bed. Ironically, therefore, it was Bazille who got some painting done, including one showing the patient staring out dolefully from between the sheets. However, Monet's preliminary work was done by October, and he returned to the studio he shared with Bazille (who, however, soon moved out). There Monet started work on the final version of the painting which had seemed far too large to execute conveniently out of doors. Only after months of effort, in April 1866, did he put it aside unfinished. The reason he gave was lack of money (which was doubtless true as far as it went), but it also seems likely that he was dissatisfied with its progress; at any rate he never attempted to finish it. Its later history was tragic. Monet carried it about with him for years, then, in 1878, left it with his landlord at Argenteuil, Alexandre Flament, as security on the back-rent he owed. He left it with Flament for six years, though he evidently preserved a kind of fondness for it: it was, he told the dealer Durand-Ruel, 'quite mediocre, but a picture I should be very happy to see again'. Unfortunately, when he did see it again large areas had been ruined by damp. After Monet had cut away the affected parts, he divided the remainder into the two large fragments that survive today. The nearest remaining equivalent to the full work is a study in oils, itself a large painting (almost a third the size of the lost *Déjeuner*), which represents a slightly earlier stage in composition, style and costume details.

In the spring of 1866, when it became clear that the *Déjeuner* would not be finished in time for submission to the Salon jury, Monet had to act quickly. After being so well received the previous year, it would have been poor tactics not to submit at all. And so, according to one account, Monet painted a full-length portrait of Camille Doncieux, the *Woman in a Green Dress*, in only four days. This, along with one of his Fontainebleau landscapes of the previous summer, was again accepted and admired.

Claude Monet. *Portrait of Madame Gaudibert.* 1868. Musée du Louvre, Paris.

Left:
Claude Monet. *The River.* 1868. Even before his decisive collaboration with Renoir at La Grenouillère, Monet was obviously fascinated by the pictorial possibilities of reflections in water. These occur again and again in later paintings until, in Monet's works, the whole world dissolves into coloured flowers, reflections and water. Art Institute of Chicago, Illinois (Potter Palmer Collection).

The result of this second success was that Monet began to be known. Working at Ville d'Avray, just outside Paris, where he had moved to avoid his creditors, he found himself able to sell some of his paintings; and now that he appeared to be on the verge of a successful career, his aunt renewed her interest in him and made him a small allowance. For the time being he was secure and could return to ambitious conceptions – though not to the recently abandoned *Déjeuner*.

Monet now carried his passion for working in the open air a stage further, adding the cityscape to his repertoire of 'scapes, and experimenting still more freely with colour and light effects. In the summer he started work on another huge canvas at Ville d'Avray. This was *Women in the Garden*, with four life-sized young women – all modelled by Camille Doncieux – picking flowers. Monet determined to paint the whole thing in the open air, dug a deep trench, and constructed some kind of pulley system that enabled him to raise or lower the picture so that he could work on the appropriate part in relative comfort.

The cost of projects on this scale – the cost in materials, living expenses, sales lost – must have been frightening; and after working on *Women in the Garden* Monet was deep in debt again. He fled from Ville d'Avray to Le Havre. Though he could not know it then, this was a turning point in Monet's fortunes, after which he was to know years of real poverty and suffering. By December 1866 things were so bad that he wrote to Bazille for some pictures he had left in Paris, which he intended to scrape clean and use for new paintings. And, to make matters worse, Camille had become pregnant.

1867 was a disastrous year. *Women in the Garden* was rejected by the Salon jury; in fact, after being relatively broad-minded for a couple of years, the jury savaged most of Monet's friends and allies. Bazille was able to help a little by buying *Women in the Garden* for 2,500 francs payable in instalments of 50 francs a month; and he also managed to sell a still life by Monet to one of his friends for 200 francs. But it was nowhere near enough. In the summer Monet was forced to take refuge with his aunt at Sainte Adresse, since bed and board was the only form of help his family were now prepared to give him. They were also glad to see him separated from Camille, who gave birth to a son, Jean, in July 1867. However, for Monet the separation was merely a financial necessity that was intended to be no more than temporary; but in the event he spent several months with his aunt or staying at Bazille's studio with his friend and Renoir.

Back in Paris, he remained miserably poor. In the spring of 1868 he returned to Le Havre, where he was awarded a silver medal at an International Maritime Exhibition to which, thanks to Boudin, he had been invited. But he remained depressed: as he told Boudin, he sold nothing at the exhibition, and emerged with a medal worth 15 francs. He did receive a commission to paint the wife of a local collector, and he also – at last – sold the *Woman in a Green Dress*. But before he left Le Havre, Monet owed so much money that his canvases were seized and auctioned off at knockdown prices.

Despite a moderate success at the Salon, things were desperate again in the summer, which Monet spent with Camille and Jean at Fécamp, about 20 kilometres up the coast from Le Havre. Late in June he wrote a desperate letter to Bazille begging for help: he had been thrown out of his inn 'naked', his family would do no more for him, he did not know where he would be able to sleep the next night; and then, in an enigmatic' coda, 'I was so depressed yesterday that I was stupid enough to throw myself in the water. Luckily there were no ill effects'. However, he went to see a patron in Le Havre – almost certainly the Monsieur Gaudibert whose wife's portrait Monet had painted – and secured enough help to spend a few months working tranquilly at Fécamp. He still owed money at the local art shop, and asked Bazille to send on any canvases of Monet's that were unused. No doubt one reason for the rock-bottom poverty that Monet and his friends so often touched was the sheer ongoing cost of their materials by comparison with, for example, a writer's or composer's; after a period without sales, artists such as Monet were confronted with the option of stopping work altogether or going without food and fuel.

In 1869 Monet's affairs were in as bad a state as ever on the material level. His submissions were rejected by the Salon jury, which seems increasingly to have identified Monet as the leading subversive of the new generation. And at Bougival on the Seine, where Monet spent the summer of 1869, he was at one time so short of food that Renoir, who was living nearby at Ville d'Avray with his parents, purloined some of their food to keep his friend going. Yet it was that very summer that the two men painted the wonderful series of riverside pictures that may be said to mark the beginning of Impressionism proper (chapter 5). Monet had worked on steadily through the years of deprivation, abandoning his ambitious attempts to render figures in a landscape when this proved (for him) a dead end, and continuing to grow in mastery of colour and effects of light. His paintings of 1869 represent the first flowering of his characteristic genius – but not, as events were to show, the end of his struggles.

Renoir

Pissarro and Monet were the most fanatical of the Impressionists, according to Renoir in his old age. He might have added that he himself was the least fanatical of them, and indeed the least inclined to bother with theories or partisanship of any sort. He threw himself into the adventure of plein-air painting from the beginning, and later stood with his friends when Impressionism became a term of abuse; but he never thought in exclusive terms about the group or felt himself committed for ever to a particular style or technique. Renoir admired the Old Masters and studied their works in the Louvre, an institution which in the eyes of Pissarro and Monet represented the dead hand of the past. He worked in the direction suggested by his experience and intuition, without much thought for popularity; but although he rejected the artistic authority of the Salon and the public, he did what he could to get their support, and was glad of it when at last it came. And while sharing Monet's fascination with effects of light, Renoir also cared for what was being lit – above all, for the human subject, for life and gaiety, for glowing skins and rich textures; and this concern was allied with a

traditionalist's feeling for solid forms and firmly structured designs, features that were eventually to be synthesised with the more fluid art of Renoir's 'pure' Impressionist period.

Pierre Auguste Renoir was born on 25 Febuary 1841 at Limoges, a town famous for its enamelwork and porcelain. Renoir was the only one of the major Impressionists whose origins were working-class: his father, Léonard Renoir, was a tailor in a small and evidently not very successful way of business in the town. Auguste was fourth of the five children who survived into adult life; the fifth, Edmond, was born in Paris, to which the family moved when Auguste was only four. Renoir therefore grew up a

Parisian, remembering nothing of his birthplace, though its artistic tradition was to have some influence with Léonard Renoir when his son came to choose a trade.

In Paris the Renoirs settled in a working-class quarter near the River Seine. Its decaying buildings were magnificently sited between the Louvre and the Tuileries Palace – an anomaly explained by the fact that the buildings had once housed the families of nobles serving in the royal guard. The site cried out for spectacular development; but spectacular developments cost so much money, and involve so many planners and schemes, that in the meantime the crumbling, proletarianised buildings on a site may remain there for decades or generations; and such was the case here. So the young Renoir grew up in the heart of Paris and played in the courtyard of the Louvre which his works were later to adorn. And – in another interesting coincidence of place and name – the road running to the river through the working-class quarter was the Rue d'Argenteuil; and Argenteuil itself was to be one of the places where Impressionism was created.

However, none of that was foreshadowed in Renoir's boyhood, except perhaps in the sketches and cartoons with which legend has decorated his (and almost every other painter's) school books. Such artistic opportunities as came Renoir's way were musical. He was a chorister at the church of Saint Eustache, where the choirmaster happened to be Charles Gounod, then quite unknown but later to be famous as the composer of *Faust*. Gounod was so impressed with Renoir's voice that he tried to persuade the boy to train as a professional singer. But without success: Renoir never lost a certain timidity and fear of public display; and about the same time – when he was 13 and ready to leave school – he was presented with a different kind of opportunity. The owner of a porcelain works in the Rue Vieille du Temple offered to take on Renoir as an apprentice. To both Renoir and his family this seemed a splendid opportunity; it would give the boy an 'artistic' career that any native of Limoges could appreciate; and it meant that Auguste would become a craftsman in his own right, with a safe, steady trade that would give him a living through bad times and good.

Renoir worked at Lévy Brothers' porcelain factory from 1854 to 1858. During that time he graduated from painting little bouquets of flowers – for which he was paid the minuscule sum of five sous a dozen – to representing fairly sophisticated figures. The

wares he decorated must have been of quite high quality, since they were fakes – pieces made for export and labelled 'Sèvres' so that buyers would take them for products of the famous porcelain centre. Renoir seems not to have minded. He earned enough to help his parents buy a house for their old age at Louveciennes, and if he had any ambitions larger than being a master craftsman, they were kept well under control. He spent his lunchtimes at the Louvre and sometimes of an evening took lessons in oil painting; but, true to his philosophy of letting life carry him along like a cork in the current of a river, he made no attempt to leave his job until events forced his hand.

Events duly obliged. In 1858 Lévy Brothers had to close down, since the firm was unable to compete with factories using the new, cheap transfer-printing method of decorating porcelain. Renoir tried to keep the workshop going as a co-operative, only to find that people actually preferred the standardised, mass-produced article. A similar fate was overtaking many traditional crafts in the 19th century, and understandably enough Renoir always retained a craftsman's mistrust of mechanisation. On this occasion at least there was a beneficial side effect: Renoir was launched into the world again. Otherwise, given his acquiescent temperament and no-nonsense approach to painting (on canvas as well as on porcelain), it seems possible that he would never have taken a step so impractical as to become a professional artist.

For some time after leaving Lévy's, Renoir lived from hand to mouth, painting fans, designing murals for cafés, and finally decorating sun-blinds. Since most of the blinds were bought by missionaries intent on converting the heathen, they performed the function of stained glass in their tropical churches, and pious subjects were much in demand. Renoir became particularly adept at these, turning them out at an amazing rate – filling in with plenty of conventionalised clouds – and started to make a very

satisfactory living. He was able to put by money regularly, and convinced his parents
that he should use it to finance a proper course of study at the École des Beaux-Arts:
when he painted a scene showing Eve being tempted by the serpent, the painter Laporte
declared that he had real talent, and Monsieur and Madame Renoir gave their consent.
Unlike other painters' parents, they seem to have been easily convinced; but then
Renoir, though only 21, had been earning his own living for the best part of eight years,
so the whole episode may have been no more than a nominal, respectful gesture on his
part. If so, it was typical of Renoir's sense of 'form', which was his equivalent to the
aristocratic codes and artistic credos held by other Impressionists.

Renoir took the entrance examination of the École des Beaux-Arts and passed it
comfortably enough, though without special distinction: the top 80 examinees were
admitted, and of these Renoir came 68th. In April 1862 he proceeded to enrol under
Gleyre, whom he remembered in later years with a certain tolerance – 'A second-rate
schoolmaster but a good man' – unlike Monet, who detested the Swiss and refused to
describe himself as 'pupil of Gleyre' at his first Salon appearance. Gleyre seems to have
taught Renoir nothing and to have disapproved of his colouristic tendencies; but he let
Renoir go his own way and even encouraged him to keep on working. Still, there was a
fundamental difference of attitude between the two men. Annoyed by the freedom with
which Renoir sketched, Gleyre said to him one day 'Young man, you are very talented,
but I suppose you only took up painting to amuse yourself'. Characteristically Renoir
answered 'That's right – if it didn't amuse me I shouldn't do it'. In his old age Renoir
confirmed the truth of this widely circulated story, but actually it seems out of
character: even in his maturity he was a rather timid, compliant man who tended to do
as he was asked rather than cause a fuss. As a student he was quiet, hardworking and

Left:
Pierre Auguste Renoir. *Alfred Sisley and his Wife.* About 1868. In his old age Renoir described Sisley as 'a delightful human being' – a man whose tender concern for women made him irresistible. In this double portrait, Sisley's protectiveness and his wife's trust are conveyed by their attitudes. A picture of cool brilliance, touching yet restrained. Wallraf-Richartz Museum, Cologne.

Right:
Pierre Auguste Renoir. *The Artist's Father.* 1869. St Louis Art Museum, Missouri.

Far right:
Pierre Auguste Renoir. *Skaters in the Bois de Boulogne.* 1868. Like Monet, Renoir painted snowpieces partly in order to analyse shadow-effects; but although he adopts Monet's high viewpoint, he also captures the bustling enjoyment of the crowd. Renoir none the less disliked working in the cold, described snow as 'the leprosy of nature', and abandoned the genre.

dutiful – which made it the more galling, as he wryly recalled, that he, hidden away in his corner, was denounced more vigorously than the rowdy 'bohemian' students, who shouted, broke the window panes and upset the teacher. He was most often in trouble with Signol, the anatomy instructor, whose fanatical conviction that line was the basis of all art led him to warn Renoir: 'You are in danger of becoming another Delacroix!' Delacroix, the great colourist, was already one of Renoir's heroes, but if he made a witty rebuttal on this occasion, it has not been preserved.

According to Renoir, the chief benefit he derived from the Beaux-Arts was being forced to draw and to make anatomical studies from the model again and again – the sort of discipline, he said, that was so boring you wouldn't put up with it if you hadn't paid fees for the privilege of doing it. But studying and copying at the Louvre meant infinitely more to Renoir. He had visited it often since the first time he had been there as a child (and neighbour), and he was to become steeped in the works of the Old Masters – particularly the Venetians (Titian, Giorgione, Veronese) and Rubens, who were colourists as well as artists with a sense of the monumental. This sense never entirely deserted Renoir, even when he was most closely involved with his friend Monet, who detested the Old Masters and painted landscapes in which the forms increasingly dissolved into a swirling play of colour and light.

Renoir also loved the 18th-century French painters – Watteau, Boucher, Fragonard – for the gaiety and delicate charm of their *fêtes champêtres* (scenes of light-hearted enjoyment in the open air) and their rosy, good-naturedly sensual nudes. These were to figure so largely in his own work that Renoir is on one level virtually a 19th-century equivalent to the earlier masters, though with a more straightforward feeling for the pleasures of the scenes than the sophisticated, self-consciously frivolous 18th century. Here too a comparison with Monet helps us to understand both artists better. Monet's *fête champêtre*, the ambitious *Déjeuner sur l'Herbe*, has many qualities but not the particular kind of gaiety, intimacy and humanity that Renoir was to achieve again and

again, and apparently without effort. Monet, vibrantly alive to light, colour and movement, was essentially a painter of nature for whom the representation of humanity became increasingly irrelevant. Renoir is a painter of humanity – above all of women – for whom open-air painting was a part rather than the whole of this art. The conflicting impulses of the 1860s – between capturing the passing moment and creating solid Old Master forms, between tradition and realism, ambition and innovation – account for the rather irregular development of Renoir's talent in the 1860s.

His effective introduction to open-air painting occurred at Chailly, thanks to Monet and the other friends he made at Gleyre's. For some months he seems to have worked at the studio in isolation; many of the more frivolous students, sporting 'arty' velvet jackets and 'wideawake' hats (low-crowned and broad-brimmed), were inclined to mock the thin, nervous-looking young workman in his porcelain-painter's smock. Then Renoir met the tall, well-bred Bazille, who became his close friend and introduced him to the wider life of Paris. The arrival of Sisley and Monet made Renoir for the first time one of a serious-minded group of artists, and further broadened his horizons. At about the same time he also met Fantin-Latour, who was working as a copyist at the Louvre and helped Renoir understand the works there. Renoir in turn dragged his reluctant friend Monet round the Louvre, and seems to have persuaded his friends to spend part of the winter working there.

At Easter 1864 Renoir went to work at Chailly with his friends, and according to his own account had an accidental meeting with the Barbizon-school painter Diaz that influenced his development. The meeting came about through Renoir's curious faculty for attracting hostile crowds. As a result of some comic misunderstandings he had already barely avoided being lynched on two occasions – once as a sexual degenerate believed to have exposed himself in public, and on another occasion as a baby-kidnapper in a park, whence he had been rescued by Bazille. At Chailly it was Renoir's smock that started the trouble: it attracted the attention of some roughs who had noticed him painting, and their horseplay was starting to get out of hand when Diaz appeared and drove them off with a big stick; it was probably a larger stick than most, since it was needed to support Diaz's wooden leg. After this he looked at Renoir's painting and told him that it was well drawn but too dark; it was faithful to academic convention but not to reality. Since Renoir was already an admirer of Diaz – he later said you could almost smell the woodland odours in Diaz's paintings – he took the older man's advice seriously and lightened his palette.

Renoir was to change styles and techniques several times in the next few years, but his experience of painting in the forest of Fontainebleau seems to have notably increased his self-confidence. A painting he had submitted to the Salon, *Esmeralda*, was accepted by the jury and shown; but despite the accolade this represented, Renoir decided it was a bad picture and destroyed it when it was returned to him. At the Salon he called himself 'pupil of Gleyre', but though he had received less than two years' formal training he decided to remain masterless after the closing of Gleyre's studio – a decision perhaps made easier by shortage of money for fees.

Renoir seems to have been very hard up during 1864-5 despite some portrait commissions. His parents had settled at the village of Ville d'Avray outside Paris, and Renoir moved about a good deal from one poor lodging to another. In 1865 his prospects seemed to improve when his *Portrait of William Sisley* and a landscape were accepted at the Salon; if his work attracted little attention, he may still have felt himself better off than Manet, whose *Olympia* was mercilessly abused. In the spring, Renoir and Sisley went to work at Marlotte, another of the little villages near the forest of Fontainebleau. They stayed at the popular Mother Anthony's Inn, and possibly at the house of Renoir's new friend Jules Le Coeur, an architect-turned-painter who lived with a woman in her twenties called Clémence Tréhot. Renoir now met Gustave Courbet for the first time and was evidently impressed by his overwhelming personality. He painted only a few pictures directly in Courbet's style, but the great Realist's influence remained visible in Renoir's conceptions for several years afterwards. Courbet's use of a palette knife to achieve his bold effects did not suit Renoir, who found the paint applied in this way impossible to rework to his satisfaction. But Courbet's monumental forms and feeling for humble realities appealed to the side of Renoir that was not content with depicting nature but sought to achieve the strong, organised forms he had admired in the Old Masters. In the '60s Renoir combined such forms, a little uncomfortably, with summery lyricism or with mythological trappings intended to placate the Salon jury.

In the autumn of 1865 Renoir and Sisley went down the Seine by boat to Rouen, and then returned to Marlotte for the winter. In January Renoir painted an interior of *Mother Anthony's Inn* which shows the influence of Courbet but has a slightly stiff, almost 'primitive' quality emphasised by the flat, depthless presentation and the china-dog poodle (with one paw missing – lost in an accident) staring out of the picture, on guard against the spectator.

In the spring Renoir met 18-year-old Lise Tréhot, the sister of Le Coeur's Clémence. She was to be his companion and chief model for the next six years, appearing in a series of portraits varying widely in mood, style and setting. Sisley made a more binding commitment: he married a young model and, apart from a month on the coast in August, henceforth saw far less of Renoir. Meanwhile Renoir's run of luck with the Salon jury came to an end: though Corot and Daubigny favoured his submissions, the majority were strongly against them. In July he moved into a studio in the Rue Visconti with Bazille, who was to be his closest friend over the next few years; it seems likely that Bazille, who at least had a regular allowance, discreetly subsidised the joint housekeeping.

They did not lose contact with Monet, who turned up in Paris from time to time and stayed in the Rue Visconti. It was Monet who inspired Renoir to paint his first cityscapes, though his versions are more picturesque and saturated with the human presence than his friend's. A picture like *The Champs Élysées during the Paris International Exhibition of 1867* has a kind of quaintness that invites comparison with Manet's painting of the Exhibition, rather than with a Monet such as *St Germain l'Auxerrois*. The differences in outlook between Monet and Renoir persisted even when they tackled the same subjects and worked side by side; yet their eventual partnership was to be a decisive one for the history of Impressionism.

In 1867, however, Renoir was still working for recognition at the Salon, for which he painted Lise as *Diana*. The picture was an uneasy compromise: on one level a Courbet-like nude, on another the goddess of the chase; the slain deer was a kind of wink to the wise, since it fitted in with the mythical subject but was also a trade-mark of Courbet's. The compromise was unsuccessful, even in material terms: the jury rejected *Diana*.

Renoir was far more successful with de-mythologised paintings of Lise such as the portrait of her with a parasol, which was accepted for the 1868 Salon. In the winter of 1867-68 Renoir and Bazille were even more short of money than usual, and used each other as models; two interesting portraits date from this time. Manet particularly admired Renoir's painting of Bazille at his easel, and Renoir's admiration for the older master is apparent in several paintings, including *Lise with a Parasol* and the double portrait of *Alfred Sisley and his Wife*, though in neither case was Renoir's personality submerged: as in his relationship with Monet, a fundamental taste for light and life always showed through.

In retrospect it seems like sheer bad luck that Renoir failed to become a commercially successful artist in the 1860s. He certainly tried hard to please, and had considerable success in getting his pictures shown at the Salons. Yet he failed to secure the regular commissions a painter needs in order to afford his art, and in the summer of 1869 he was in such straits that he and Lise went to stay with his parents, who had retired to the village of Ville d'Avray; and even there he was often so poor that he could not afford to buy paints. As it happened, Monet and Camille were not far away, at Bougival, and they were even worse off than Renoir; on occasion it was not a question of buying paints but of Renoir taking bread from his parents' house to feed the Monets. Yet between miseries the two painters managed to work whenever they had sufficient materials, making advances in the rendering of nature that were to be central to the history of Impressionism. As far as Renoir is concerned, the freer style and purer colours of this period were to be the basis for the splendidly festive open-air paintings of the 1870s, which are his best-known, and for most people his greatest, works.

Bazille

Frédéric Bazille. *The Pink Dress*. 1865. A
singularly charming and poetic early work. It is
interesting to compare this with the figure
paintings done by Bazille's friend Monet at
about the same time. Musée du Louvre, Paris.

Frédéric Bazille has been the unluckiest of the Impressionists in terms of his
posthumous reputation. The youngest of the entire group, he was the first to die,
before his art had reached even the earliest phase of maturity; and his life was
uneventful – free from the scandals, and also from the dramas of poverty and suffering,
that are the stuff of legend. As a result, Bazille is a somewhat neglected figure, rarely
discussed as a painter in his own right: he appears in memoirs and biographies as an
extra – as the companion and financially helpful friend of the principal actor, whether
he be Monet or Renoir. Yet even as its stands, Bazille's achievement is by no means
negligible, and hints at a distinctive outlook that might have given him his own special
place in the history of Impressionism.

Above:
Pierre August Renoir. *Portrait of Frédéric Bazille at his Easel*. 1867. Painted while Renoir was sharing his friend's Paris studio; Bazille returned the compliment by painting Renoir. Manet was the first owner of the portrait, though it is not clear whether he bought it or received it as a gift from the artist. Musée du Louvre, Paris.

Right:
Frédéric Bazille. *La Toilette*. 1870. Submitted to the Salon jury in 1870. It was rejected – ironically, in view of the success of Bazille's less conventional *Bathers*. The exoticism of the picture, and the prominence given to colourful, meticulously rendered fabrics, suggests that it was painted specially for the Salon. Musée Fabre, Montpellier.

Frédéric Bazille. *L'Ambulance Improvisée*
(Monet after his Accident). 1866. A pathetic
little picture of Monet confined to bed just
when he was about to start an enormously
ambitious picnic painting to rival Manet's
Déjeuner. Bazille, who had studied medicine,
improvised some kind of drip contraption to
ease the pain in Monet's injured leg. Musée du
Louvre, Paris.

Bazille was born on 6 December 1841, in the South of France: at Montpellier, the chief town of Languedoc. His family were wealthy and cultivated, and Bazille studied medicine at Montpellier University before moving to Paris. He was supposed to study medicine in the capital too, but soon began to devote much of his time to painting. Fortunately his parents were more understanding than Monet's: they agreed to let him divide his time between medicine and painting, and in 1864, when he failed his medical examinations, acquiesced in his choice of an artistic career. Though his allowance does not seem to have been princely, Bazille was never in actual want; at most he may occasionally have pawned his watch to pay his bills – or his friends' bills, which are among the major topics of Impressionist correspondence surviving from the 1860s.

At Gleyre's according to Renoir, it was Bazille who struck up an acquaintance with him one evening, when the two men were going home in the same direction. Renoir, or his son Jean, who tells the story, may well have telescoped several events into a single walk, which otherwise must have been singularly action-packed. Walking through the Luxembourg Gardens, Bazille had barely managed to begin a majestic dictum – 'The big classic compositions are finished' – when Renoir exercised his fatal gift for attracting a hostile crowd. He started rocking the unattended pram of a howling baby, and succeeded in pacifying it; but the nurse, who was presumably conditioned to noise, at once came to find out what was wrong; and when she saw a strange man leaning over her charge, she called on her hussar boyfriend and the assembled mothers to lynch the inoffensive Renoir. The tall, well-dressed Bazille calmed them down, presented his card to the park attendant, and carried off his proletarian friend unscathed except for a fright and a reprimand.

The incident illustrates quite clearly the gulf that separated the 19th-century gentleman from the rest of the population (not only workers but shopkeepers and all but the most important functionaries). It went beyond income – or rather, differences in income were so great that the full-fed, groomed, dressed and educated lady or gentleman behaved, looked, sounded, and even felt to the touch like a separate and superior kind of animal. Bazille, like Manet and Degas, possessed this quality; unlike them, however, he had a strong vein of camaraderie that prompted him to minimise differences rather than remain aloof and distant. On his first meeting with Renoir he is supposed to have proclaimed the necessity of painting contemporary daily life, rescued his new friend from the mob, and also, over a beer, confessed that he sought Renoir out because he had seen him draw and 'felt that he was somebody'. Not a bad way to start a friendship.

In fact, Bazille seems to have been a kind of link-man between the Impressionists in the 1860s, and especially between Renoir and Monet, whose friendship appears to have

been rather in abeyance between about 1864 and 1869. After the trips to Chailly in 1863-4, Bazille painted with Monet in Honfleur in 1864; he also met Monet's parents at Sainte Adresse, perhaps because Monet hoped his so-presentable friend would give his parents a more favourable idea of painting as a career. In the following year Bazille shared a studio with Monet, painted his friend lying dolefully in a bed at Chailly after injuring his leg, and then posed for two of the figures in Monet's version of *Déjeuner sur l'Herbe*. The sharing of a studio was, among other things, a way in which Bazille could help his friends; and Renoir moved in with him in 1866, and again in 1867, joined for a while by Monet. (It was towards the end of Renoir's second stay that he painted his portrait of Bazille.) The four friends from Gleyre's were briefly united, since Sisley lived at the same address, though his means presumably allowed him to have a separate studio. Apart from this discreetly helpful 'sharing', Bazille effectively gave Monet an allowance by buying *Women in the Garden* for the (then) inflated price of 2,500 francs, paying in monthly instalments of 50 francs. And on numerous occasions he responded to his friends' direct requests for supplies of money or painting materials – though Monet was often so desperate that Bazille's slowness of response made him indignantly angry. It says a good deal for Bazille that he never tired of his friends' importunities, however justified; and it says as much for them that they forgave him his money and forbearance.

So much for Bazille the friend. As an artist he seems to have had advanced ideas at least as early as most of the Impressionists. Right at the beginning of his friendship

82

with Renoir he was asserting his faith in nature and the present; and as early as 1866, while waiting for the Salon jury's decision on his first submissions, he wrote to his parents: 'the subject is not very important provided what I do is interesting as painting. I chose the modern era because that is what I understand best, what has most life in it for people who are alive.' He adds, pessimistically, 'that's why I shall be rejected', which proved correct as far as *Girl at the Piano*, a work of which he thought highly, was concerned. But he had also shrewdly submitted a more conventional still life, and that was accepted.

Even before this, Bazille had painted some interesting land- and seascapes around Chailly and Honfleur. *The Pink Dress*, another painting done in 1865, shows more of Bazille's personal style. The colours are as bright as those used by any Impressionist at that time, but they are used to give a more jewel-like decorative effect. This is reinforced by the clear forms and the firmly established mood of tranquillity. The picture gains a mysterious charm from the girl's pose, half-turned from the spectator so that her face is averted, and this perhaps makes it more effective than the otherwise similar *View of the Village*, with a girl in the foreground and the village rising up the hillside behind her, which was painted three years later. Bazille's best-known painting, *The Artist's Family*, displays a similar mood of tranquillity verging on sadness. The 'composed' grouping and utter stillness of the scene – life suspended as if for the photographer – is quite un-Impressionist in effect. By contrast, one of Bazille's last paintings, *The Artist's Studio, Rue de la Condamine*, shows Bazille and his friends,

Frédéric Bazille. *The Artist's Family*. 1867. Shown at the Salon of 1868. It was painted in the open air, though retouched in 1869; the faces in particular have a 'superimposed' quality in marked contrast to the natural setting. Bazille's father and mother are seated on the bench; the painter himself stands on the extreme left. Musée du Louvre, Paris.

including Manet and the novelist Zola, ranged about the room in the free-and-easy manner of people who are thoroughly at home and occupied – perhaps an involuntary comment on the pleasures of bohemian as contrasted with family life.

On the evidence of his surviving works, Bazille remained more concerned with mood and structure than his friends did in the later 1860s. Though he painted in the open air, for example, he did so after making plans and sketches in the studio; and if his landscapes are rendered increasingly 'Impressionistically', the human figures stand out firmly against the backgrounds, giving the picture its predominant mood.

Had he lived, Bazille would probably have been swept away by the joyful surge of experiment and discovery among the Impressionists in the 1870s which made plein-air painting their central concern – and then, perhaps, like Cézanne, he would have integrated the general discoveries into his distinctive approach, going beyond anything that could be called Impressionism. Constructing a posthumous career for Bazille in this fashion would be a pointless exercise if it were not necessary to deny that he is only an aborted Impressionist.

1870 promised to be a good year for Bazille. In May his *Bathers* was accepted at the Salon and, he told his parents, it was well hung and much talked about; not all the comments were flattering, but Bazille felt that he was now known as an artist who could not be ignored. Then, in July, the Franco-Prussian War broke out. A few weeks later Bazille volunteered and was accepted into the Zouaves, one of the most romantically fierce of cavalry regiments. He served through three drearily unromantic months of defeats, and was killed in November during the French retreat from Beaune-la-Rolande. In old age, Renoir remembered him with a pained and wistful affection – the chivalrous Bazille, so pure in heart; 'the friend of my youth'.

Frédéric Bazille. *Summer Scene, Bathers.* 1869. Shown at the Salon of 1870, where it was well received. To the very end, human figures were important in Bazille's art: by contrast with Monet's and Renoir's La Grenouillère paintings, the figures dominate the landscape, not vice versa. Fogg Art Museum, Harvard University, Cambridge, Massachusetts (Gift of M and Mme F. Meynier de Salinelles).

Sisley

Alfred Sisley. *Avenue of Chestnut Trees near La Celle-St Cloud.* 1867. Southampton Art Gallery.

Alfred Sisley's was the quietest, steadiest talent among the Impressionists. He devoted himself almost exclusively to landscapes, executed with a touch of poetry that might have been expected to appeal to people unable to sympathise with Monet's more 'objective' outlook. Yet in his lifetime Sisley received almost no encouragement outside his immediate group of friends, and his pictures sold for prices that were often ludicrous.

In the first half of Sisley's life this was relatively unimportant, since his family was wealthy. His father and mother were English, and Sisley himself never acquired French nationality. But he was born in Paris (on 30 October 1839), and was brought up in the city until he reached the age of 18. Then his father sent him to London to learn English and get some commercial experience. Like most future painters he neglected business and spent much of his time in the galleries and museums, where he saw and admired works by Constable and Turner; so if English painting influenced the Impressionists, directly or indirectly, in the 1860s, it is most likely to have been through Sisley.

After four otherwise uneventful years in London (1857-61), Sisley returned to Paris and persuaded his parents to let him study painting. In 1862 he enrolled under Gleyre and quickly struck up a friendship with Monet, also a newly arrived pupil; then, through Monet, he met Renoir and Bazille, and these four formed a common artistic front. Although the oldest, Sisley had nothing of Monet's flamboyance, and left to himself might have been a docile enough student; he apparently planned to compete for the Rome Prize, an enormously prestigious award involving a five-year studentship in Rome. However, when Gleyre's studio closed, Sisley went off to Chailly with his friends and worked there in the open air. He made no further attempt to meet the deadline for the Rome Prize, and he also steered clear of the teaching studios, though

his means would presumably have allowed him to pick his own master. Like his friends, Sisley now resolved to learn from Nature herself.

For a year or two before his marriage, he and Renoir were particularly close, and Sisley probably helped Renoir to earn a little money by having him paint a portrait of his father, William Sisley (1864). The two artists confronted Nature together: they put up at Mother Anthony's in Marlotte in the spring of 1865, took a trip down the Seine together in the autumn, and then wintered back at Marlotte. Although they were less intimate after Sisley's marriage, Renoir evidently continued to admire his friend. His affection shines out of the double portrait he painted of Sisley and his wife in about 1868. The Sisleys are shown as an elegant, well-groomed pair, and their finery is lovingly rendered; but the predominant sensation given by the picture is one of exquisite tenderness: protective on the part of Sisley, trusting on that of his wife. In old age, Renoir's feelings remained unchanged: Sisley, he remarked, was 'a delightful human being'.

Although Sisley was committed to working in the open air, his technique remained relatively conservative all through the 1860s, despite his trips with Renoir and contacts with Monet at Honfleur. Whereas both his friends were experimenting with a lighter palette and brush-strokes of pure colour, Sisley continued to paint in the more sombre style of Corot. This was evidently a matter of temperament rather than lack of revolutionary ardour. Two of Sisley's paintings were accepted by the Salon in 1866; he married in the same year and became a father in 1867. But if he was tempted to think of himself as a worldly success, rejection by the Salon of 1867 must have disillusioned him, and he was one of those who signed the petition for a new Salon des Refusés. Though he was intermittently successful at the official Salon, around 1870 he was beginning to practise an unmistakably Impressionist technique, abandoning the dark tones and sharp outlines of such paintings as *View of Montmartre, Painted from the Cité des Fleurs* (1869). His views of the Canal St Martin and similar subjects of 1870-72 represent an abrupt advance. The palette is lighter, the colours are purer, and the pictures are now suffused with a sense of atmosphere. As such works indicate, Sisley's temperament was already formed, and would persist through any subsequent changes of technique (his subject matter – landscape – was never to change). His melancholy, poetic art seems to have been an accurate reflection of his personality, so reticent and fastidious that he has always been the least documented of the major Impressionists.

Sisley's slow development may reflect a lack of full commitment to painting. According to Renoir, Sisley, though socially shy, was irresistible to women – a pleasant if time-consuming distraction from art; and his wealthy background seems to have encouraged him to retain an essentially amateur outlook. If so, the Franco-Prussian War – a financial and personal disaster for Sisley – may actually have come as a heavily disguised blessing to the artist in him.

Above:
Alfred Sisley. *View of Montmartre, Painted from the Cité des Fleurs.* 1869. When this was painted, Montmartre was a little village on a hill just outside Paris, which was in fact about to swallow it up. Manet and his friends moved to the nearby Batignolles quarter at about this time, and later in the century Montmartre itself became the favourite haunt of rebellious artists such as Toulouse-Lautrec and Utrillo; their music-hall and street scenes increased the fame of the area. After the First World War the artistic community moved south of the River Seine, though Montmartre remained popular with tourists. Musée Municipale, Grenoble.

Above right:
Alfred Sisley. *The Canal St Martin, Paris.* 1870. This and the *Canal St Martin* of 1872 are among a number of peaceful, unpretentious canal studies by Sisley. Musée du Louvre, Paris.

Below right:
Alfred sisley. *The Canal St Martin, Paris.* 1872. Musée du Louvre, Paris.

Morisot

As a group, the Impressionists were to be the most abused painters of the 19th century. In the circumstances it must have seemed unlikely that a woman – and especially a woman who was well born and well off – would join them. But Berthe Morisot was such a woman: she joined the group, and she stayed with it through thick and thin.

Berthe Morisot was born on 14 January 1841 at Bourges, the capital of the Cher department some 200 kilometres south of Paris. Her father was the Prefect (administrative head) of the department, a position of considerable eminence; so Morisot was brought up in ease and comfort, and never in her life experienced money worries. In 1855 the family moved to Passy, on the western edge of Paris, and this gave her a chance to study painting, for which both she and her sister Edma had already shown some talent; Edma was Berthe's constant companion until 1869, when she married and gave up painting for good.

Over the next few years Berthe Morisot studied under reputable teachers and dutifully copied Old Master paintings at the Louvre, where she met Manet's friend Fantin-Latour. But she was already finding her own way, suggesting to her current master, Guichard, that she should start painting out of doors. Though a pupil of Delacroix, Guichard was shocked – but perhaps on sexist rather than artistic grounds.

Berthe Morisot. *The Harbour at Lorient*. 1869. The lady with the parasol is Morisot's sister Edma. Manet, who had quite recently used Berthe Morisot as the model for one of the group in his *Balcony,* was so delighted with the picture that Morisot made him a present of it. National Gallery of Art, Washington, DC (Ailsa Mellon Bruce Collection).

He was soon to warn Berthe's mother that the girl was in danger of becoming too passionately involved in painting, which he evidently considered would be a disaster. Since she would not have to earn a living by whatever she did, Guichard presumably objected on the grounds that professional painters were not suitable company for a well-brought-up young lady (which was not complimentary to his own trade), or that the female sex was too delicate to endure the rejections and harsh criticisms that were part of a painter's existence. If so, time was to prove Guichard wrong on both counts.

In 1861 Berthe Morisot found the teacher she needed in Camille Corot, who, after long neglect, had become an established master in the 1850s. Corot normally refused to accept pupils, but he was evidently charmed by the Morisot sisters: he allowed them to work with him at Ville d'Avray where he lived, and became a regular dinner guest at the Morisots' house. A little later the Morisots studied under one of Corot's pupils, Achille François Oudinot, met the famous masters Daubigny and Daumier and the fashionable Carolus-Duran, took up sculpture, holidayed in the Pyrenees, in Brittany, in Normandy ... At this point in her life Berthe Morisot gave every indication of being a highly successful young woman, with a circle of distinguished friends and an enviable but not-too-excessive reputation as a painter who had one or two canvases accepted each year at the Salon from 1864.

Then in 1868 Fantin-Latour introduced her to Édouard Manet while she was copying in the Louvre. They rapidly became close friends, and in the autumn of that year Morisot posed for one of the figures in Manet's *The Balcony*, which was shown at the Salon in 1869. She appears in several of Manet's paintings, notably a black-clad head and shoulders and a fresher, more youthful full-length portrait. Although never Manet's pupil, she now looked to him for guidance, having quarrelled with Oudinot. And when Manet did take as a pupil the striking-looking young painter Eva Gonzalès, Berthe Morisot was distinctly jealous, remarking bitterly that 'all his [Manet's] admiration is concentrated on Mlle Gonzalès', and deriving a good deal of satisfaction from the difficulties Manet was experiencing in painting the other woman's portrait. A little later she noted with satisfaction that Manet was praising her fulsomely: 'It seems that what I do is decidedly better than Eva Gonzalès'. Whether these excitements and jealousies extended beyond the professional sphere remains a matter for speculation.

At the Salon of 1870 Berthe Morisot showed two pictures. One was *The Harbour at Lorient,* which was probably a kind of epithalamium: the girl in it is Berthe's sister Edma, who married a naval officer stationed at Lorient in the year the work was painted (1869). Manet praised it so enthusiastically that Berthe Morisot gave it to him; it was one of several of her pictures that he owned. Her other Salon entry, a portrait of her mother and sister, fared less happily at Manet's hands. She was so uncertain of its quality that she asked Manet's advice; and he helpfully offered to retouch it – which he did so extensively and with such abandon that she was torn between her fears of showing a 'caricature' and her reluctance to wound Manet's feelings by withdrawing the picture altogether. Eventually she decided to show, and was relieved to find that the picture attracted little attention.

Although Manet's influence on Berthe Morisot was a powerful one, she continued to make other artistic friends whose opinion she valued – notably Puvis de Chavannes, whose vein of hieratic historical fantasy was out of step with all the movements of the time, and only came into its own with the advent of Symbolism. Berthe Morisot's own style remained free, fresh and distinctively light-toned, and it is possible that she had some influence on Manet; at any rate it was a year after meeting her that he made his first sustained experiments in open-air painting at Boulogne. They were to remain close over the coming years, but it was to be the pupil, not the master, who threw herself wholeheartedly into the Impressionist movement.

Edouard Manet. *Portrait of Berthe Morisot.* 1872. Berthe Morisot was close to Manet from 1868, and he painted her several times. Private Collection.

Right:
Paul Cézanne. *Portrait of the Artist's Father Reading L'Événement.* 1866–68. The emphasis on the title of the newspaper is a compliment to Cézanne's friend Emile Zola, who worked for *L'Événement* as its art critic; his collected articles were published in book form with a dedicatory letter to Cézanne. National Gallery of Art, Washington, DC (Collection of Mr and Mrs Paul Mellon).

Cézanne

Above:
Pierre Auguste Renoir. *Portrait of Paul Cézanne.* 1880. As always, Renoir softens his male portraits. Even the cantankerous Cézanne is made to look quite benign. This pastel, which pre-dates Renoir's break with Impressionism, has a modelled fullness that anticipates Renoir's later manner.

Of the painters discussed so far, most experienced some degree of difficulty in breaking with the academic style, but then developed steadily, without abrupt changes of direction. Cézanne is the exception: until he was past 30 he painted in a violent, morbid, late-Romantic style that seemed to have no connection with the art of the academies or the development of contemporaries such as Monet. Cézanne arrived at Impressionism in a leap, at the eleventh hour, finding in nature the stabilising, objective element his personality needed to interact with; and in time he was to work his way out of Impressionism to a still more radical art.

Paul Cézanne was born on 19 January 1839 at Aix-en-Provence in the South of France. His father, Louis Auguste Cézanne, had succeeded in business as a hat merchant, and made himself one of the town's leading bankers. He was the domineering, self-righteous type of man who plays the tyrant at home while keeping outsiders at a distance. Even when Cézanne was a grown man, Louis Auguste opened his letters; and Cézanne remained dependent on his father financially – and was, it seems, dominated by him personally – right down to Louis Auguste's death in Cézanne's 47th year. The psychological and material influence of this relationship was probably responsible for some of the stranger aspects of Cézanne's character: the sudden bursts of temper, the secretiveness, the alternations of affection and mistrust in his relations with friends and fellow-artists.

His schooldays were brightened by the companionship of two boys with whom he swore an oath of life-long friendship in true 19th-century sentimental style. The friends were the novelist-to-be Émile Zola and Baptistin Baille, who became a polytechnic professor. Zola later described their expeditions into the countryside in idyllic terms: friendship, swimming, the poetry of Victor Hugo and Alfred de Musset, dreams of love, life and glory. In 1858 Zola left for Paris, and Cézanne wrote to him regularly, including quantities of humorous verse and schoolboy Latin that make touching reading in the light of his later development. He was already working at the drawing academy at Aix, but also obeyed his father's wishes by studying law at the university.

By 1860 Cézanne knew he wanted to be a painter, but he was unable to make much headway against his father's opposition. For month after month Zola – himself lonely and struggling in Paris – expected Cézanne's arrival, intermittently plying his friend with a judicious bystander's advice about how to handle his father. In the event it was not until April 1861 that Cézanne gave up his law studies and moved to Paris. He worked at the Académie Suisse, where he met Pissarro, but he found his progress there so disappointing that he went back to Aix within a few months. Zola has described the despairs and resolutions, packings and unpackings that preceded his friend's departure; they indicate an inner turmoil – and an inner uncertainty – apparently more intense than existed in any other major artist among Cézanne's contemporaries.

For a time Cézanne seems to have given up painting in disgust, though, while working in his father's bank, he occupied himself by scribbling and sketching in a ledger. By the summer of 1862 he was painting once more, and by November he was ready to try again in Paris. This time he persisted, painting on through rejections and periods of poverty; his father seems to have kept him on a short rein, and occasionally we hear the cry of the really poor artist – 'paints are scarce here, and very expensive, misery, misery!' In order to cope with life, Cézanne developed a deliberately bearish and eccentric manner, thickening his Provençal accent, boasting of his dirtiness and defying the artistic authorities; his paraded rebellions may have been caused by the rejections he endured, but they also made future rejections more certain. He, who in 1861 had written of the Salon as the proper place for a clash between all styles and tastes, was boasting in 1865 that he would send in canvases 'which will make the Institute blush with rage and despair'. Not surprisingly, Cézanne's paintings were consistently rejected by the Salon jury, and despite the advocacy of Zola his public

Left:
Paul Cézanne. *Uncle Dominique (The Man in the Blue Cap).* About 1865–66. Metropolitan Museum of Art, New York (Wolfe Fund, 1951, from the Museum of Modern Art, Lizzie P. Bliss Collection).

Below:
Paul Cézanne. *Head of an Old Man.* About 1865–68. In early works such as this one, Cézanne's use of paint anticipates by decades the work of Van Gogh and many later Expressionists. The thick paint and vigorous, unconcealed brush-strokes contribute to the impression of the man's age and strength. Musée du Louvre, Paris.

Right:
Paul Cézanne. *Portrait of Marie Cézanne.* About 1867–69. A portrait of the artist's sister, done in his early manner. St Louis Art Museum, St Louis, Missouri.

record throughout the entire 1860s was one of unrelieved failure.

Cézanne's actual work during this period tells us much about his inner turmoil but contains almost no hint of his later development. His paintings are violent, sombre, haunted, and soaked in erotic fantasy. The technique reinforces the violence, especially in 1865-7, when Cézanne adopted Courbet's practice of working with a palette knife. Cézanne's palette strokes, however, have a slashing violence that is foreign to Courbet, and they are built up in thick, irregular layers of paint more suggestive of a future Van Gogh than of the mature structure-making Cézanne. Orgies, rapes and murders abound in this nightmare period, and even innocent subjects such as picnics, portraits and still lifes have an air of the grotesque, the dark, or the doom-laden. Cézanne puts himself

94

into many of these canvases in the role of balding voyeur, making overt the direct
personal emotions involved. Erotic violence can be sensed in much Romantic art (in the
paintings of Delacroix, for example), but in Cézanne's early work it is presented far
closer to its source in private strains and fantasies.

This was an unusual path for an artist to take in the 1860s, when the rest of the
younger generation was advocating objectivity – submission to nature rather than the
expression of either conventional or introspective responses to the world. As early as
1866 Cézanne himself spoke fervently in praise of painting from nature, but in his
practice he seems for some years to have remained virtually uninfluenced by Monet,
Renoir, or even his respected older friend Pissarro. He rarely appeared at the Café
Guerbois, partly because he had little taste for theoretical discussions and partly
because he spent long periods away from Paris, at home in Aix. He therefore remained
somewhat isolated, and was probably unaware of the breakthroughs being made
around 1869.

The following year found him hiding out at L'Estaque, a village near Aix on the
Mediterranean coast. He was hiding from his father, who was unaware that Cézanne
had set up house with a model called Hortense Fiquet; and he was hiding from the
military authorities, who might feel inclined to call up a healthy 31-year-old to fight the
Prussians. At L'Estaque, perhaps inspired by the sea, Cézanne did paint some
landscapes in a less 'personal' style that suggests he had begun to look for a new way of
working. He was detained in the South by the war, the Commune, and finally the birth
in January 1872 of a son, Paul, whose existence was another secret that had to be kept
from Cézanne senior. Only after this did Cézanne go north. He settled at Pontoise,
where Pissarro was working, and in effect made himself the disciple of the older man.
So, belatedly, Cézanne became part of the Impressionist movement.

96

The
Impressionist Years
The Impressionists Before 1869

Previous chapters have shown the gradual development of opposition to academic art, with its historicism, inflated sentiments, moral tone, and reliance on formulas. The most important thing the opposition artists had in common was a taste for the contemporary scene, rendered with respect for its everyday, casually 'uncomposed' quality; otherwise there was a variety of approaches to subject and treatment, ranging from the spontaneity of Monet to the carefully planned 'casualness' of Degas. And there seemed to be no certainty about the direction anti-academic art would take in the immediate future. Few people would have predicted the role assumed by open-air painting, for example: in the 1860s only Pissarro and Sisley – both strongly influenced by Corot – were entirely committed to landscape painting. Manet, Degas, Renoir, Bazille, and Corot's pupil Berthe Morisot were all at least as interested in figure painting, and even Monet was lured away from land- and seascapes to ambitious figurative compositions such as the *Déjeuner sur l'Herbe*. Only around 1870 did a style and a subject matter emerge that were common for a time to most – though still not to all – of the group.

The subjects were 'scapes: land-, sea- and cityscapes, painted in the open air and with a common technique; paintings in which nature, the environment, the atmosphere and light played a shaping role, though human figures might be admitted and even, by their dress and gestures and activities, establish the mood as opposed to the appearance of the moment. The moment was all: the Impressionist painting captured the scene as it had never quite looked before and would never quite look again ... Or so one might describe a kind of model Impressionist painting, impossible of achievement even in a sketch, but most closely approached in works like Pissarro's *Diligence at Louveciennes,* or Monet's *Gare St Lazare* series, or Renoir's *The Swing,* which are situated in the very centre of the spectrum of Impressionist art.

The early biographical sections in this book have shown the gradual coming together of the Impressionist painters. Pissarro, Cézanne and Guillaumin met at the Académie Suisse in 1861. Monet, Renoir, Bazille and Sisley became friends at Gleyre's in the winter of the following year. Pissarro was the link between the two groups: he had known Monet since the latter's abortive visit to Paris in 1859, and in the mid-60s visited the friends when they worked at Marlotte. The two older men, Manet and Degas, seem not to have met before 1862, and to have had little or no contact with the others before about 1866.

By the time this occurred, however, Manet had clearly become the leader of the new 'realist' or 'naturalist' school: he had earned the title through his achievements and sufferings, dating back to 1863 – the year of the Salon des Refusés and *Déjeuner sur l'Herbe* – and maintained by *Olympia* in 1865. Émile Zola, newly arrived at the newspaper *L'Événement* as a reviewer, launched a ferocious attack on the Salon of 1866 and was soon predicting that 'M. Manet's place in the Louvre is marked out'. His articles lambasted the jury system as reactionary and corrupt, and he singled out Monet and Pissarro for praise alongside the older painters Corot and Daubigny. He put in a strong plea for a new Salon des Refusés, echoing the sentiments of his friend Cézanne, who had just written to the Superintendent of Fine Arts, Count Nieuwerkerke, dissociating himself from the jury system (as well he might, since he was always turned down) and proclaiming his desire to appeal to the public. Zola probably had a large hand in this production too. His own articles were curtailed after they had provoked an outcry, and *L'Événement* gave equal space to a critic of more orthodox taste.

In 1867 Manet was again cast in the part of reluctant rebel, holding his own show during the International Exhibition, albeit with a conciliatory, almost apologetic notice insisting on the painter's sincerity and that 'M. Manet has never desired to protest'. As a matter of fact, none of the Impressionists was radical in temperament except, perhaps, Monet: even Pissarro, whatever his politics, was content to be known as the

pupil of Melbye and Corot, and to exhibit at the Salon. Lack of recognition created first a rebellious group and then a break with the system. The idea of an independent group show was first discussed in 1867, which was a particularly bad year for the Impressionists at the Salon, leading Pissarro, Renoir, Sisley and Bazille to petition for a new Salon des Refusés. Bazille described the proposed independent exhibition in letters to his parents which may well have been intended as hints that financial assistance would not be unwelcome. If so, the hints were not taken, and the project fell through for want of funds. It then lay dormant for several years, probably because the Salon juries were relatively lenient towards everybody but Monet and (of course) Cézanne.

The following year, 1868, the group drew together still more closely. Bazille moved to the Rue de la Paix in the Batignolles area, where Manet lived and held court at the Café Guerbois; it seems quite likely that the move was a deliberate gesture of affiliation. Renoir shared the studio with Bazille, and both men became well acquainted with Manet, who particularly admired paintings by Renoir, such as his *Portrait of Bazille at his Easel*. Alfred Sisley came to live in the same building as Bazille and Renoir. Monet stayed with Bazille when he was in Paris, but he seems not to have come to the Guerbois until 1869. The existence of the group as more than a casual gathering was driven home by Zola, now writing in *Le Figaro*. When the Salon of 1868 came round he devoted a separate article to Manet, whom he treated as a being apart, and one who was about to force his way to the front – a natural enough belief on Zola's part, since Manet's portrait of him was currently on show at the Palais d'Industrie with the other successful entries. In his second article – on Pissarro, whom he described as 'probably the least known, but [a] ... characteristic talent' and one of 'masterly greatness' – he describes 'the Naturalists' as a group, mentioning all the chief Impressionists except Sisley, and associating them with Jongkind, Boudin, Corot and Courbet – which was not quite right as a grouping, but not bad at all as art history. Zola even mentioned Berthe Morisot, a young woman painter who was only just about to enter the history of Impressionism by meeting Manet and falling under his influence.

Manet's stature in these years is summed up in Fantin-Latour's *Studio in the Batignolles Quarter*, often called 'Homage to Manet' by analogy with Fantin's *Homage to Delacroix*, painted six years earlier. The difference was that the tribute to Delacroix was painted just after his death, whereas Manet's apotheosis took place while he was still in his prime. There was some sharp comments about it from ill-wishers, and one cartoonist mocked the rather solemn, reverential quality of the picture with a caricature of 'Jesus Painting among His Disciples'. Degas also found the 'Homage' a bit too much to take: he was supposed to appear on the left-hand side of the picture, but evidently withdrew and was replaced by some oriental curios. The formality of Fantin's painting quite certainly exaggerates the master-disciple relationship between Manet and the rest:

98

Henri Fantin-Latour. *A Studio in the Batignolles Quarter*. 1870. Exhibited at the Salon of 1870. Manet is shown painting the writer Zacharie Astruc. The others are (left to right) the German painter Otto Scholderer, Renoir, Zola, Edmond Maître, Bazille and Monet. Fantin-Latour was a friend of Manet who seems to have understood the new painting but elected for a conventionally successful career as a portraitist and flower painter. Musée du Louvre, Paris.

the easy camaraderie of Bazille's *Artist's Studio, Rue de la Condamine* has a more authentic feeling.

No detailed accounts of the Guerbois meeting exist, despite the fact that several of the habitués were literary men. The café was in the Grande Rue des Batignolles (now the Avenue de Clichy), in the Batignolles quarter which had become identified with Manet and his sympathisers. Meetings were held regularly on Thursdays, but some members of 'Manet's gang' were usually present on any given evening. Manet himself seems to have been most at home in the friendly, relaxed atmosphere of a café: before frequenting the Guerbois he had used the Tortoni and the Café de Bade, both on the Boulevard des Italiens, and in the later '70s he was to move on to the Nouvelle-Athènes. No doubt café society gave him what society at large denied: acceptance and respect based on recognition of his talent. His literary friends included Zola, Théodore Duret, Zacharie Astruc, Armand Sylvestre and Edmond Duranty. Among the artists were Henri Fantin-Latour, the engraver Félix Bracquemond, well known for his book illustrations, Antoine Guillemet – a friend of Pissarro and Cézanne, but also a distinctly career-minded painter – as well as Degas, Monet, Renoir, Bazille, Sisley, Pissarro and Cézanne. Of the younger men, Bazille seems to have attended most often, perhaps because he was best equipped by temperament and education to take part in the discussions that arose. Renoir came quite often, though he affected to be sceptical about the value of discussion, perhaps because he, like Monet, was rather poorly educated. As we have seen, Monet benefited, and late in life he was still prepared to acknowledge that the meetings had been intellectually stimulating as well as useful in keeping up morale.

Pissarro and Cézanne spent more time away from Paris than the others, and though they occasionally turned up at the café there is no evidence that its discussions loomed very large among their activities. Degas is known to have played odd man out at these gatherings: he was unclannish by temperament, and his ambivalent attitude towards Manet probably encouraged him to assert his independence in an atmosphere politely dominated by the painter of *Olympia* and his admirers. Socially, Manet was in command – urbane and charming, though not incapable of cruel irony. But as an artist he was less assured, his confidence shaken by a long run of failures broken only by half-successes. One sign of this was that he began to show the influence of those who looked up to him: the young painters who were making a cult of working in the open air.

Frédéric Bazille. *The Artist's Studio, Rue de la Condamine*. 1870. A small picture, of less documentary but more atmospheric value than Fantin's *Studio in the Batignolles Quarter*. The identities of the figures are not certain; one plausible interpretation has Zola on the stairs chatting to Renoir, and Bazille standing by the easel while Manet talks about the picture and Monet listens. The pianist is the amateur musician Edmond Maître. Musée du Louvre, Paris.

Summer 1869: Breakthrough

Manet spent the summer of 1869 at Boulogne, painting the beach and the Channel steamers. Though he was still working from sketches and doing the actual painting in his studio, his manner at this time represents a significant movement towards the style of the younger generation. The characteristic and brilliant contrasts between light and dark colours are still present, but the feeling of timelessness that pervades even 'historical' paintings such as *The Execution of the Emperor Maximilian* has vanished. Instead there is a new 'outdoors' feeling in, for example, *The Departure of the Folkestone Boat*, and with it the hint of movement and change which gives the picture its captured-moment quality.

Above left:
Édouard Manet. *Moonlight over the Port of Boulogne.* 1869. Painted at a time when Manet was beginning to feel the first stirrings of an interest in outdoor painting. But the dramatic night effects he obtains here are very different from the aims of Monet and Renoir at this period.

Left:
Parisian Pleasures: Boating at Joinville le Pont around 1880. Engraving by M. Sahib. An amusing variation on a subject dear to the Impressionists. This boating scene, though more crowded and chaotic, clearly belongs to the same world as Renoir's *Boating Party* and the stories of Guy de Maupassant.

Above:
Pierre Auguste Renoir. *At La Grenouillére.* 1869. This should be compared with Monet's almost identical painting of the same subject on the next page. Renoir uses brighter colours and, characteristically, gives more prominence to the bustle of human life. Nationalmuseum, Stockholm.

At roughly the same time, Monet and Renoir were exploring new ways of capturing the moment. Monet was living with Camille Doncieux and his son Jean at Bougival, close to the Seine north-west of Paris; Renoir was staying nearby with Lise Tréhot at his parents' house at Ville d'Avray. Both men were utterly impoverished – short of paints and, in Monet's case, sometimes short of food. Yet, as Renoir later recalled, it was Monet who never lost heart and gave Renoir the courage to go on. At this time he was the more daring of the two, and Renoir, though working independently, had tended to find himself following a trail blazed by Monet whenever he ventured outside the field of figure painting. Thus he had painted cityscapes a little later than Monet, and then investigated snow scenes after his friend – and despite his own intense dislike of snow. But in the summer of 1869 this near-parallel development was to turn into a close working relationship.

In summer, the area on the right bank of the Seine around Bougival was thronged with visitors from Paris; most of them were day-trippers who came by train for the sunshine, boating, bathing, and meals in the open air. A particularly popular spot was called La Grenouillère (the Frog Pond), an intimate, leafy place on an arm of the Seine where there was a restaurant as well as the other facilities. It became a favourite place for Monet and Renoir too, when they had materials to work with, and the small group of canvases they painted at La Grenouillère marks a turning point in the history of Impressionism. Before considering the technique employed on these paintings, it is worth emphasising that their subjects are important too. Even within open-air painting, there is a wide choice of possible subjects, and Monet's and Renoir's choice – people enjoying themselves in friendly open-air surroundings – embodied what was to be the predominant Impressionist mood of the 1870s. For many people, in fact, this innocent sunshine mood – in Monet's *Beach at Trouville*, Renoir's *Moulin de la Galette*, Sisley's *Small Meadows in Spring* – constitutes the supreme achievement of Impressionism and the justification of its technical experiments.

The virtues of working in the open air were known to earlier generations than the Impressionists, though by no means universally accepted. Monet's first teacher, Eugène

Boudin, put it succinctly: 'Everything painted on the spot has a strength, a power, a vividness that can't be recaptured in the studio'. The rapid, spontaneous work needed to catch fleeting effects did not lend itself to the kind of smooth finish demanded by the academies, and controversy raged for years over what was a 'sketch' and what a proper painting. Many masters compromised in one way or another, 'finishing' their painting in the studio or using plein-air sketches as the basis for a picture executed in the studio; often the result has been that the sketches and studies have worn better than the paintings.

The young Impressionists took over this open-air tradition, drawing on the Corot-Daubigny landscape school, the Boudin-Jongkind coastal school, and also the modern-life tendency represented by Manet and Degas, which encouraged them to sweep away both classical trappings and Romantic atmosphere in the interests of depicting 19th-century ordinariness. It is tempting if not particularly meaningful to see the La Grenouillère paintings – leafy, watery, casually inhabited – as a kind of synthesis of the three 'ancestors' of Impressionism. Actually, the younger men had already made distinctive contributions in their peopled city- and snowscapes. The study of snow effects confirmed them in a belief that was central to their technical development: that there were no black shadows – just as, for that matter, there was no white snow, but a range of colours and tones influenced by everything around it, including the sky. Shadows, similarly, were influenced by all the surrounding colours and by the light and atmosphere prevailing at any given moment. And so Impressionists like Monet and Renoir did not convey the transition from shadow to light simply by a change of tone, as convention prescribed: they put in the lights and colours they saw present in the shadow itself. One important effect of this was to unify the picture in a new way: instead of being divided into light and dark areas, it became a colour-continuum, expressing a single mood in a fashion that would not otherwise have been possible using a range of bright colours. The unity was not one of grand design, so to speak, but of impact: the picture became the 'impression' it was intended to be – a place and a moment, apparently recorded on the instant and apparently possible to apprehend on the instant.

Advances in the science of optics evidently played a part in the further development of Impressionist practice. The most important influence was certainly Eugène Chevreul's treatise on colour harmonies, published in 1839, which may also have been known to the pioneer colourist Delacroix. Chevreul had pointed out that shadows were coloured, and also proposed a theory of optical mixture on which Monet's and Renoir's painting at La Grenouillère could be said to be based – if, that is, the theory suggested the practice rather than justified it after the event, which seems just as likely.

Optical mixing denotes the eye's activity in mixing juxtaposed but separate colours, which is one of those ways in which we automatically supply the 'sense' of information that seems incomplete. A similar example is the mental filling-in of a letter omitted from a printed word: we see what we know – or think we know – is there. Exploiting this phenomenon, Monet and Renoir began applying small brush-strokes of vivid colour instead of colours mixed on the palette. The technique (chromatic division) lent itself to rapid open-air work as well as making for a far more brilliantly coloured picture. The setting in which Monet and Renoir were working was probably conducive to taking this final step: the sunlight falling through the leaves, the ripples of the river, did part of the job by breaking up light and reflections into coloured facets – which is not of course to say that the job would not have been done.

The small brush-strokes, the vivid colours, the absence of 'drawn' outlines, created a light-saturated world in which not only atmosphere but motion seemed to have been caught and frozen for a moment. (The slight blur or tremor on people and objects in Impressionist paintings, which contributes to the sense of life and movement, may have been suggested by contemporary photographs of objects in motion – if so, an interesting example of a technical deficiency in one discipline suggesting a useful device in another.) The technique also left a picture surface that was unlike any seen before – far 'rougher' than anything Courbet had ever produced, with the marks of the brush-strokes visible to the naked eye. Later painters such as Cézanne were to make the marks themselves part of the picture pattern. But though Monet and Renoir had no such idea in mind, the novel picture surface they created was sufficient to disconcert the orthodox critic, accustomed to seeing the picture subject as if through a pane of glass. And as if that were not enough, the new pictures had coloured shadows and, when viewed from close up, dissolved into dabs and dashes of colour – not like the Old Masters, in whose works every square inch remained identifiable even under a

Claude Monet. *The Jetty at Le Havre.* 1870.

104

magnifying glass … With a little imagination it is not difficult to understand the
consternation these pictures were to cause, even among critics who were sympathetic to
realism and experiment.

It was a substantial achievement for one summer – except, perhaps, for the painters
themselves, whose productivity had been so severely restricted by lack of funds, and
who were no nearer earning a reasonable living. In October Monet went off to
Normandy, while Renoir returned to Bazille's studio. Over the next few months the
two men may have discussed their discoveries with friends in Paris, but any
developments that might have taken place were deferred by the terrible events of
1870-1, which were temporarily to scatter 'Manet's gang'. All the same, though it had
not yet acquired a name, Impressionism had been born.

The
Franco-Prussian
War and the
Commune

In July 1870, outmanoeuvred diplomatically by the wily Bismarck, Napoleon III declared war on Prussia. Crowds poured into the streets shouting 'To Berlin! To Berlin!' Confident in her great military tradition – despite some less-than-convincing performances over the previous few years – France plunged into a conflict for which neither the army nor its commanders was equipped. A series of defeats in August was followed by the catastrophic defeat of the French army at Sedan on 2 September. Louis Napoleon, suffering agonies from a kidney stone and rouged to conceal his pallor, rode frantically over the field hoping a stray bullet would end his humilation. But even this form of escape was denied him, and he was taken prisoner by the Prussians.

Louis Napoleon was a self-made emperor, and when his defeat and capture was known, the Empress Eugénie and her son slipped away from the Tuileries Palace by a side door, and the Second Empire vanished with them. Under the Third Republic, resistance to the Prussian advance went on with a determination that might have won the war if it had been manifested earlier. By mid-September the Prussians were

Above:
Parisians suffer during the Prussian siege of the city in the war of 1870-71. As the shop sign indicates, this is a dog-and-cat-butcher's; and the customers are desperate enough to queue for the meat.

Left:
Prussian shells bursting within the Port d'Auteuil during the siege of Paris. Illustrated London News, 28 January 1871.

Right:
Prussian victory march, 1871. By insisting on this march, and passing under the Arc de Triomphe and along the Champs-Elysées, the Prussians insulted the Napoleonic past and inflicted a deep humiliation on Parisians.

Left:
The Vendôme Column immediately after its demolition. The column, crowned with a figure of Napoleon I, was regarded as 'a symbol of brute force and false glory' that insulted conquered peoples. A red flag was raised on the broken base. The ninth figure from the right, the heavily bearded man in a cap, is the painter Gustave Courbet, who was later sentenced to pay for the restoration of the column. Most of the monuments and buildings destroyed during the Commune were restored exactly as they had been before – defects and all; in the bitterness of class war, the victorious government hoped to wipe out all traces that the Commune had ever existed.

Below left:
The defenders of the Commune: a woman guiding artillerymen, Place Taranne, 22 May 1871. Paris was besieged by troops of the government based at Versailles, and was resolutely defended by the Communards. In this bitter class war, working-class women were among the most ardent and active Communards.

investing Paris itself, but the defenders held on. The radical politician Gambetta escaped from the city by balloon, formed a government of national defence at Bordeaux, and began to raise new armies. But the armies were beaten back; Parisians ate dogs, cats, and rats; and when the capital at last surrendered on 28 January 1871, the war was effectively over.

The artists reacted to the war in various ways, but certainly not with overwhelming ardour. Bazille joined the colours and was killed in November, when it was already clear the war was lost. Renoir, true to his philosophy of letting fate decide, made no attempt to join up but allowed himself to be conscripted; since he was a townsman who knew nothing of horses, military logic sent him to train them in the Pyrenees. Manet, Degas, Berthe Morisot and possibly Sisley remained in Paris. Degas and Manet joined the artillery section of the National Guard (roughly speaking a middle-class militia); according to Berthe Morisot, Manet spent most of the siege changing uniforms, perhaps as consolation for having to serve under one of the idols of the Academy of Fine Arts, the facile military painter Ernest Meissonier. Cézanne hid at L'Estaque to make sure he was not called up. Monet, who was staying at Le Havre when war broke out, quietly slipped across the Channel when things began to go badly, leaving Camille and Jean behind. Pissarro, who had abandoned his house at Louveciennes as the Prussians approached, stayed in Brittany for a time and then

Right:
The Hôtel de Ville in flames. It was fired by the Communards as they were falling back before the Versailles government troops.

Below right:
Édouard Manet. *The Barricade.* 1871. Manet returned to Paris during the last days of the Commune; this lithograph records the summary 'justice' meted out to the Communards. Museum of Fine Arts, Boston, Massachusetts (Gift of W. G. Russell Allen).

followed Monet's example. Many painters who were not Impressionists also behaved as though the war was a kind of natural disaster it was best not to get involved in: Daubigny and the academic artist Gérôme were among the considerable number of painters who took refuge in London, while Boudin and Diaz found a haven in Brussels.

The agony was not yet over. Before many of the self-exiled artists could return, Paris rose against the new Republican government and proclaimed herself an independent Commune. Since the French Revolution the capital had been more radical than the rest

Left:
Camille Pissaro. *Penge Station, Upper Norwood.* 1870. Here the railway track has the same function as the road in so many other works by Pissarro. Nearby was the Crystal Palace (then still standing in the area now called after it), which Pissarro also painted. Courtauld Institute Galleries. London.

Below right:
Camille Pissarro. *Street in Upper Norwood, London.* 1871. A pleasingly warm picture forming an interesting contrast with the snow scene in *Lower Norwood, London.* Neue Pinakothek, Munich.

of the country, in which the majority were peasants; now, inflamed by the hardships of the siege, aware of the shortcomings of 'bourgeois' rule, and at odds with the new government, a mixed bag of journalists, working men and returned political exiles – they were quicker about it than the artists – set up a government under the banner of 'Social Revolution, Equality, Justice'. Though not socialist or communist in the modern sense, the Commune was undoubtedly *for* the workers and *against* the bourgeoisie. As such, it is part of the history (and myth) of the Left, and therefore still too politically contentious to admit of easy generalisations. All that need be said here is that the class struggle proved more ferocious than the one between nations; that the Prussian army was able to look on while French artillery pounded Paris and French regulars fought their way into the capital, barricade by barricade; and that after the city had fallen, at least 25,000 Communards were killed in retribution.

Most of the artists escaped the worst rigours of the second siege of Paris. Manet, Degas and Berthe Morisot had all left the capital to recuperate after the capitulation, though Manet returned during the last days of the Commune and drew lithographs of its bloody suppression. Zola had returned to the city earlier, and as ex-secretary to a cabinet minister believed himself in some danger from the Communards; he remained hidden till it was all over. But Courbet, long notorious for his socialism, joined the revolutionaries and presided over an assembly of artists that briefly dismantled the École des Beaux-Arts and the rest of the official art establishment. He also instigated a literal demolition job – the destruction of the Vendôme Column which, with its idealised, laurel-wreathed Napoleon at the top, had come to symbolise political and artistic tyranny in Courbet's mind. After the fall of the Commune, Courbet was imprisoned for this 'crime' and fined so heavily that he fled to Switzerland, where he died in exile.

Renoir, like Zola, returned to Paris in time to be trapped; he had been invalided out of the army after almost dying of dysentery, and had made his way back via Bordeaux. When the Commune ordered the conscription of all able-bodied men, Renoir was able to get a pass out of the city because the police commissioner, Raoul Rigault, turned out to be an ex-student agitator he had helped to escape from Napoleon III's police some years before; meeting Rigault while painting in the forest of Fontainebleau, Renoir had put a smock on the student and passed him off as a fellow-painter.

Renoir's actual escape conveys the atmosphere of the times. When Rigault gave him the pass, he warned Renoir that though it would be honoured by Communard patrols, government troops would probably shoot him if they found it on him. Furthermore, if he had no government pass he would still be in trouble; and in any event it would not be easy in the middle of the night to tell which side was which. Thanks to his aristocratic patron Prince Bibesco, Renoir was able to acquire a government pass too. Finally, by using one pass while he hid the other in a tree, he managed to get through the lines and join his mother at Louveciennes.

Monet and Pissarro missed all these dramas by staying in England until life in France returned to normal. Inevitably, both were short of money, though Pissarro's situation was the worse since he had Julie Vellay and their two sons with him. Monet had the good luck to meet Daubigny, who already admired his work to the point of resigning from the Salon jury in 1870 when it refused to accept Monet's entries. Daubigny introduced Monet to the dealer Paul Durand-Ruel, and urged him to buy the younger painter's work; he even offered to let Durand-Ruel have one of his own works – now fetching high prices – for every painting by Monet that failed to sell. But Durand-Ruel needed no such incentive. Already the leading dealer in paintings by the Barbizon school, he was to prove a godsend to the Impressionists, buying as many of their pictures as he dared, even in the worst times, and several times coming close to bankruptcy as a result.

Neither Monet nor Pissarro knew that the other was in London until Pissarro left one of his paintings at Durand-Ruel's gallery in New Bond Street. Durand-Ruel was delighted with the picture, arranged to buy it, and also put Pissarro in touch with Monet. The two painters were pleased to see each other, and apparently met frequently during their stay in London. They were not able to work together much, since Monet lived in Kensington, close to the heart of London, while Pissarro stayed with his family in Lower Norwood, which is now part of London's southern sprawl but was at that time an attractive, countryfied place on the edge of the city. Monet's works included atmospheric studies of Hyde Park and Westminster; Pissarro painted views of Penge Station, Dulwich College and other south-of-London spots. It is possible that this contact with Monet, however limited, was decisive in Pissarro's development. His London paintings are certainly among his best, with a fluency and brightness not often found in his previous work. However, it is also possible that they represent the culmination of earlier experiments with the small-brush-stroke manner, whether discovered independently by Pissarro or used in response to ideas aired before the war at the Café Guerbois; the mastery of a pre-war painting such as *Diligence at Louveciennes* suggests that Pissarro – an artist much given to self-doubt – needed technical help less than the kind of moral support that Monet's driving personality provided.

Both men derived encouragement from the pictures they saw in London's museums and galleries: Constables, Turners and Cotmans, and even works of the 18th-century English and French schools, which made them feel they were part of a significant development in painting. But on the material plane, neither Pissarro nor Monet had much success in London. Durand-Ruel failed to sell any of their work, and their submissions for the Royal Academy exhibition were rejected. The only consolations were acceptances for the International Exhibition at the South Kensington Museum, where their canvases were shown in good company, alongside works by Corot, Courbet, Daubigny and Jongkind. Writing to the critic Théodore Duret, Pissarro none

Above:
Claude Monet. *The Thames below Westminster.*
1871. National Gallery, London.

Right:
Claude Monet. *Madame Monet on a Sofa.*
1871. In 1870 Monet regularised his
relationship with Camille Doncieux, who had
shared his life since 1865. Her rather worn
appearance probably reflects the severity of their
struggle to survive. Musée du Louvre, Paris.

Above left:
Camille Pissarro. *Lower Norwood under Snow.*
1870. At this time, Lower Norwood, where
Pissarro and his family took lodgings, was
outside London. More freely handled than most
of Pissarro's earlier pictures, though he
continues to lean on his favourite compositional
device of a road running away into the distance.
National Gallery, London.

Left:
Camille Pissarro. *The Crystal Palace, London.*
1871. This building, one of the 19th-century
marvels of iron-and-glass engineering, housed
the Great Exhibition of 1851. Later it was
removed from Hyde Park and re-erected at
Sydenham; in 1870–71 Camille Pissarro lived
nearby at Norwood, and the Crystal Palace
appears in the painting above. It was destroyed
by fire in 1936. Art Institute of Chicago, Illinois.

the less complained bitterly of English inhospitality ('There is no art here; everything is
a question of business.') though he had to concede that his ill-success was not peculiar
to residence in England ('it follows me everywhere'). Equally to the point, his family
followed him everywhere; and Julie Vellay, who had not been improved by a life full of
privations, made no effort to adjust to England and complained endlessly. In spite of
this, Pissarro belatedly married her – she was pregnant for a third time – just before
leaving England in June 1871. He returned to his house at Louveciennes to discover
how much damage the Prussians had done (far more than his landlady had dared to tell
him). Monet had quitted England slightly earlier, but spent the rest of the year in
Holland. By the time he returned, all the Impressionists (all except for poor Bazille)
were again in or around Paris, and the gatherings at the Café Guerbois had resumed.

The First
Impressionist Show

Camille Pissarro. *Entrance to the Village of Voisins.* 1872. Also known as *The Edge of the Village.* A bright and peaceful spring day, with trees evidently about to burst into life. The shadows lying across the road help to break the near-symmetry of this quiet but subtle work. Musée du Louvre, Paris.

Life returned to normal in France with surprising speed. As often happens after periods of suffering and disaster, people wanted to forget about the past and enjoy the present. And in 1872-3 they were helped to do so by a post-war boom as the French economy picked up again.

For the Impressionists too these were good years. Durand-Ruel came to know them one by one, and was bold enough to buy a considerable number of their paintings. He made a particularly large investment in Manet's works (acquiring still unsold masterpieces such as *The Spanish Guitarist, Concert in the Tuileries Gardens,* and *The Engagement of the Kearsarge and the Alabama*), but at his London exhibitions Pissarro, Monet, Degas, Sisley and Renoir were also well represented.

Renewed contacts seem to have diffused knowledge of new technical points and also to have stimulated a general vivacity and experimental spirit. It is difficult to pinpoint the moment when any individual made a decisive advance: Sisley, for example, shed much of his dependence on Corot and lightened his palette without sacrifice of subtlety; but whether working with Pissarro at Louveciennes had more influence on him than working with Monet at Argenteuil would be hard to say. Having left Louveciennes for Pontoise in 1872, Pissarro himself undoubtedly influenced Cézanne, who painted alongside the older artist and even copied one of his pictures. Two lesser figures, Armand Guillaumin and Édouard Béliard, also worked with Pissarro. These were golden years for him, and he painted with a confidence and freedom that he was

Right:
Camille Pissarro. *Portrait of Paul Cézanne.* 1874. Painted at a time when Cézanne was very much Pissarro's protégé; it was only through the older man's efforts that Cézanne's paintings were accepted at the first Impressionist exhibition in the same year. Private Collection.

Below right:
Paul Cézanne. *Dr Gachet's House at Auvers.* 1872–73. Cézanne met the art collector Dr Gachet after moving to Auvers to be close to his friend and tutor Pissarro. During these years he created his most Impressionist works. R. Staechelin Collection, Basle.

to lose in a few years' time and not to recover until late in life; Cézanne said, 'If
Pissarro had continued to paint as he did in 1870 he would have been the strongest of
us all'. Degas, as always, went his own way, apparently no more influenced by his
friends and acquaintances than by a six-month trip to New Orleans. He was
discovering life backstage and the world of dancing, subjects that he was to exploit so
brilliantly and completely that other major artists have avoided them ever since. Manet,
by contrast, was doing a good deal of open-air painting, perhaps influenced by his old
friend Berthe Morisot, who was painting in an increasingly freer, lighter manner;
however, Manet's course was very uncertain during these years, and he also visited
Holland to study the Dutch Old Masters.

Monet spent much of his time in Holland during 1871-72, but outdoors, painting
barges and windmills and the permutations of water and sky that held such an
attraction for him. He returned to take a house at Argenteuil, another pleasant little
place on the banks of the Seine, but this time on the main course of the river, where
there were barges and bridges and sailing boats. Monet's experience of Holland may
have influenced him in his choice of home, as it may well have influenced the subject of
paintings such as *Unloading Coal at Argenteuil.*

Renoir remained in Paris but saw Monet often at Argenteuil. Sisley too was a visitor.
He remained true to his preference for long views, for example painting the wooden
bridge at Argenteuil and the town square. Monet and Renoir combined this sort of
subject with more intimate studies including a number done in Monet's garden. Here
their brush-strokes grew even smaller, so that in a painting like Renoir's *Monet
Working in his Garden* the dense, brilliant rendering of flowers and plants creates an
effect of intense vibration and growth.

At the Salon, the change of political régime had no visible effect on the art
establishment. There were adjustments from year to year, alternations of reaction and
liberalism – in 1873 there was even another Salon des Refusés – but the basic situation
remained: the Impressionists and their friends were forced to submit themselves for
judgement by men who neither understood their aims nor sympathised with their
experiments. In fact they had grown so tired of the struggle that by the early '70s only
Manet, Renoir and Berthe Morisot regularly submitted works to the Salon.

By 1873 it seemed just possible that 'Manet's gang' would gain general success and
recognition, with or without the approval of the Salon. In Durand-Ruel they had a
dealer who believed in them; they had been taken up by a few perspicacious collectors
like Ernest Hoschedé, Dr Paul Gachet and the opera singer Jean Baptiste Faure; and
their prices were starting to rise. Durand-Ruel even began to prepare a lavish three-
volume catalogue of works in his possession, grouping the Batignolles painters with the
Barbizon school and indicating that the younger men were the legitimate successors of
Rousseau, Daubigny and Corot.

In these circumstances, when Zola's disciple Paul Alexis suggested that the

Alfred Sisley. *Wooden Bridge at Argenteuil.* 1872. Shown at the third Impressionist exhibition in 1877. This is a rather more peopled view than is usual with Sisley. It is interesting to compare this with the Argenteuil paintings of Monet, Manet and Renoir. Musée du Louvre, Paris.

'naturalists' should hold an independent exhibition, Monet eagerly took up the idea, which had lain dormant since the discussions of 1867 had come to nothing. Pissarro, Sisley and Guillaumin rallied to Monet. So did Renoir, who was not notable for his partisan spirit but seemed incapable of pleasing the Salon jury with even his most innocuous canvases. Even more surprising was the adherence of Degas, who was by no means in entire sympathy with the rest and, for all his originality, quite successful at the Salon. The outstanding absentee was the presiding figure of the whole group: Manet refused to exhibit with the rest, insisting that 'the Salon is the real field of battle'. He had just had his first success there since 1861, and had persuaded himself that the battle was being won. Actually the admired picture, *Le Bon Bock*, was an uncharacteristic and not particularly inspired portrait of a merry old toper, so much in the style of the Dutch Old Masters that it is closer to plagiarism than many of Manet's better-known 'borrowed' compositions. The Salon public was prepared to accept Manet, but only when he was not being Manet; his splendid full-length portrait of Berthe Morisot, also shown in 1873, was ignored. However, Manet's absence from the Impressionist show was not a mere miscalculation on his part: he was by temperament the cautious, conventional *haut bourgeois*, just as Degas was by temperament the disdainfully independent *haut bourgeois*: the decisions of the two men are surprising only at first sight. Despite Manet's protests, his close friend Berthe Morisot decided to join the Impressionists, although she had hitherto been a regular exhibitor at the Salons. Since she was neither unsuccessful nor short of money, this was a risk she was not forced to take (participants in an exhibition rivalling the Salon were not likely to be favourably considered by future juries). But once committed, she was to show a similar resolution ever afterwards.

Before the new group had even organised itself properly, their prospects took a sharp turn for the worse. At the close of 1873 the post-war boom suddenly collapsed. Durand-Ruel, whose very excellence of taste put his business constantly at risk, found himself for the time being unable to buy any more of his friends' paintings. Prices fell steeply, and survival again became a problem at the very time when the Impressionists were planning to desert and offend the artistic establishment. But in spite of these portents the preparations for an independent exhibition went ahead.

The group did not call itself 'Realist' or 'Naturalist', let alone 'Impressionist', a term that had not yet been invented. It was simply 'The Anonymous Society of Painters, Sculptors, Engravers, etc.' – which gave nothing away. The composition of the group was intended to be equally unspecific. Degas in particular insisted that the widest possible cross-section of artists should be invited, so that the exhibitors would not be looked upon as a collection of Salon failures; he also argued that the public would be more likely to accept a mixed show than a concentrated exposure to the most advanced modern art. He got his way, though probably for financial rather than tactical reasons: the more artists exhibited, the lower the costs would be per head. Once the point was gained, Degas threw himself energetically into organising the

Above:
Pierre Auguste Renoir. *The Pont Neuf.* 1872.
Monet and Renoir both painted the bridge from
almost the same angle but in different
atmospheric conditions; Renoir,
characteristically, chose fair weather that gives
the scene an air of bustling good temper. His
brother Edmond stopped passers-by and
engaged them in conversation so that Auguste,
working at a window facing the bridge, had
time to sketch them into the picture. National
Gallery of Art, Washington, DC (Ailsa Mellon
Bruce Collection).

exhibition and trying to persuade friends to contribute. His general view of the event is neatly summed up in a letter to James Tissot, a painter who had settled in London: 'The realist movement no longer needs to fight with others. It is, it exists, it has to show itself *separately*. There has to be a *realist Salon*'.

In the event, there were 30 exhibitors. Degas brought in some of his friends and managed to persuade a handful of painters with established reputations to show – men like Stanislas Lépine and Giuseppe de Nittis, who are now remembered only for their participation. Boudin was an exhibitor, probably as a result of Monet's persuasion. Pissarro insisted on the inclusion of Cézanne, who was regarded with suspicion by the rest of the group as the wildest of wild men. Félix Bracquemond joined of his own volition. Finally, there were lesser figures and 'Sunday painter' friends, such as Astruc, who felt more or less sympathy with the aims of the 'Impressionist' nucleus; and the numbers were made up by some little-known artists and one or two older men. Revered older painters such as Corot and Daubigny were not asked to exhibit, possibly because they were known to disapprove of the venture. When Antoine Guillemet decided not to join them, Corot is said to have congratulated him, saying 'You did well to get away from that bunch!'

The 'Anonymous Society' was a properly constituted business association. Those who wished to do so could become members by paying their dues (60 francs) without exhibiting at the show itself – which was one way of discreetly sympathising without offending the powers-that-were. Everything was arranged on a fraternal basis. A tenth of all sale prices was to go as commission into the society's funds, and the hanging of works was divided by drawing lots. The actual work of hanging was less equally divided: most of it was left to Renoir.

The exhibition was held on the Boulevard des Capucines, in the studio vacated shortly before by the photographer Nadar; he was a well-wisher, and seems to have allowed the artists to use his rooms free of charge. The place was a well-known one, since it had a large sign outside and was painted red. The entry fee for the exhibition was a franc; the catalogue, prepared by Renoir's brother Edmond, cost 50 centimes. In order to secure maximum public attention, the exhibitors arranged the first evening sessions ever put on as part of a show. Opening day was 15 April 1874.

The outcome is well known: the Impressionists as a group received a sustained

Right:
Pierre Auguste Renoir. *Parisian Women Dressed as Algerians.* 1872. Strongly influenced by Delacroix, this exotic painting was rejected by the Salon jury of 1872. National Museum of Western Art, Tokyo.

Above:
Édouard Manet. *Le Bon Bock*. 1873.
Philadelphia Museum of Art, Pennsylvania (Mr
and Mrs·Carroll S. Tyson Collection).

Right:
Pièrre Auguste Renoir. *Monet Working in his
Garden at Argenteuil*. 1873. Painted on the spot
while Monet was actually working on a picture
of his own: the garden view he is said to have
been recording still exists. Wadsworth
Atheneum, Hartford, Connecticut (Anne Parish
Titzell Bequest 1957).

Pierre Auguste Renoir. *The Meadow*. 1873.
Collection of Peter Nathan, Zurich.

Right:
Claude Monet. *Le Déjeuner* (Luncheon). 1873.
A bright, charming version of a favourite
subject. Musée du Louvre, Paris.

critical battering far worse than anything they had suffered as individuals. If the public
were ever inclined to enjoy the show – which seems doubtful – they soon learned the
proper attitude, and went along only to laugh. The worst and most widely read review
was Louis Leroy's 'The Exhibition of the Impressionists', published in *Charivari*. It
took the form of a funny story – sadly unfunny today – in which the critic visits the
exhibition with a respectable landscape painter who suffers one traumatic experience
after another in front of atrocious, scrappy 'impressions' – a *Dancer* by Renoir with
'cottony' legs, dirt-spattered landscapes by Pissarro, 'black tongue-lickings' instead of
people in Monet's *Boulevard des Capucines*. The unfortunate landscapist's mind
collapses under these shocks, and he begins to think of himself as an 'Impressionist'. He
picks Monet's *Impression: Sunrise* as his favourite (because it is less finished than the
crudest wallpaper), and criticises the unnecessary detail in the rendering of a municipal
guard's face – the said guard being a real man, on duty at the exhibition. Finally he
gibbers and dances in front of the guard before, presumably, being led away.

As well as pillorying the Impressionists, Leroy gave the group its name. His article
was full of jokes on 'impressions' (conveying the idea of daubs instead of accurate,
detailed renditions), and the title of Monet's painting was a journalistic godsend that
clinched the matter. Degas in particular detested the name, but it was taken up by a
slightly more sympathetic critic, Jules Castagnary, and it stuck; and most of the group
accepted it. On one level this was pure accident: Edmond Renoir had complained about
Monet's monotonous and pedestrian titles, so on the spur of the moment Monet
suggested *Impression*, which Renoir 'improved' to *Impression: Sunrise* in the catalogue.
However, the word 'impression' had cropped up again and again in previous reviews
and conversations, for example when Odilon Redon wrote that Daubigny was 'the
painter of a moment, of an impression'. This, after all, was just what most of the
important painters at the show of 1874 were trying to be. No name covers every
tendency in a group or movement; but if groups must have names, then 'Impressionists'
was at least as good as any for this one.

In this and other respects Leroy knew his job. He singled out for his sneers all the

Above:
Claude Monet. *Wild Poppies*. 1873. The fresh-air feeling is very strong in this picture, with its emphasis on depth and distance set off against the tumbling poppies in the foreground. People making their way across a field was a recurrent Impressionist subject. Musée du Louvre, Paris.

Right:
Pierre Auguste Renoir. *The Dancer*. 1874. This was the figure whose legs were described by the hostile critic Louis Leroy as 'cottony'. The subject is reminiscent of dancers by Degas and Manet. National Gallery of Art, Washington, DC (Widener Collection 1942).

Below:
Paul Cézanne. *The House of the Hanged Man*. 1873. Painted at Auvers while Cézanne was working with Pissarro, the picture was shown at the first Impressionist exhbition. It is Impressionist but hardly an 'impression': instead of the fleeting moment Cézanne offers ordered masses that look as though they will endure for geological ages. Musée du Louvre, Paris.

Pierre Auguste Renoir. *La Loge.* 1874. Shown
at the first Impressionist Exhibition in 1874. The
sitters were a well-known model called Nini and
Renoir's brother Edmond. Renoir managed to
sell this now world-famous picture — but only
for the 425 francs he owed in rent. Courtauld
Institute Galleries, London.

painters now regarded as masters: not one was omitted, whereas the lesser figures and artists working in different styles were (with the exception of Degas's friend Henri Rouart) hardly mentioned – damned with faint damns. The best works in the show by Monet, Renoir, Sisley, Pissarro, Degas, Morisot were unerringly picked for ridicule; so was Cézanne's monumental *House of the Hanged Man* and, rather more understandably, his extraordinary *Modern Olympia*, which must have stood out in this company like a scream at a picnic. Somehow or other, though, Leroy managed to overlook Renoir's *La Loge*, superb though it is.

In the short run, at least, the exhibition of 1874 proved a disastrous tactical error on the part of the Impressionists. After all, their paintings were becoming more, not less, difficult for the public to appreciate – more 'sketchy' in finish and unconventional in the way colour was used. At such a moment it was not worldly-wise to defy the established system, in which the advanced artist could still hope to gain a degree of acceptance. At the Salon an occasional Impressionist painting brightening the room might have been approved or overlooked or pardoned by the critics; at a small show in which Impressionist paintings could be seen in such numbers, hung with such prominence – in spite of Degas's partial success in broadening the show's membership – the unmistakable, violent, wilful eccentricity of the new art was bound to be apparent at once to both critics and public; and the resultant outcry would be full-throated and general. Manet may well have reasoned in some such fashion, finding that the logic of the situation reinforced his temperamental aversion to radical measures. He must have remembered the reception of his *Déjeuner* at the Salon des Refusés, which unquestionably proved it was a forlorn hope to appeal to the public over the heads of the Salon jury. On the prudential level this attitude was unchallengeable, though it ignored the morale-raising effect of breaking with a system in which one could never achieve more than mediocre success. Like dissident groups of all kinds, the Impressionists gained in strength and perseverance by turning their dissent into a public stance, even though they failed to win public approval.

Paul Cézanne. *A Modern Olympia*. 1872–3. This curious picture can be seen as Cézanne's farewell to his wild earlier manner; however, with typical audacity he showed it at the first Impressionist exhibition (1874), where it aroused such fury that it was feared the crowd might tear it to pieces. Whether the joke is on Manet or on Cézanne himself is not clear. Cézanne is certainly the portly *voyeur* for whom this sprawling, pinkly amorphous Olympia – the opposite in every way to the contained, cool young woman in Manet's *Olympia* – is being unveiled. The whole painting trembles in a kind of jokey erotic rapture; even the flowers – here transformed into an erupting urnful – and the electric-shocked cat are part of it. Cézanne seems to have been obsessed with this subject, of which he painted several versions. Musée du Louvre, Paris.

The Years of Struggle

After the fiasco of their show, the Impressionists went their ways again. For most of them the next few years were to be difficult ones. At Argenteuil, Monet was evicted from his house, but found a new one thanks to Manet's help. This seems to have brought the two men into closer contact, and Manet spent long periods at Argenteuil during the summer of 1874. He worked with Monet, and with Renoir, who was also a frequent visitor. A whole group of splendid river and yachting scenes came out of this association – Monet's *Bridge at Argenteuil*, Renoir's regatta scene, and a series of pictures by Manet that have a fresh-air quality more marked than anything in his previous paintings of outdoor subjects. The high key of the colours and the impressionistic handling of the paint is astonishing in the master who created *The Fifer* and *Déjeuner à l'Atelier*: they might be two different men.

None the less Manet remained determined to conquer the Salon rather than exhibit with his friends. He also held aloof from the auction of works by Monet, Renoir and Sisley at the Hôtel Drouot, though Berthe Morisot, who was also well off, put a group of paintings, pastels and watercolours up for sale as a gesture of solidarity with her three friends. The auction, held in March 1875, was a disaster – a near-riot during which the works on sale were knocked down for ludicrous prices; ironically, it was Berthe Morisot who made the most money.

The auction confirmed that the Impressionists were worse-thought-of, in financial terms, than they had been before the Franco-Prussian War. Their circle of admirers was growing, but painfully slowly; the most chronically impecunious members of the group – notably Monet – found themselves time and again trying to borrow money from (or sell pictures to) the same few people. One of Monet's luckiest encounters at Argenteuil had been with Gustave Caillebotte, a young man who had just inherited money and who was himself a painter; he became an important patron of Monet and Renoir, and was to play a significant part in the movement as an organiser. Another, less wealthy enthusiast was Victor Chocquet, who had managed to build up a collection of paintings

Claude Monet. *The Bridge at Argenteuil.* 1874. One of Monet's most joyfully summery works, in which he again demonstrates his mastery as a painter of water reflections. Musée du Louvre, Paris.

by Delacroix before discovering the younger masters at the Hôtel Drouot auction. He was to become the special patron and friend of Cézanne.

When the second Impressionist exhibition was held in April 1876 at Durand-Ruel's gallery, Chocquet spent his time there arguing with visitors and pointing out beauties in the works on display. To no avail: there were fewer visitors than two years before, and the press remained hostile or contemptuous. At this time Manet, rejected at the Salon, took the unusual step of opening his studio to the public so that they could judge the canvases for themselves. Since this amounted to abandoning the 'battlefield' of the Salon – if only temporarily – it is strange that he should have exhibited alone rather than with his friends; presumably Manet saw his gesture as an appeal for justice rather than a challenge to the fundamental authority of the Salon, which the Impressionist exhibitions had become. His friends had a new nickname – the 'Intransigents' - which Manet must have found much more distasteful than 'Impressionists'. His chosen course of action was not a despicable one, since it must have taken courage to submit alone, and be rejected alone, year after year, just as it took courage to fight the whole system as part of a group. Whether Manet's tactics were sound is another matter: the critics rarely failed to mention the connection between him and the 'Anonymous Society', with strong hints that he should join his 'followers' in Outer Darkness; and as the Salon jury was hostile for year after year, Manet's resolution smacks of a bad decision persisted in out of pride.

Despite their material setbacks, the Impressionists produced some notable work at this time. Renoir was particularly creative, perhaps because he was able to paint with relative peace of mind. He had been introduced to Zola's publisher, Georges Charpentier, who was proving a generous and hospitable patron. It was probably

Claude Monet. *The Bridge at Argenteuil*. 1874. Another view of the bridge over the Seine at Argenteuil. Neue Pinakothek, Munich.

Charpentier's help that enabled Renoir to take a spacious house with a garden at Montmartre, where he painted some of his most joyous pictures. The gaiety of the *Moulin de la Galette, The Swing* and similar works is intensified by the sun-dappling effects Renoir captured so successfully – though the critic Albert Wolff could see no more than signs of putrefaction in the green-tinged shadows that fell on one of his nudes. Sisley too advanced, painting a series of pictures of the floods at Marly, where he had been living since the previous year. These have always been placed among his finest works, executed with a characteristically quiet lyrical intensity. By contrast, Monet began painting one of his most famous series, of the great Parisian railway station, the Gare St Lazare. He may well have been responding to criticisms that the Impressionists' techniques were suitable only for the limited purpose of rendering landscapes in sunlight. At the same time the station, with its moving monsters flinging out tremendous clouds of steam, did provide the challenge of fugitive effects.

130

Pierre Auguste Renoir. *Regatta at Argenteuil.*
1874. A dazzling, Turneresque picture in which
forms dissolve and melt into one another under
the impact of light; at this point Renoir seems to
have gone even further in this direction than
Monet, who was to become the great virtuoso
of light. National Gallery of Art, Washington,
DC (Ailsa Mellon Bruce Collection).

In the spring of 1877 the friends managed to organise a third exhibition, largely
thanks to Gustave Caillebotte, who advanced the money needed to rent premises in the
Rue Le Peletier. This show marks a hardening of the Impressionists' resolve. For the
first time they actually applied the name to themselves, describing the event defiantly as
'The Exhibition of Impressionists'. They also agreed that no one would henceforth be
allowed to exhibit unless he foreswore the Salon; Degas, who had once pressed for a
less provocative, widely-based show, was now the most ardent of the separationists. A
sympathetic young critic, Georges Rivière, even published a periodical called *The
Impressionist* which ran concurrently with the show. The group of friends now
dominated the show itself, since they put on display large numbers of their works,
while the number of non-Impressionist exhibitors had fallen considerably. The
paintings by Renoir and Sisley mentioned above were shown; so were no less than eight
of Monet's *Gare St Lazare* series and a range of typical works by Degas, now achieving
full mastery in such chosen subjects as dancers and women washing.

While the Impressionists entrenched themselves, the press showed no signs of coming
over to them. Critics and cartoonists took up Albert Wolff's remarks about a
putrefying nude and made one joke after another in this vein. Leroy commented on the
Impressionists' studies at the morgue; a police commissioner supposedly asked for the
addresses of their models so that he could arrange for their burial; a caricatured painter
bemoaned his inability to capture the *smell* of a corpse. But one cartoon did achieve
genuine humour: in it, a gendarme rushes to stop a pregnant woman going into the
exhibition: 'Madame, it would be unwise to enter!'

The next few years were a time of bitter disappointments. For Impressionists like
Monet, Pissarro and Sisley, with large families and no private incomes, survival itself
often seemed in question. Year after year Monet found himself writing begging letters
to Manet, to Zola, to Gachet, unable to pay the rent or the removal men, unable even
to buy back his dead wife's pawned bracelet without a loan from one of these friends.
The economic climate remained as unfriendly as the critical one, prices were low,
Durand-Ruel was still in difficulties. The collector Hoschedé was ruined and his
collection auctioned at low prices, at one stroke depriving the Impressionists of a buyer
and flooding the market so that their unsold works were worth even less. And then, in
1878, Renoir decided to submit work to the Salon again.

This was the first serious defection from the Impressionists – ironically, not by one
of the hard-pressed family men in the group but by the bachelor Renoir. The following

Above:
Pierre Auguste Renoir. *The Seine at Argenteuil.*
1875. After his Argenteuil period, Renoir seems
to have lost interest in the painterly possibilities
of water (unlike Monet, who remained obsessed
with it to the end of his life), and turned back to
studies of the human figure. Portland Art
Museum, Portland, Oregon (Bequest of
Winslow B. Ayer).

Above right:
Édouard Manet. *The Seine at Argenteuil.* 1874.
This glowing canvas was executed at a time
when Manet was in very close contact with
Monet and was doing a great deal of painting in
the open air. But even here, Manet is not a
landscapist in the same sense as Monet: the
human presence is vital to the mood of the
picture. The Dowager Lady Aberconway.

Right:
Pierre Auguste Renoir. *The Angler.* About 1874.
Put up for auction at the disastrous Hôtel
Drouot sale of March 1875. It was bought for
only 180 francs by Georges Charpentier, who
became one of Renoir's most important patrons.
Private Collection.

year Sisley and Cézanne followed his example, and all three could therefore not show
at the fourth Impressionist exhibition, also held in 1879. Actually the word
'Impressionist' was dropped, on Degas's insistence, and the exhibitors simply called
themselves 'Independent Artists'. More people than ever before turned up at the
Avenue de l'Opéra to see the show, which actually made a profit through entrance fees;
but sales were poor and the press was still hostile – though lethargically so, since the
Impressionists were now stale news. Two newcomers among the exhibitors were to be
of some note: the American painter Mary Cassatt, introduced by Degas, and a young
man who worked for a stockbroking firm named Paul Gauguin, whose entry was
admitted at the last moment.

At the Salon of 1879 Renoir had an important success with a large painting of
Madame Charpentier and her children. It had proved an important commission for
him. He had been paid 1,000 francs for it – not an enormous price, but substantial
enough by comparision with the 100 francs or so that many of his old friends' paintings
were fetching. And thanks to the Charpentiers' influence the painting was well hung
and favourably received. It seemed as though Renoir had arrived at last.

The following year Monet, the initiator of the group exhibitions, cut himself off
from them by submitting canvases to the Salon; dispirited by his wife's death the
previous autumn, and by years of utter poverty, he hoped for a success like Renoir's.
Degas was scathing about this betrayal, and broke off relations with Monet; but then
he had never been poor, though some family disasters had for several years made him
partly dependent on sales in order to live comfortably.

The 'Independents' were now sadly reduced, and tended to split into two camps.
Berthe Morisot, Pissarro, his pupil Gauguin, Guillaumin, Caillebotte and others
represented the 'Impressionist' element; Degas – once in a virtual minority of one –
now had an equally large collection of friends and supporters, including Mary Cassatt
and an increasing number of artists such as the up-and-coming Jean François Raffäelli,
whom the rival faction regarded as completely irrelevant to the movement.

This was the situation during the fifth show of 1880, held in the Rue des Pyramides;
and it was virtually unchanged for the sixth show of 1881, back in the Boulevard des
Capucines, though not in Nadar's old studio where the whole venture had begun. With
bickerings between the two camps, defections, an unexcited public response, and
increasingly lukewarm support from old friends such as Zola, the Impressionists
seemed about to disband.

Any progress being made was outside the shows. In 1879 the Charpentiers had set up

a weekly review, *La Vie Moderne*, which sponsored occasional one-man shows – an idea that was still a tremendous novelty, and one that for the first time made it possible for the public to gauge an individual artist's development. The Salon had been reorganised, and in the more liberal atmosphere that prevailed, bright open-air painting was becoming accepted – provided the end product was not too adventurous in disregarding 'finish'. Manet, now a sick man, achieved the distinction of a second-class medal. And Durand-Ruel's fortunes improved (if only for a short time), enabling him to buy regularly and bring the Impressionists to public attention.

In spite of all difficulties a seventh show was arranged – and, such is the perversity of arrangements, it turned out to be a galaxy of Impressionist talent, less mixed with alien elements than any previous show. The exclusion of Degas's supporters was the culmination of the dissensions between the two groups of 'Independents'; and as a result, Degas himself, supported by Mary Cassatt, refused to exhibit. But Renoir, Monet and Sisley all returned – not as a matter of simple decision, but after a frantic, several-sided, last-minute correspondence, riddled with Ifs and Buts, which miraculously came out right in the end. There was even an appearance of whole-hearted enthusiasm in the abundance of canvases shown – an appearance only, since most of them were lent by Durand-Ruel, who was again in difficulties and wanted the group to have as much good publicity as it could get; some exhibitors, notably Renoir,

Pierre Auguste Renoir. *Nude in the Sunlight.* 1875–76. Shown at the second Impressionist exhibition in April 1876, and therefore earlier than other sun-dappled paintings such as the *Moulin de la Galette* and *The Swing.* The influential critic Albert Wolff wrote of this picture 'Try to explain to M. Renoir that a woman's torso is not a mass of rotting flesh covered with violet-green spots . . .'. Musée du Louvre, Paris.

Edgar Degas. *Portraits at the Bourse*. About 1878. Shown at the fourth Impressionist exhibition in 1879. The central figure is Ernest May, a Jewish banker and art collector who owned a number of Degas's works. However, this picture of the Parisian stock exchange is not entirely friendly. Musée du Louvre, Paris.

allowed their canvases to be shown mainly to oblige the dealer. Manet yet again decided not to show, as did Cézanne. But the final list was still impressive: Pissarro, Monet, Renoir, Sisley and Berthe Morisot, with their friends and followers Gauguin, Guillaumin, Caillebotte and Vignon. The show, held in the Rue St Honoré, was reasonably well received, and though there were still hostile press notices, it was becoming clear that by sheer persistence the Impressionists were making a place for themselves.

Above:
Berthe Morisot. *Woman at her Toilet.* About 1875. Shown at the fifth Impressionist exhibition in 1880. The combination of intimate subject, light tones and very free brush-work gives the painting its delightful romantic glow. Art Institute of Chicago, Illinois (Stickney Fund).

Left:
Edgar Degas. *Little Dancer, Aged Fourteen.* About 1880. A bronze cast from Degas's original wax model, which was shown at the sixth Impressionist exhibition of 1881. The tutu and ribbon are real fabric objects on both wax and bronze versions. Tate Gallery, London.

Paul Gauguin. *Snow. Rue Carcel.* About 1883.
This is Gauguin at his most Impressionist,
painting the kind of snow scene we expect from
Pissarro and Sisley. The subject is the painter's
own garden at 8 Rue Carcel, Paris. Ny Carlsberg
Glyptotek, Copenhagen.

The Break-up

Even before the Impressionists had achieved full acceptance, challenging new tendencies had begun to appear in French art. Odilon Redon began to exhibit paintings of a fantastic character that heralded the Symbolist and 'decadent' movements, so different in spirit from the everydayness of Impressionism. In 1884 the artists rejected by the Salon formed the nucleus of a Society of Independent Artists, which permitted anyone to exhibit who paid his membership dues. And the show of these new Independents – who perhaps, as rejected artists, even hoped the public would confuse them with the Impressionists – also marked the appearance of works by Georges Seurat, who was to take Impressionist colour theory and use it for his own somewhat different purposes. None of these phenomena would of course have been possible had not the Impressionists broken the monopoly of the Salon and partly prepared the public for new things.

But the Impressionists themselves no longer existed as a group, for all the deceptive unity of 1882. They increasingly lived apart and worked apart. Monet moved to Giverny and Pissarro to Eragny, some 60 to 65 kilometres from Paris and about 35 from each other; Sisley settled at Moret, even further away in the opposite direction. Manet died, Renoir travelled, Degas secluded himself in Paris, and Cézanne stayed for longer and longer periods in Aix. Impressionist unity was now reduced to monthly 'Impressionist dinners' – the sort of institutionalisation that only becomes necessary when genuine ésprit de corps has disappeared.

More important than personal disaffections were the work crises that began to afflict the individual Impressionists. A mood of dissatisfaction seems to have been general, but whereas Monet and Sisley eventually worked their way through it – becoming, if anything, more 'Impressionist' in their devotion to colour and light – Renoir and Pissarro changed course dramatically. Renoir renounced Impressionism altogether, for a style he claimed was a continuation of the 18th-century tradition; Pissarro embraced the theories of Seurat (see page 167) and became what he termed a 'Scientific Impressionist' as opposed to his old friends, who remained 'Romantic Impressionists'.

Pissarro had been the heart and soul of the group shows, respected by all and as friendly with Degas as with Renoir and Monet. Now he was himself part of a faction, and one disapproved of by all the rest. Nevertheless, in 1886 an eighth and final group show was patched together after a good deal of quarrelling. Since the term 'Independents' had been appropriated, the show was simply called 'The Eighth Exhibition of Paintings' – a title that did, however, insist on the show's continuity with the Anonymous-Impressionist-Independent development. In fact, the 1886 show was almost the reverse of the previous one, four years earlier. Degas and his friends returned; Renoir, Monet and Sisley stayed away. Berthe Morisot was the last of the Old Guard working in the central Impressionist tradition; Pissarro exhibited in a separate room with his 'Scientific Impressionist' friends Seurat and Signac. Their works – not anything that might conceivably have been termed 'Impressionist' – now attracted attention, ridicule, and the sarcasms of the press. If not exactly *passé*, Impressionism was no longer at the heart of controversy in France, though it was only just beginning to be known in London and New York. As chance would have it, Zola pronounced a kind of epitaph on the movement a month or so earlier in his novel *L'Oeuvre,* a brilliant evocation of the Impressionist adventure, despite the failure and madness of the central character, and the author's obvious conviction that Impressionism had only half-fulfilled itself.

In so far as it is ever possible to be categorical about such things, Zola was wrong in his general view. But with the closing of the last show in June 1886, Impressionism as a cohesive movement did cease to exist. Its practitioners, however – and its influence – were to live on for decades.

Mary Cassatt. *Girl Arranging her Hair.* 1886. Shown at the eighth Impressionist exhibition in 1886. Degas owned the painting, which owes something to his off-centre method of composition. But Mary Cassatt brings affection to the subject as well as her eye for truth. National Gallery of Art, Washington, DC (Chester Dale Collection).

Above:
Georges Seurat. *Bathers, Asnières.* 1883–84.
One of several paintings by Seurat, including
the celebrated *Sunday Afternoon on the Grande
Jatte,* in which he treats typical Impressionist
subjects in a quite un-Impressionist spirit: a
scene that would have been full of noise and
movement in reality is transformed here into an
eternal moment of mystical stillness. National
Gallery, London.

Below:
Vincent Van Gogh. *Outskirts of Paris: Road with
Peasant Shouldering a Spade.* 1887. This
delightful springtime study is perhaps the most
successful of Van Gogh's landscapes done in
the divisionist manner. He worked a good deal
out of doors with Seurat's disciple Signac.
Karen Johnson Hixon Collection, Fort Worth,
Texas.

Pierre Auguste Renoir. *The Luncheon of the Boating Party.* 1881. A record of simple, open-air pleasures that is reminiscent of the *Moulin de la Galette* and similar works of the mid-1870s. It might almost be considered Renoir's farewell to Impressionism, and indeed the treatment is rather more mannered. The girl with the dog is Aline Charigot, Renoir's future wife; the man in the T-shirt at the right is Gustave Caillebotte. Phillips Collection, Washington, DC.

Later Lives
Manet

The 1870s were a period of continuing disappointments for Manet. They had started promisingly: in 1872 Durand-Ruel bought, for 51,000 francs, a large batch of his paintings – including masterpieces such as the *Concert in the Tuileries Gardens,* which had lain in Manet's studio since 1862; and a year later his conventional *Bon Bock* was widely praised at the Salon, leading Manet to suppose that he was at last close to victory on 'the real field of battle'. In 1874 too he had an encouraging sale, when the singer Faure bought half-a-dozen of his paintings. Not that Manet badly needed to sell; but he desperately needed encouragement.

This was to be the last he received for some years. Despite his steady refusal to take part in the Impressionist group shows, Manet continued to be linked with the exhibitors by name in the hostile reviews; so he received the same abuse as they did without the glory of having made a stand. Nor was his moderate, conformist line rewarded at the Salon: from 1874 most of his entries were rejected by the jury, which also identified him with the rebels in the Boulevard des Capucines.

There was some show of reason in the jury's attitude, since Manet had in fact moved closer to the prevalent open-air style of his juniors – much closer than in the days when they were supposed to be 'Manet's gang'. This development had been foreshadowed by his Boulogne paintings of 1869, and may have been influenced by his relations with Berthe Morisot – not that Manet is likely to have been unaware of what stronger talents such as Monet were doing; but it is easier to learn from a lady admirer than from an equal or rival, however friendly. By 1874 Manet was painting open-air scenes in company with Monet and Renoir at Argenteuil, and certainly without any feeling of discipleship. *Argenteuil*, for example, has a gusty atmosphere as fresh as anything painted during the 1870s; even the couple posing rather self-consciously in the foreground contribute to the holiday feeling. Later in the summer of 1874 Manet visited Venice, where he painted in the same style with very free brush-work and a much lighter palette than he had employed in earlier years.

Even in this, his most plein-air 'Impressionist' period, Manet never painted with the small brush-strokes Monet and Renoir were using, or developed an equivalent obsession with the play of light. In fact Manet soon turned away from the regular practice of the open-air style, which was perhaps not wholly congenial to the more formal side of his genius. Something of the Impressionist mood and technique quite often appears in later paintings, and some were done on the spot, like the various versions of the *Rue Mosnier Decorated with Flags* (1878) and the superb *Chez le Père Lathuile* (1879), at first also known as *In the Open Air*; but most of Manet's work in the later 1870s was of quite a different character.

Or rather it was of several different characters: Manet's painting after about 1870, though still often displaying his splendid gifts, seems rather lacking in certainty and direction. Manet was highly sensitive to criticism as well as conventionally ambitious, and the Salon scandals and rejections seem to have made him doubt the value of his work. In 1873-4 we find him almost simultaneously painting a conventionally sombre 'Dutch' picture for the Salon and working swiftly and loosely in bright colours with his younger friends at Argenteuil. Later he was to range from a jewel-like brilliance seen, for example, in *In the Conservatory*, to a kind of lumpy expressionism that is vaguely reminiscent of the young Cézanne; and on occasion he even treated the same subject in radically different styles, as in the two versions of *The Beer Waitress (La Servante de Bocks)*.

The distinctive quality of Parisian life is captured in this last subject, as in *Nana* and *The Bar at the Folies-Bergère*. These may represent an effort on Manet's part to re-establish himself as 'the painter of modern life' championed by his dead friend Baudelaire, and so to give his work the cohesion it seemed to lack. This view gains support from Manet's uncharacteristic proposal to the Municipal Council of Paris,

142

Edouard Manet. *Chez le Père Lathuile*. 1879.
Shown at the Salon of 1880. A superb painting
which combines the Impressionist feeling for
open-air pleasures with a glimpsed relationship
between two people: its tension is felt although
its exact nature remains unknown. Musée des
Beaux Arts, Tournai (Collection H. van
Cutsem).

made in 1879: he asked them to commission him to execute a series of paintings for the
new Hôtel de Ville (town hall) that would capture the life of Paris in all its variety: Les
Halles (the food market), the railway, the racecourse, the parks, and so on. A project
on such an epic scale was not likely to have suited Manet's refined talent, and it may
have been just as well that the municipality refused his offer.

The idea for the project may have been suggested to Manet by the cumulative success
of Zola's Rougon-Macquart cycle of novels, which was doing for France in literature
what Manet proposed to do for Paris in painting. Zola, with his documentary approach
to the arts, would probably have approved. He and Manet remained on good terms,
and Manet's *Nana* is clearly related to Zola's novel of the same name; as the picture
was finished before the publication of the novel, Zola must have told Manet something
of the plot, which describes the career of a Second Empire sex-symbol-cum-courtesan.
The Salon jury rejected *Nana* on the grounds that it was immoral – doubtless because
the girl was in her underwear in the presence of a man (presumably her protector) fully
dressed in evening clothes. This, even more than *Olympia* 12 years before,
demonstrated the sinfulness of modernity in the academicians' eyes: Nana, revealing
nothing, was more immoral than the most lasciviously naked goddess of antiquity. And
Nana, like Olympia, sinned by looking at the spectator (and in rather more friendly
fashion than Olympia) so that he was drawn into the scene.

Whatever his private uncertainties, Manet kept up a front of extroverted amiability
in the evenings. From about 1876 he and his friends moved from the Café Guerbois to
the quieter Nouvelle-Athènes, just off the Place Pigalle. Renoir often put in an
appearance, and Degas usually turned up, though quite late; but the other painters in
the old Guerbois group, now somewhat scattered, were more rarely seen; the habitués
of the Athènes tended to be sympathetic critics and writers, but generally sufficiently
numerous to fill the two tables reserved for Manet and his friends.

From the public point of view, the years 1876-78 were the worst in Manet's career.
Only one of his paintings – a portrait of Faure as Hamlet – was accepted at the Salon.
In 1876 Manet held a private show of the rejects at his studio, and in 1878 he was so
discouraged that he omitted to send in any paintings at all for the jury's consideration.

At two auctions of Manet's works – one of Faure's collection, the other of the ruined Hoschedé's – the bids were discouragingly low. And at the new International Exhibition held at Paris in 1878, Manet's paintings were not considered worthy of being shown as representatives of French art.

The situation improved in 1880-81, with a one-man exhibition at *La Vie Moderne*, Salon acceptances, and finally the award of a second-class medal. However absurd such an award may seem for an artist of Manet's stature, it marked a real practical advance, since medallists' paintings were not submitted to the jury but were automatically admitted to the Salon. The following year, 1882, found Manet's friend Antonin Proust as Minister of Fine Arts in Gambetta's cabinet; and thanks to Proust, Manet at last received the Légion d'Honneur. Unfortunately these tokens of recognition came too late

Édouard Manet. *The Bar at the Folies-Bergère*. 1882. Shown at the Salon of 1882. By the time he painted this famous picture, Manet was so ill that he worked sitting down. It was done in his studio, with a real barmaid as the model, standing behind a table covered with bottles, glasses and fruit. Courtauld Institute Galleries, London.

Left:
Édouard Manet. *La Servante de Bocks* (The Beer Waitress). 1878-1879. Part of a larger painting that was cut in two. There is another version of the subject in the Musée du Louvre, Paris. National Gallery, London.

to give Manet the pleasure he would have felt as a younger man. By this time he was mortally sick, though still painting. Trying to recuperate at Versailles in 1882, he painted some outdoor scenes as exquisitely fresh and brilliantly coloured as anything he had ever done. On the other hand – a living contradiction to the last – he also did a large number of pastels in his last years which are rather pretty-pretty in a conventional, sentimental manner; like Degas, Manet found pastels easier to handle than oils when he was in poor health, but his works did not significantly advance the use of the medium. In the spring of 1883 his condition grew worse. His left leg became gangrenous and had to be amputated, but he failed to recover. He died on 30 April 1883, aged 51.

In January 1884 a memorial exhibition of Manet's work was held at the enemy headquarters – at the École des Beaux-Arts itself. The catalogue introduction was written by Manet's old friend Zola. The exhibition was well attended and was followed by an auction of the contents of Manet's studio, which fetched excellent prices. 'I should like to read the enthusiastic notice you will write about me – after my death', Manet had told the caustic Albert Wolff, whom he had tried so hard in life to conciliate (he even started to paint Wolff's portrait). The sequel, however, did not follow story-book lines: Wolff professed to be delighted with the high prices Manet's paintings had brought – but only for the sake of his widow . . . Proper recognition came five years later, at the International Exhibition held in Paris, where a group of Manet's works were widely seen and admired. In 1890 Claude Monet raised a subscription to buy *Olympia* and succeeded in having the picture installed in the Musée du Luxembourg, which was (so to speak) the antechamber of the Louvre: in the 19th century, pictures by distinguished contemporaries or near-contemporaries stayed in the Luxembourg until they had aged sufficiently to be transferred to the Louvre itself. Finally, in 1907, with a little help from Monet's friend, the politician Georges Clemenceau, who had once sat for Manet, the shameless Olympia found herself enshrined in the Louvre.

Édouard Manet. *Portrait of Clemenceau*. About
1879. Georges Clemenceau (1841-1929) was a
doctor and rising Radical politician when this
was painted. He became one of the most
prominent of the Dreyfusards who worked to
reverse the unjust conviction of Dreyfus for
spying. Later, as a prime minister of France, he
led the country during the First World War. He
was a particularly close friend of Claude Monet.
Manet's painting remained unfinished, since
Clemenceau was too busy to continue the
sittings. Musée du Louvre, Paris.

Degas

After the suppression of the Commune, Degas returned to Paris and his career resumed its quiet, laborious course. However, the 1870s were to be more eventful than any other period of his life. On the public level there was his involvement with the Impressionist group shows, which has already been described. Privately, there were shocks. Some aspect of Degas's military service seems to have caused – or revealed – a serious weakness in his eyesight, which was always afterwards a subject of worry. And after the death of Degas's father in 1874 the family finances suffered reverses; René Degas ended up owing a great deal of money he could not pay, and Edgar sacrificed much of his own fortune – and his collection of works of art – to meet the debts. This action was evidently required by Degas's strict sense of what constituted good form, as was his refusal to discuss his misfortunes, let alone complain of them. He does remark in one letter that he was 'obliged to do something to earn money every day', but this was probably an exaggeration: Degas seems to have remained fairly comfortable but perhaps did need to make occasional sales – which, fortunately, he found not too difficult.

Degas's artistic development was seemingly unaffected by these reverses. In 1872 he began the studies of dancers that were to become the most widely known of all his works. Once more there are the characteristic 'cut-off' effects, the subtle 'unfocused'

Below:
Edgar Degas. *The Pedicure.* 1873. An interesting paradox in Degas's art: the subject is daringly 'modern' and workaday, yet it is treated with a 'classical' detachment. Musée de Louvre, Paris (Camondo Collection).

Right:
Photograph of Degas with his housekeeper.

Left:
Edgar Degas. *The Cotton Market, New Orleans.*
1873. A typical Degas composition, with the
apparently accidental quality of a photograph.
This was the only picture Degas painted on his
American trip except for family portraits – and,
again typically, he chooses not an exotic scene
but an interior that might equally well have been
Parisian. The old gentleman in the foreground is
Degas's uncle, Michel Musson. One brother,
Achille, leans against the partition window; the
other, René, reads a newspaper. Musée des
Beaux Arts, Pau.

Right:
Edgar Degas. *Absinthe,* 1876. Sometimes taken
as a description of the dangers of alcohol; but
this was almost certainly not in Degas's mind.
The man is Marcellin Desboutin, whose less-
than-polished appearance was bohemian rather
than drink-induced. He was a writer and artist,
exhibiting with the Impressionists in 1876. The
woman is the actress Ellen Andrée. Musée du
Louvre, Paris.

compositions, the unusual angles. Once more there is a deliberate avoidance of drama,
which in this case means the actual performance. The dancers are shown rehearsing,
resting, lacing their pumps, adjusting their dresses, limbering up. Or, if there is a
performance, its significance is often minimised and the emotion defused: we see the
dancers over the heads of people in a box, or de-glamorised by a glimpse of figures
waiting in the wings, or in close-ups that emphasise the purely physical nature of the
action. Degas, in fact, avoids emotion just as much as he avoids drama. This explains
his choice of subjects, which otherwise seems random. He concentrates on people
whose lives are spent in disciplined physical effort, which makes for a maximum of
physical grace and a minimum of personal emotion. Two men racing their horses may
yell with exhilaration; a couple dancing may be moved by lust or joy; but jockeys and
ballet dancers are first and foremost efficient bodies which evoke more emotion than
they display.

Seen in this way, Degas's next new subject was a logical choice: the hard-worked
washerwoman, physically larger than the dancer, a top-heavy presence with her
muscled shoulders and arms, but still absorbed in physical performance and not much
given to expressing any feeling beyond fatigue. Degas's nudes too, though often
sensual, are entirely absorbed in physical processes (washing, combing their hair),
during which they show no consciousness of the artist's presence. Degas himself likened

Below:
Edgar Degas. *At the Seaside.* About 1876. Done
with oil thinned with turpentine on paper. This
is about as close as Degas ever came to the
spontaneous, open-air side of Impressionism –
not really very close. This is still a very
deliberately designed work with bold colour
contrasts and the characteristic Degas 'cut-off'
at the edges. National Gallery, London.

his approach to spying on the subject through a keyhole. Even a thoroughly unusual subject such as *The Pedicure* is a simple physical transaction that carries no particular emotional weight – unlike, say, the extraction of a tooth.

For Degas, the distillation of physical poetry from a given subject was a specialised task that required endless study and was capable of yielding endlessly varied results. He would quite certainly have approved Goethe's famous line 'In limitation only is the master manifest'. His attitude was most clearly revealed during the trip he made in 1872 to visit his brother Achille, who was a cotton merchant in New Orleans. The colourful life of Louisiana inspired him with no more than some vague plans: the main product of the visit was an interior – *The Cotton Market, New Orleans* – that might have been painted in Paris. Yet Degas was far from unresponsive to this new environment: characteristically, he was impressed more by the people than by their

surroundings, and above all by the pictorial qualities they embodied – the black women carrying white children about, the fascinating mixture of races in shops, offices and imposing colonial-style buildings, the exotic orange groves. True, Degas complained that it was hard to work because the light was too strong for his sensitive eyes; but he also reiterates in his letters that the wonders of New Orleans are irrelevant because thorough familiarity is essential for the production of good art. And he makes the revealing comment that 'Instantaneous impressions are merely photographic' – which puts in a nutshell the progressive elimination of the inessential that forms so large a part of his endeavours.

So in April 1873 Degas returned to Paris, and to dancers, singers, jockeys, washerwomen, milliners, nudes. He was fortunate in that his work was appreciated by

a circle of friends and acquaintances such as the de Goncourt brothers – writers and
well-known connoisseurs – and also attracted less hostile attention than that of his
fellow-exhibitors at the Impressionist/Independent shows.

The first substantial defence of the exhibitors was *The New Painting* (1876), a
pamphlet by Degas's friend Edmond Duranty which stressed the 'modern-life' aspect of
the movement and made Degas its hero. Degas's worst notice came from the
implacable Albert Wolff, who classed the painter as a 'lunatic' like Pissarro (who used
crazy colours) and Renoir (who painted women as masses of rotting flesh). 'Just you
try to make M. Degas see reason – tell him art includes such qualities as drawing,
colour, technique and control, and he will laugh in your face and label you a
reactionary.' Degas is said to have commented 'How could he possibly understand? He
arrived in Paris by way of the tree-tops!'

In any case, Degas thrived on opposition; at the Café Guerbois and at its successor,
the Nouvelle-Athènes, he was as disputatious as ever. In 1877 his friend Halévy wrote
and staged a play called *La Cigale*, featuring an 'Impressionist' whose landscapes
looked just as good (or bad) whichever way up they were hung; Degas agreed to design
the studio set, doubtless enjoying the joke against his fellow-exhibitors.

From about this time Degas made increasing use of pastel – at first, it seems, because
pastels were quick and easy to do, and sold well, thus making light work of the money-
earning that he now found necessary. They were also useful for on-the-spot notations
that could be worked up in the studio – about as close as Degas ever got to the plein-
air methods of his colleagues. Deteriorating eyesight soon gave him a reason for
working seriously with pastel, though he had to devise new technical procedures to
obtain the surface richness and the variations in texture he desired. One method was to
mix the pastel with water and apply it to the paper with a brush; another, which
permitted more varied effects, was to blow steam on to the picture and then work over
the dampened areas to create smooth or hatched surfaces that contrasted effectively
with the 'dry' untouched pastel areas. The evolution of Degas's techniques and mastery
over the years can be traced through *Café-Concert at the 'Ambassadeurs'* and *At the
Milliner's* to the late *Woman Drying Herself*, each representing an advance in
elimination of detail and enrichment of the picture surface.

As might be expected of such a superb draughtsman, Degas left a splendid collection
of graphic work. In some of these – and especially in his monotypes (single-copy prints)
– he worked with a freedom and emotional expressiveness deliberately excluded from
his more formal productions. Around 1880 he made an interesting series of brothel-life
and sexual scenes (many of the latter apparently destroyed by Degas's family after his
death); the subject was very much in the air, since the de Goncourts, Zola and Guy de
Maupassant were all writing sensational stories about prostitutes at about the same

Edgar Degas. *Miss Lala at the Cirque Fernando.*
1879. Circus pictures have been popular since
the later 19th century, attracting artists as
diverse as Seurat, Toulouse-Lautrec, Picasso
and Rouault. Degas ignores the human setting
and concentrates on the performer's strength
and skill. National Gallery, London.

Left:
Edgar Degas. *Miss Lala at the Cirque Fernando*.
1879. Another version in pastels. Tate Gallery,
London.

Below:
Edgar Degas. *Jockeys in the Rain*. About 1881.
One of the artist's favourite subjects, this time
rendered in pastel. Glasgow Art Gallery (Burrell
Collection).

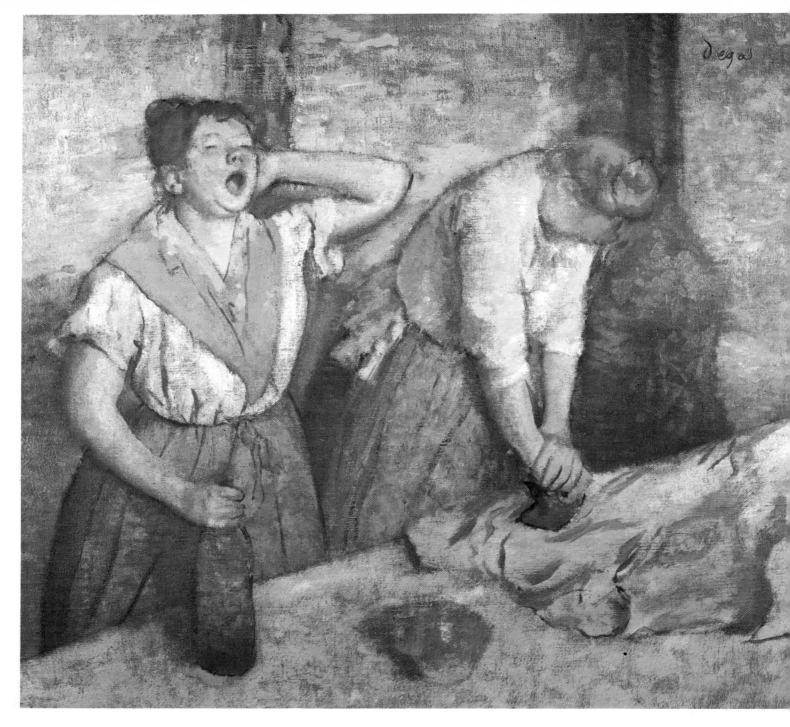

time. The feeling in these prints is generally grotesque, though sometimes very sensual too, bringing to mind later artists such as Henri de Toulouse-Lautrec (virtually Degas's disciple) and Georg Grosz. Still later, in the 1890s, Degas made a series of colour monotypes of landscapes – not the humanised countryside of his nature-loving Impressionist companions-in-arms, but with a slightly sinister quality reminiscent of the backgrounds in Symbolist paintings. Degas's works verge on abstraction without losing this underlying feeling.

This quality may be partly accidental in origin, since Degas's eyesight was giving him more and more trouble. By the 1900s it was almost impossible for him to work except with sculpture, where he could still create by relying on his sense of touch. He had experimented intermittently with modelling from as early as the 1860s, and had exhibited his *Little Dancer, Aged Fourteen* at the 1881 show. His work in this medium quickly won admirers, and indeed Renoir was to claim that Degas was the first great sculptor 'since the days of the cathedrals'.

Even in old age Degas remained cantankerous; Renoir said, justly, that he quarrelled with everybody in the end. During the Dreyfus Affair, Degas became a fierce anti-Dreyfusard and anti-semite, breaking with Jewish friends such as Halévy and Pissarro, and going so far as to dismiss models he suspected of being Jewish – or Protestant, since he believed the Protestants were part of the Dreyfus 'conspiracy'. To the end he was loyal to his own narrow social circle, and to the code he derived from it (and interpreted rigidly enough to provide the occasion for antagonisms).

Degas's limited sympathies, the impersonality of his approach to his subjects, impoverished his life while they gave his art its strength. Though unable to work after about 1908, he survived through to the First World War, and could occasionally be seen wandering about on the boulevards and being helped by gendarmes to avoid the motor cars he detested and feared. He died on 27 September 1917 and was buried in Montmartre, whose women and cabarets he had done so much to make famous.

Above:
Edgar Degas. *Women Ironing*. About 1884. Perhaps the best known of a series in oils and pastel on this subject. Degas was unsurpassed in his ability to combine accurately-captured movements with the requirements of picture composition: the horizontal line of the yawning woman's arm, and the self-contained vertical stance of her companion, are as formally satisfactory as they are natural to the situation. Musée du Louvre, Paris.

Above right:
Edgar Degas. *Le Tub*. 1886. One of the finest of the great series of pastels on this subject, which obsessed Degas in the 1880s and '90s. The sense of intimacy, of being an unnoticed presence, is heightened by the unusual viewpoint. Musée du Louvre, Paris.

Right:
Edgar Degas. *Woman Drying Herself*. About 1890-95. In a rather different, more richly sensual mood from *The Tub*. National Gallery of Scotland, Edinburgh (Maitland Gift).

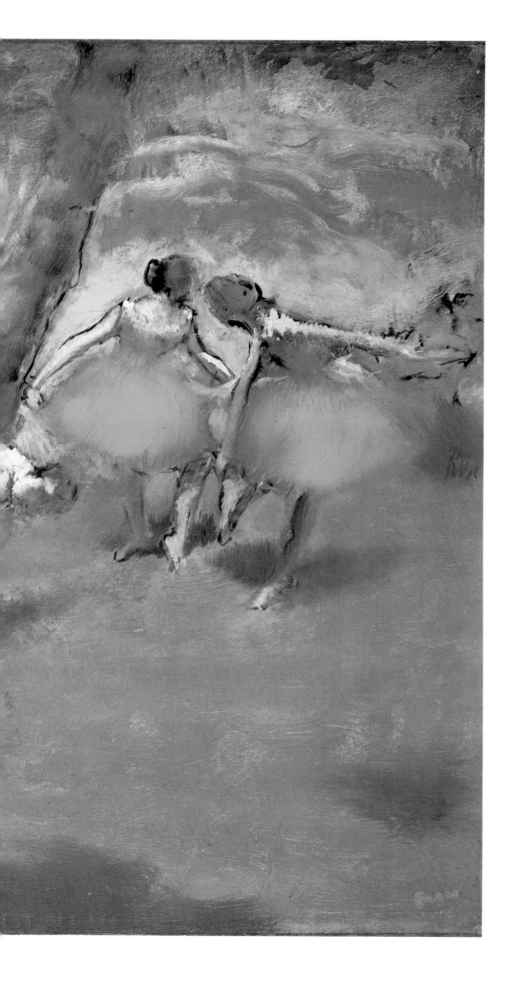

Edgar Degas. *Before the Performance*. About
1896-98. A sort of Impressionism of the
indoors, with the dancers merging into the set
under the strong artificial light – though even
here, at his most summary, Degas does not
abandon outlines altogether. National Gallery of
Scotland, Edinburgh.

Pissarro

After 1870 Pissarro's stature grew rapidly, both as an artist and as a presence within the Impressionist group. Now in his forties, he became a kind of benevolent father-figure, almost universally liked, and willing and able to combine his own work with organising exhibitions and making up quarrels – two activities that amounted to much the same thing, as Pissarro's letters show quite clearly. And despite his conciliatory organisational tactics, Pissarro himself was the only painter who showed his work at all the eight Impressionist exhibitions between 1874 and 1886. Having made up his mind not to seek official recognition in any circumstances, he held to his course without wavering, despite periods of extreme poverty that brought his wife close to suicide.

But Pissarro was far more than an organisation man or partisan: Cézanne, as we have seen, never ceased to admire him, called him 'humble and colossal', and thought that he might have been 'the strongest of us all'. Curiously enough, Pissarro, so firm in his anti-Establishment convictions, was the most susceptible of the Impressionists to artistic influence, and changed his style several times – an unusual characteristic in an artist so preoccupied with theoretical questions, which generally indicates a dogmatic, novelty-resistant temperament. Pissarro's susceptibility went beyond the early eclecticism of Renoir, and must have stemmed from an inner uncertainty that occasionally led him down blind alleys.

In 1870 all this lay in the future. Pissarro himself remarked that though by this date he was a zealous propagandist for open-air painting, he still had no conception of the implications and consequences. His exile in England lasted until June 1871: whatever his political convictions, Pissarro missed not only the war but the Commune too, returning only when bourgeois 'order' was restored. In England, as we have seen, he reached a late but impressive artistic maturity, perhaps completed by his contacts with Monet. On the material plane he was less successful, though his meeting with the dealer Paul Durand-Ruel held out some promise of better things to come. And he married Julie Vellay, who was henceforth the dominating matriarch of Pissarro's growing family.

Back at Louveciennes, Pissarro resigned himself to the Prussians' triumphant vandalism and set to work again. For a time he was joined by Alfred Sisley, who was living in the same town. Pissarro had a profound respect for Sisley, perhaps reinforced by the fact that both had been followers of Corot, and both confronted nature with a passion quieter and less flamboyant than, say, that of Monet and Renoir; even the layout of their paintings had points of resemblance, since both at this time favoured scenes with roads or rivers running away from the foreground into the distance. However, once Pissarro left Louveciennes he seems to have seen relatively little of Sisley; after Sisley's death he called him 'a beautiful and great artist'.

In the spring of 1872 Pissarro moved further north and across the Seine to Pontoise. In September Cézanne joined him, living in or near Pontoise until early 1874. Nothing better illustrates Pissarro's gift for teaching without condescension than his successful relationship with Cézanne, who was touchy to the point of paranoia. Part of this gift was a capacity for learning that kept Pissarro's friendships – even with very much younger men – on a basis of equality. To Cézanne he demonstrated the virtues and technical skills of open-air working; but contact with Cézanne served to strengthen Pissarro's feeling for picture structure and the solid forms on which the light falls. The temperamental basis for this already existed: whereas Monet's element was water, perpetually moving and breaking up reflections so that reality tended to dissolve, Pissarro was primarily a painter of domesticated landscape, bathed but not drowned in light. If his forms never have quite the weight of Cézanne's, they are still further from the mirage-like objects that appear in Monet's or Renoir's works of the early '70s. There is perhaps a hint of Cézanne's influence in a picture such as *Red Roofs, Edge of a Village*, painted as late as 1877. At the time, however, it was Pissarro's influence on

Cézanne that was most evident, and Cézanne even solemnly carried off one of Pissarro's paintings of trees at Louveciennes in order to learn by copying it.

During this period Pissarro, like the other Impressionists, was optimistic. At the Hoschedé sale in 1873, one of his pictures fetched 950 francs, and he proudly claimed that this was an amazing sum for 'a mere landscape'. Then, with the economic recession and the failure of the first Impressionist show, Pissarro, like the rest, fell on hard times again – with the additional grief of the death of his nine-year-old daughter Minette only a few days before the show opened on 15 April 1874. Pissarro's unspectacular art became so unsaleable that the dealer Père Martin – the dealer of the

Pissarro and his wife. Pissarro met his companion and eventual wife, Julie Vellay, when she worked as a maid for his family after their return to France. Years of poverty and ill-success understandably did nothing to help her appreciation of art; but though she ruled the Pissarro household, she failed to turn her husband into a practical man, or to stop their children from becoming artists.

Below:
Camille Pissarro. *Harvest at Montfoucault*. 1876. Montfoucault was a farm in Normandy that belonged to Pissarro's painter friend Ludovic Piette. Pissarro and his family were frequent visitors, and Montfoucault often served as a refuge when they were desperately short of money in the 1860s and 1870s. Piette died in 1877. Pissarro captures admirably the Breton landscape, with brighter, fresher colours than those of the Pontoise area. Musée du Louvre, Paris.

Camille Pissarro. *The Village of Pontoise.* 1872. Kunstmuseum, Basel.

Camille Pissarro. *Red Roofs, Edge of a Village.*
1877. The dense, screened quality of this
painting is reinforced by the mass of small
brush-strokes, which form a thick, rich, brilliant
paint surface. Musée du Louvre, Paris.

last resort for the Impressionists, paying a miserable 50 francs or so for a painting – refused even to handle his work. And though he was not involved in the disastrous Hôtel Drouot sale of 1875, Pissarro did allow four of his paintings to be auctioned after the 1876 group show. The results were no more encouraging: the highest price he commanded was 230 francs.

The reverses of these years sapped Pissarro's confidence; for a short time in 1875 he even tried to change his style, using a palette knife again as he had in the mid-1860s when most under Courbet's influence. Yet in spite of his difficulties Pissarro was at the height of his powers: like most of his colleagues, in the 1870s he was exploiting the new possibilities revealed by the Impressionist vision and technique, as yet unaware that it might have any limitations. His palette was appreciably lighter than in the past, as in *Red Roofs*, and his composition was more subtle; instead of the slightly monotonous 'long-shots' of subjects, there were skilfully chosen medium-distance views, or views half-concealed by trees in the foreground. In other pictures, such as *Orchard in Pontoise*, Pissarro's joy in nature achieves full expression. It was painted during one of Cézanne's visits, when the two men worked side by side, ostensibly recording the same subject; but where Pissarro sees a mass of flowering trees, Cézanne sees the geometric masses of houses on the hillside, with a rather sparse and relatively insignificant group of trees at the foot. Even in the objective art of the Impressionists, what Zola called 'the medium of a temperament' affected what was seen as well as how it was seen.

In these years Pissarro worked mainly around Pontoise, or at Montfoucault, his friend Piette's farm in Normandy. In 1877 he rented a room in Paris on the Quai d'Anjou, where his friends Cézanne and Guillaumin were staying, but much of his time in the capital was spent in desperate efforts to sell 50-franc paintings to dealers like Georges Petit. Even a sympathiser like Eugène Murer was either unwilling or unable to give substantially more; and in 1878 Pissarro was forced to appeal to Père Martin, who had actually run down his work. He wrote gloomily, 'Soon I shall be an old man, my sight will fail, and I shall be no better off than I was twenty years ago'.

One tragi-comic incident summed up public indifference to Pissarro's art. Eugène Murer ran a lottery from his pastry shop, with a painting by Pissarro as first prize. The event attracted so little interest that it had to be postponed; but when the draw was eventually made, the winner was a local girl who opted for a cream bun instead of Pissarro's picture. Murer obligingly gave her the bun.

Pissarro's role as an exhibition organiser was most important in the shows of 1879-1882; Monet and Renoir seem to have been at least as energetic during the early shows, until Renoir defected and Monet became discouraged. In 1879 and 1880 Pissarro and Caillebotte were the chief organisers; in 1881 Caillebotte, who had become increasingly hostile to Degas and his followers, dropped out. Pissarro, though artistically quite dissimilar to Degas, was on excellent terms with both Degas and his friend Mary Cassatt. All three worked together at etching, and Mary Cassatt later painted beside Pissarro at Pontoise; she said of him that he was such a good teacher he could have taught the stones to draw. These friendships were not disrupted by the 1882 exhibition, from which Degas and Miss Cassatt withdrew, though Pissarro was otherwise successful in bringing together the other leading exhibitors of the 1874 show in a deceptive display of unity.

One of the new exhibitors in 1879 was an amateur called Paul Gauguin who had become a pupil of Pissarro – another difficult character, and one about whom even the uncensorious Pissarro had reservations. The old pupil and the new met a couple of years later when Cézanne came to Pontoise; though Gauguin admired Cézanne's work, the younger man's thrusting, caustic manner was too much for the ultra-suspicious Cézanne, who was ever afterwards convinced that Gauguin had stolen his way of registering his painterly sensations.

Pissarro's life was no easier in the 1880s than it had ever been. His wife had never thought much of painting as a way of earning a living, and she scolded all the more intensely as the Pissarros' eldest son, Lucien, showed signs of wanting to become an artist instead of bringing money into the house. Julie, as one observer noted, 'wore the trousers'. She got her way in everything except the thing that mattered: unresisting yet unmoved, Pissarro practised his art, and one after another his sons followed suit. In fact, Pissarro had the gift of immersing himself in his work so thoroughly that he became oblivious to his miseries; his moments of gloom seem to have been shortlived, and when commenting on Guillaumin's reluctance to give up his regularly paid job, Pissarro declared that for all his sufferings he would have done the same again. Julie Pissarro, who had no such consolation, and who besides had to manage the money and grow vegetables in the garden, can hardly be blamed for feeling differently. She also had to look after and feed the children; and by 1884 there were five of them alive and a sixth on the way.

Since 1882 the Pissarros had been living at Osny, very close to Pontoise. Now they found a house with room enough for them all at Eragny, a village of a few hundred souls about 60 kilometres north-north-west of Paris. The large ramshackle house and huge garden, and the closeness of the River Epte, seemingly made the place ideal for a painter with a large family. Eragny did indeed become Pissarro's home for the rest of

Above:
Camille Pissarro. *The Path across the Fields.* 1879. A typical Impressionist subject, treated in homely fashion by Pissarro. Musée du Louvre, Paris.

Above left:
Camille Pissarro. *Orchard in Pontoise, Quai de Pothuis.* 1877. Shown at the fourth Impressionist exhibition in 1879. The orchard was just behind Pissarro's house, and he and Cézanne painted the same view. Musée du Louvre, Paris.

Left:
Camille Pissarro. *Grey Day on the Banks of the Oise.* 1878. A quiet, subtle picture. The view shown through a screen of trees was one of Pissarro's favourite devices, giving interest and formal complexity to a subject that might otherwise have been dull. Musée du Louvre, Paris.

his life, though mainly because Julie refused to move despite Pissarro's later restlessness.

Though his work had begun to fetch better prices, Pissarro was dissatisfied with it. The feeling was common to most of the Impressionists in the early '80s, though their consequent decisions were widely different. In Pissarro's case, meeting two young men – Paul Signac, and later Georges Seurat – led to his conversion to divisionism or Neo-Impressionism. As formulated by Seurat, this reduced the small Impressionist brush-stroke to a dot, and took optical mixture to its seemingly logical conclusion: seen close up, the divisionist canvas is a swirling multi-coloured mass of dots; at a distance its colours have a singular luminosity, as Pissarro tried to point out to his sceptical Impressionist colleagues. On the other hand, the dot technique was so laborious that it made working out of doors virtually impossible. Seurat himself produced pictures conveying a mood quite different from Impressionist works, despite the technical relationship between them. His art has a formal, slightly mysterious, timeless quality, as in the famous *Sunday Afternoon on the Island of the Grande Jatte*; this is Impressionist in subject while not attempting to capture light, atmosphere, movement or a feeling of relaxed Sunday enjoyment.

The rejection of these qualities may have been consciously emphatic in the *Grande Jatte*, which has been interpreted as a deliberate anti-Impressionist manifesto. It was shown at the 1886 exhibition along with divisionist paintings by Signac, Pissarro and Pissarro's son Lucien; these were only included after fierce arguments, and were shown in a separate room. Pissarro, once the conciliator, was now a party man, rowing furiously with Eugène Manet over the inclusion of Seurat and Signac, and irritating his old friends by attempts to convert them. Monet was angry, Degas scornful, Renoir blandly unconcerned; having not yet received much in the way of recognition, none of them was inclined to believe that 26-year-old Seurat had discovered a scientific approach to painting that relegated them to romantic 'forerunners'.

It says a good deal for Pissarro's humility that he was willing to become a follower at the age of 56. On the other hand, his letters make it quite clear that he thoroughly enjoyed himself as a fighting member of a new movement: the theorising, the discussions of exhibition results, and the range of fresh contacts with the younger generation of painters and critics seem to have given Pissarro a kind of second youth – perhaps a painter's version of the last fling of middle age. Now and later he seems to have been glad of an excuse to stay away from home – which was probably all the less welcoming a place since his change of style had reduced the family to penury again. In April 1887, according to a letter she wrote to her son Lucien, Julie Pissarro was in such a state of despair that she had taken her two younger children to the river with the intention of drowning herself and them; but her courage had failed her.

Pissarro began to fall out of love with Neo-Impressionism as early as 1888, when he complained that working with dots was too laborious and entailed a loss of movement and life; his impatience is shown by the fact that even his most divisionist pictures are painted with rather larger dots – more like commas – than Seurat employed. By 1890 Pissarro had abandoned the technique, and in March 1891, while he mourned Seurat's tragically early death, he wrote that divisionism too was 'finished'.

Pissarro's break with Neo-Impressionism was well timed, since the reputation of his Impressionist work was beginning to rise very quickly. A retrospective show put on by Durand-Ruel in January 1892 established Pissarro once and for all: it was well received by the critics, and over 50 paintings were sold. Although Julie almost immediately made him buy the house at Eragny, giving her the security she had lacked for so many years, Pissarro appears to have had no serious financial problems from this time. One advantage of this was that he could travel – to Rouen, which had become one of his favourite working places, to London, or even just to Paris. The truth was that he had exhausted Eragny as a place to work, and was always glad to be away from it.

Pissarro's trip to Belgium in June 1894 was apparently prompted by other considerations. A series of anarchist bomb attacks and assassinations culminated in the stabbing of the French president, Sadi Carnot, and Pissarro's connections with anarchism were sufficiently strong for him to believe it was prudent to leave the country until the repressive backlash had exhausted itself. Anarchism is a form of socialism that advocates the abolition of the state – not the seizure of power by socialists but the abolition of all state power and its replacement by a society of free men living and working in co-operation by choice. By all accounts Pissarro had long been in sympathy with such ideas: in 1874, for example, he had wanted to organise the Impressionist 'Anonymous Society' on the lines of a bakers' co-operative he was

familiar with. But his active involvement with anarchist groups seems to have begun only late in life, perhaps as a substitute for the lost conspiratorial stimulus of Neo-Impressionism: he joined a debating club, subscribed to an anarchist journal, and contributed occasional lithographs: no more. Much has been made of his political views, but his statement that 'only painting counts' tells us more about his life: it seems that he was interested in events – from the Commune to the Dreyfus case – rather than involved in them: there is no record of his taking part in a march, let alone throwing a bomb. Pissarro's anarchism was of the peaceful-constructive rather than the terrorist type, and his 'flight' was the most political of his recorded acts – though not, it should be said, an unreasonable one, since a number of his friends were arrested for a time. However, when the furore died down Pissarro allowed his 'exile' to turn into a leisurely vacation before he returned to the bosom of his family.

From 1889 Pissarro had serious trouble with his right eye, and it was never completely cured. An infection caused the tear duct to become inflamed and made it impossible for him to work in the open for long periods. Like other Impressionists towards the end of the century, he came to value the work – and reworking – that could be done in the studio, without wishing to abandon spontaneous impressions recorded in the open air. Pissarro discovered a compromise solution that also helped to preserve his eyes: he rented a series of hotel rooms from which he painted the splendid views of the boulevards which are among the best works of his later years. In summer he managed to work on the coast, most often in or near Dieppe. He was still in general and creative good health when a prostate abscess, wrongly treated (or rather, it seems, neglected by a homeopathic practitioner), turned into blood poisoning. Pissarro died, aged 73, on 13 November 1903.

Monet

Monet's life in the early 1870s was virtually synonymous with the history of Impressionism. We have already seen the importance of his relationships with Renoir at La Grenouillère and with Pissarro in London; his visits to the Netherlands; and his part in organising and naming the Impressionists as an exhibiting group. As in the 1860s, he was the most aggressive of the Impressionists as well as the most technically adventurous. Later on he shared in the further struggles of the group – in the Hôtel Drouot auction of 1875 (in which 20 of his paintings grossed a mere 4,655 francs) and in the second, third and fourth shows.

For Monet as an individual, his private struggles were even more bitter than the public ones. As an artist he was in his prime, producing the splendid Argenteuil paintings and the Gare St Lazare series. But poverty was beginning to wear him down: in 1875 he was still proclaiming his faith in the future while begging a 20-franc note from Manet; but by the late '70s he several times remarked in despair that, approaching 40, he had completely failed to make his mark. In 1878 one of his chief supports fell away: the financier Ernest Hoschedé, Monet's patron and a generous host at his château, went bankrupt. At the auction of Hoschedé's collection that followed, 12 of Monet's paintings sold for a miserable average price of 184 francs – an even worse result than at the Hôtel Drouot auction three years before. This was all the more depressing since Monet's second son, Jean, had only just been born, and Camille seemed unable to recover from the birth. The only bright spot was that the Monets were now established – apparently with help from Manet – at the peaceful village of Vétheuil, about 55 kilometres below Paris on the River Seine. Madame Hoschedé left her husband and arrived at Vétheuil soon afterwards to look after Camille, bringing her six children with her; so Monet was now responsible for a household of patriarchal dimensions. In September of the following year, Camille died; Monet later confessed with a certain self-disgust that he had become so much a slave to his art that he found himself carefully noting the colours cast by death on his wife's face.

Although the receipts at the fourth Impressionist show of 1879 were quite encouraging, Monet seems to have taken more notice of the 'renegade' Renoir's success at the Salon. This, together with the death of Camille – who had been his companion in years of poverty and nothing but poverty – may have inclined Monet to compromise with the established system and submit paintings to the Salon once more. He evidently felt guilty about defecting from the Impressionist camp, since he tried to shift the blame on to his former associates. 'I am still and always intend to be an Impressionist ... but I see only very rarely the men and women who are my colleagues. The little band [of Impressionists] has become a club which opens its doors to the first dauber' – which was hardly a reasonable comment, since painters were certainly not rushing to join the Impressionists in 1879-80, and any dilution of the Impressionist element in 'the little band' might equally well have been put down to the capitulations of Renoir, Sisley, Cézanne and Monet himself.

Monet's remarks were made at a one-man show of his works on the premises of *La Vie Moderne* in June 1880. His return to the Salon had only been partly successful (the more important of his two submissions, a study of floating ice on the Seine, had been rejected), and he was soon to break with the Salon for good. He failed to sell a single painting at his one-man exhibition; but after it Madame Charpentier – the wife of *La Vie Moderne*'s proprietor – bought the rejected *Floating Ice on the Seine* for the substantial sum of 1,500 francs.

Such windfalls were no doubt welcome, though they were no substitute for public acceptance and the security which came from regular commissions and sales. From that point of view a more genuinely encouraging sign was Durand-Ruel's financial recovery and consequent resumption of buying. It was largely through Durand-Ruel's efforts that the Impressionists came together again for the exhibition of 1882, to which Monet

170

Claude Monet. *Self-Portrait.* 1917. Musée du Louvre, Paris.

Above:
Claude Monet. *Jean on his Wooden Horse.*
1872. From the collection of Mr Nathan
Cummings, New York.

Right:
Claude Monet. *The Gare St Lazare, Paris.* 1877.
Monet painted a whole series of pictures with
this famous railway station as their subject. True
to form, he is not interested in making any kind
of 'modern life' comment, but concentrates on
capturing the effects of shooting steam and
light filtered through begrimed glass. Musée du
Louvre, Paris.

contributed 30 paintings. But he had now begun to feel that the group shows were
boring the public without winning over the press, and he gladly agreed to Durand-
Ruel's plan to hold a series of one-man shows instead. Monet's show was held in
March 1883, and his complaints that it had not been properly mounted can probably be
taken as indicating a return of confidence in his own powers: when not depressed by
failure Monet was tough and unsentimental in his dealings with others. This was made
still clearer in 1885, when he had an exhibition at the gallery of Durand-Ruel's great
rival, Georges Petit, much to Durand-Ruel's consternation; Monet disarmingly
explained that Impressionist paintings had to be more widely shown so that the public
would become convinced that the movement was something more than a particular
idiosyncrasy of Durand-Ruel.

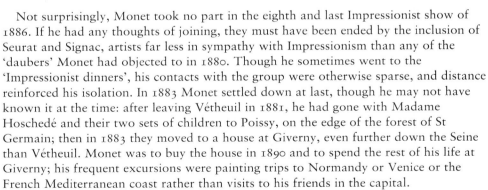

Claude Monet. *Lady with a Parasol*. 1886.
Musée du Louvre, Paris.

Left:
Claude Monet. *The Rue Montorgeuil Decked
out with Flags*. 1878. A brilliant evocation of a
Parisian street during France's national holiday,
14 July. Musée des Beaux-Arts, Rouen.

Above right:
Claude Monet. *Floating Ice on the Seine*. 1880.
Exhibited at Monet's one-man show under the
auspices of the Charpentiers' periodical *La Vie
Moderne*. The painting was bought by Mme
Charpentier for 1,500 francs. Calouste
Gulbenkian Foundation, Lisbon.

Below right:
Claude Monet. *Lavacourt in Winter*. 1881. Also
known as *Sunshine and Snow, Vétheuil*.
Painted at a period when Monet was evidently
fascinated by snow and ice. National Gallery,
London.

Not surprisingly, Monet took no part in the eighth and last Impressionist show of
1886. If he had any thoughts of joining, they must have been ended by the inclusion of
Seurat and Signac, artists far less in sympathy with Impressionism than any of the
'daubers' Monet had objected to in 1880. Though he sometimes went to the
'Impressionist dinners', his contacts with the group were otherwise sparse, and distance
reinforced his isolation. In 1883 Monet settled down at last, though he may not have
known it at the time: after leaving Vétheuil in 1881, he had gone with Madame
Hoschedé and their two sets of children to Poissy, on the edge of the forest of St
Germain; then in 1883 they moved to a house at Giverny, even further down the Seine
than Vétheuil. Monet was to buy the house in 1890 and to spend the rest of his life at
Giverny; his frequent excursions were painting trips to Normandy or Venice or the
French Mediterranean coast rather than visits to his friends in the capital.

After a short trip to the Côte d'Azur with Renoir in December 1883 Monet became
more convinced than ever that he no longer derived any benefit from working with
others. He wished to confront nature entirely on his own. Nature – or rather his
sensations in the face of nature – became the sole source of Monet's art. Until the mid-
1880s he had occasionally painted or drawn portraits and figure studies; his still lifes
were even more infrequent. Later, such items disappeared altogether (with the
exception of a few family records), and even small incidental figures became rare:
Monet records an unpeopled world in which boats or houses are more like natural
objects than products of the human world. He now took fidelity to the appearance of
the moment as far as it was humanly possible to do so, carrying about several canvases
in a specially partitioned case; as the light changed he put one canvas away and worked
on the next.

In this way Monet captured the seasons, nature's moods and the changing effects of
light in series of similar or identical subjects. He painted Vétheuil extensively, most
notably in the grip of snow and ice; *Vétheuil in Summer* and *Floating Ice on the Seine*
are typical examples. Etretat on the Normandy coast, with its dramatically sculptured
rocks, prompted a series in which Monet succeeded in capturing the violent movement

Top:
Claude Monet. *Fishing Nets, Pourville.* 1882.
One of a number of similar paintings done at
this spot, near Dieppe. At this period Monet was
again becoming interested in the sea as a
subject – or, to be more exact, in the problems
involved in capturing swift and violent
movement. Haags Gemeentemuseum, The
Hague.

Above:
Claude Monet. *Rocks at Belle Île.* 1886. This
study of waves breaking over rocks was done
on a small island about 48 kilometres from the
south coast of Brittany. A tendency to eliminate
the sky from his pictures was already becoming
noticeable in Monet's work. Musée du Louvre,
Paris.

of the waves. The brilliant, sunlit Côte d'Azur inspired paintings that were far more boldly – some said garishly – coloured, whereas Monet showed the Creuse country in all its starkness. Though reality can only be known as filtered through a human consciousness, in these years Monet came as close to objectivity as anyone is ever likely to: his moods, finances or opinions could never be guessed from the subjects he chose or the way he painted them.

Meanwhile, success came at last. In the 1880s there were quite frequent shows of Monet's paintings, not only in France but in Holland, Germany, Britain and the United States. (Monet, good Frenchman that he was, found it hard to take seriously any artistic event that took place outside Paris.) In 1889 Georges Petit put on a joint show of works by Monet and the sculptor Auguste Rodin, who was himself sometimes called an Impressionist because of his concern with the play of light on the surfaces of his figures. The success of this show established Monet once and for all. In the same year

Claude Monet. *Meadow in Giverny.* 1888.
Hermitage Museum, Leningrad.

he showed three canvases at the Paris International Exhibition, where the paintings of his dead friend Manet were also winning belated recognition. Monet's new authority in the world of art was shown in practical terms by his success in placing Manet's *Olympia* in the Musée du Luxembourg. In 1890 Monet bought the house in which he lived at Giverny; in 1892 he married Madame Hoschedé, who had been sharing his home since before Camille's death.

Financial security made it possible for Monet to travel widely. But though he visited some new places – notably Norway and Venice – he displayed a liking for familiar scenes, returning to the Netherlands and England as if he was not satisfied that he had exhausted their painterly potential; the Thames in particular obsessed him, combining water with mist, and he returned to London again and again, even in extreme old age.

In the 1890s Monet painted some of his most famous series: of poplars on the Epte in 1890-91, haystacks, and Rouen Cathedral. The cathedral series points the direction of Monet's later work particularly clearly: the dissolution of solid forms has already begun and is blatant in the paintings of this great stone edifice, which in bright sunlight seems to be writhing or melting in the heat.

This tendency reached its climax in Monet's paintings of his garden at Giverny. He had devoted great care to altering the house to suit him, and laboured long to create a garden that should be a demi-paradise; his paintings celebrate the achievement of his ambition, and photographs taken at the time and later confirm that these lush and colourful paintings are no mere fantasies. The heart of the garden was a pool which Monet created by diverting the waters of the River Epte; its surface became covered in

176

Left:
Claude Monet. *Poplars on the Epte.* 1891. An
example from one of Monet's famous series of
same-subject paintings, done in varying light
and weather conditions. Monet's house at
Giverny was on the River Epte, so he was able
to work close to home; all the same, the stamina
of a day-labourer might have been sorely tried
by the practice of men like Monet and Cézanne,
who spent day after day in the open air at all
times and in all temperatures. National Gallery
of Scotland, Edinburgh.

Below left:
Claude Monet. *Rouen Cathedral in Bright
Sunshine.* 1894. Monet painted many pictures
of Rouen Cathedral between 1892 and 1894,
spending months at a time in a rented room
from which he could see the facade. As with the
Gare St Lazare series, he seems to have wanted
to prove that Impressionist techniques were
applicable to subjects not taken from the natural
world. However, the dissolving, almost dripping
stonework in this picture goes beyond the
objectivity the Impressionists sought, and closer
to the 'imagination in the face of nature' that
Gauguin praised. Musée du Louvre, Paris.

a burgeoning mass of flowers which completed the world-within-a-world of the garden,
turning it into a dazzling, shifting expanse of water, leaves and plants. In his last years
this became Monet's only subject, painted with ever-greater freedom so that the forms
of trees, flowers, even bridges, virtually dissolved. The sky disappears from these
canvases, making their contact with everyday reality still more tenuous. Eventually
Monet painted nothing but the water lilies on his pool, finding more than sufficient
inspiration in the patterns of their growth and movements. During the First World War
he received his first public commission, to paint the water-lily murals now in the Musée
de l'Orangerie, Paris. All these works seem like the records left by a man disappearing
into his dreams – a dream of colour, and nothing but colour. Monet once remarked
that he would have liked to see the world as a blind man might if his vision were
suddenly restored – as a brilliant play of colours on unrecognisable forms.

This dissolving of the solidities of the world represents an unmistakable long-term
tendency of Monet's art, though its final phase may owe something to the purely
physical phenomenon of his failing sight, which became serious in the early years of the
20th century. By 1923 Monet was suffering from a double cataract, and seemed
doomed to total blindness. His old friend Clemenceau finally succeeded in convincing
him that it was worth undergoing an operation; this was successful, and enabled him to
work until the end of his life three years later – years devoted to the inexhaustible
subject of water lilies. Monet died at Giverny on 26 December 1926, aged 86. The last
of the major Impressionists, he had lived into the Jazz Age, and had become as much a
classic as the museum-enshrined painters whose works he detested.

Left:
Claude Monet. *Bridge over the
Thames.* 1903. Museum Solothurn.

Below:
Claude Monet. *Water Lilies.* About
1916–20. Monet became obsessed
with this subject, partly at least
because the ever-changing,
brilliantly coloured surface provided
an inexhaustible flow of pictorial
ideas in his own home. National
Gallery, London.

Renoir

Renoir was at the heart of the Impressionist movement right from the early days at Gleyre's and the group painting trips to the forest of Fontainebleau. His close relationship with Monet at Bougival and La Grenouillère in 1869, and again at Argenteuil in 1872-74, was crucial in the development of plein-air painting techniques. On the more formal level, he was one of the leading organisers of the first Impressionist show in 1874, and remained closely involved with the second and third shows (1876, 1877). Yet Renoir was also the first Impressionist to return to the fold and exhibit at the Salon, and also the first to break with Impressionism as a style or technique.

The War and the Commune were more hair-raising events for Renoir than for any of

Renoir in old age, his hands twisted horribly by arthritis. The last six years of his life were spent in a wheelchair, but he carried on painting to the end.

Pierre Auguste Renoir. *Portrait of Claude Monet*. 1875. A splendidly elegant and affectionate portrait. This is a less tough Monet than the pipe-smoking figure in Renoir's *Claude Monet Reading a Newspaper*. Musée du Louvre, Paris.

his colleagues: as already related, he almost died of dysentery at Tarbes in the Pyrenees, and on his return to Paris might well have been shot by either government troops or by the Communards. In 1872 his long relationship with Lise Tréhot came to an end; she married a young architect and never saw Renoir again. Then began another period of close contact with Monet, which often involved working side by side, painting city views, landscapes (for example, with people making their way through long grass), and river scenes with sailing boats. This is Renoir at his most Impressionist, with the forms of things on the point of dissolving into a rich harmonious blur in a manner we are more used to considering typical of Monet. Images of Monet, and of his wife Camille, are frequent in these years, and appropriately enough: Monet's role in their lean years together was so important that Renoir later said simply, 'Without him I should have

given up'. Renoir's fortunes hit rock bottom with the Hôtel Drouot sale of March 1875, which he himself had suggested: his 20 paintings fetched only 2,250 francs, making him the worst failure among a group of failures.

In 1875-76 Renoir painted the famous pictures in which dappled sunlight lends enchantment to his subjects, giving them a kind of spangled gaiety. Although this device is essential to the mood of *The Swing* and *Le Moulin de la Galette*, it is not in itself the subject of the pictures, as it would be in a painting by Monet. Renoir's feeling for the human presence has reasserted itself; by contrast with his Argenteuil paintings, in which the play of the light tends to be more important than what it plays upon, the true subject of *The Swing* and *Moulin de la Galette* is the joy of life. In this sense, these scenes of *la vie Parisienne* represent Renoir's emergence from Monet's influence and his renewed awareness of traditional values. Unlike Monet, Renoir had always admired the old traditions, copied the Old Masters, enjoyed the 'sweetness of life' that Talleyrand claimed for France before the Revolution, and which survives in the paintings of Watteau, Boucher, Fragonard, and other 18th-century artists. Renoir defined his position vis-à-vis tradition forcefully and clearly: he revered it and wished to continue it, not to copy it slavishly. It does not seem too fanciful to interpret *The Swing* as a tribute to the famous painting of the same name by Fragonard, and the *Moulin de la Galette* as a 19th-century version of the *fêtes galantes* in which aristocratic ladies and gentlemen, often in fancy dress, disported themselves in the open air. But here the tradition is thoroughly reworked, as Renoir claimed it should be. Instead of ladies and gentlemen, he gives us ordinary Parisians out to have a good time; and the amorous glow in the atmosphere is a world away from the self-consciously naughty games that passed for love in the last days of the Ancien Régime.

Only a little later, Renoir was to paint a number of portraits in a more directly 18th-century manner; the combination of cool colour and warm feeling in *Madame Henriot*,

180

Left:
Jean Honoré Fragonard. *The Swing.* 1768. A famous and typical example of one side of Fragonard's art – charming if rather silly in its self-conscious naughtiness. Renoir greatly admired 18th-century French painting, and it is interesting to compare Fragonard's painting with his *Swing.* Wallace Collection, London.

Above:
Pierre Auguste Renoir. *The Swing.* 1876. Shown at the third Impressionist exhibition in 1877. This is the predecessor and companion piece to the larger *Moulin de la Galette,* but it has a more tranquil charm. Musée du Louvre, Paris (Caillebotte Collection).

for example, has suggested comparisons with the pastel artist Jean Baptiste Perroneau. Renoir's growing success as a portraitist may have tended to separate him from his fellow-Impressionists; the separation was made tangible by his decision to submit *The Cup of Chocolate* to the Salon of 1878, which automatically excluded him from the Impressionist show the following spring. Renoir later tried to justify himself in a letter to Durand-Ruel, written while he was visiting Algiers: 'There are scarcely fifteen collectors who can appreciate a painter not approved by the Salon. There are eighty thousand of them who wouldn't buy a single thing if the painter hadn't shown it at the Salon. That's why I send in two portraits every year ... Besides, I don't want to find myself taking up the stupid view that a thing must be bad or good just because it is hung in a particular place. In short, I don't want to waste my time bearing a grudge against the Salon ... If I were accused of neglecting my art, or sacrificing my beliefs to some stupid ambition, I could understand my critics; but as that isn't so, there's no more to be said ... My submission to the Salon is purely a matter of business.' This was a rather ingenuous defence since his abandoned colleagues could well have retorted that Renoir was familiar with such arguments long before he joined them in taking an independent stand. However, Renoir's proved to be the first of several defections from the Impressionist camp, and this rather diffused and diluted any ill-feeling that it may have caused. In Renoir's case it was obviously true that programmes and ideas meant little to him: he had the strengths, and also the weaknesses, of people who accept things as they are.

Renoir was painting an increasing number of portraits in the later 1870s, including two of the customs official Victor Chocquet. Renoir and Chocquet met at the Hôtel Drouot sale in March 1875, and Chocquet became a valued friend and patron, though his greatest enthusiasm was reserved for Cézanne's paintings. An even more important contact was the publisher Georges Charpentier, to whose family Renoir became a sort of official portraitist. *Madame Charpentier and her Children* was his first great success at the Salon when it was shown in 1879, partly at least because of the sitter's influence, which ensured that it was well hung. Madame Charpentier had the ambition of becoming a great hostess in the French tradition, with a circle of writers and artists regularly gracing her salon. So through the Charpentiers Renoir was introduced to the

Pierre Auguste Renoir. *The Moulin de la Galette*. 1876. A large (131 × 174 cm) work, shown at the third Impressionist exhibition in 1877. The Moulin de la Galette was a well-known open-air establishment in Montmartre, not far from Renoir's studio in the Rue Cortot. The picture was painted on the spot; the men are friends of Renoir's, but the girls were genuine customers who happened to turn up while he was working. Musée du Louvre, Paris.

opulence and cultivation of upper-middle-class life, which he seems to have taken to effortlessly. He became an intimate of the household, writing frequently to both husband and wife, alternately boasting of his numerous commissions and urgently asking for money. Perhaps his naivety is seen in its most attractive light when he enthuses about being able to paint the Charpentiers' two little girls, since he will be able to use them as models – without even having to pay!

The Charpentiers' new weekly magazine, *La Vie Moderne*, was an important outlet for Renoir, who had a one-man exhibition on the premises. The magazine itself was run by his brother Edmond, and so carried favourable and detailed criticism as well as drawings by Renoir – who, however, complained that the arrangement, whereby he would be paid out of the profits, was equivalent to not paying him at all.

By 1880 Renoir seemed to be establishing himself as a fashionable portrait painter.

Pierre Auguste Renoir. *The First Outing.* 1875-76. It is interesting to compare this with *La Loge.* Here the more feathery brush-work and tender blue of the girl's head-dress point up her youthful vulnerability. National Gallery, London.

Pierre Auguste Renoir. *Madame Charpentier.*
1878. Musée du Louvre, Paris.

Through the Charpentiers he had met – and painted – such distinguished people as the actress Jeanne Samary and Madame Alphonse Daudet, wife of the famous writer. He had also stayed with a new friend and patron, the embassy secretary Paul Bérard, who in 1879 invited Renoir to spend the whole summer at his country house near Dieppe, painting members of Bérard's family and working in the surrounding countryside. Bérard was to become an intimate friend, and Renoir went back to the estate, Wargemont, over several summers.

He was still often short of money, or at least short enough to work for the pastry-shop owner Eugène Murer, who seems to have given Renoir and his friends vol-au-vents in part payment for their efforts. Murer also helped Renoir to draft a scheme for running the Salon more fairly; it was published in 1880. Renoir and Monet were still only grudgingly accepted at the Salon, and had protested against the bad hanging of

Pierre Auguste Renoir. *Spring Landscape.*
About 1877. This looks like an anticipation of
the divisionist painting of Seurat, in which the
picture surface is entirely covered by tiny dots.
But if so, Renoir never followed up the idea; and
when divisionism did arrive on the scene, he
scoffed at it. Musée des Beaux-Arts. Algiers.

their pictures at the Salon exhibition earlier in the year.

If, at this period of his life, Renoir can be called a fashionable portraitist, the phrase should be used without the customary pejorative implications. Though fashionable, Renoir's portrait work was never merely slick. He muted his colours and smoothed his manner to conciliate his sitters, but he seems to have preserved a certain sincerity of attitude that was perhaps the happy result of his naivety. It has been well said that Renoir avoided the emptiness of the run-of-the-mill flattering portrait because his flatteries were always motivated by a deep and genuine desire to please: there was no contempt or cynicism hidden behind them.

All the same, Renoir began to be worried about his own facility. More seriously, he was becoming dissatisfied with Impressionism, which sacrificed everything – including the traditional disciplines of drawing and composition – to capturing the effects of light through on-the-spot working.

Some of Renoir's restlessness was taken out in travel, which he was now better able to afford. In February 1881 he spent a few weeks in Algiers, which had inspired one of his great heroes, Delacroix. Renoir painted some exotic subjects including mosques, banana trees and the blazing-coloured *Kasbah of Algiers.* But, unlike Delacroix, he had no real taste for the exotic: like Degas, with whom he otherwise had so little in common, he found inexhaustible inspiration in the familiar.

A more important event in this period was Renoir's meeting with the woman who was to become his wife. At 40, he found in 19-year-old Aline Charigot the sturdy common-sensical home-maker he needed. She was also an enchanting model, with the kind of snub-nosed, cat-eyed beauty Renoir loved; she appears in *The Luncheon of the Boating Party,* which is very close in mood to the paintings of the *Moulin de la Galette* period, in *Dancing in the Country,* and later, breast-feeding her first son, Pierre, in *Maternity* (1886).

In 1881 Renoir also toured Italy, which was more profoundly important than Algiers in his artistic development. He studied frescoes by Raphael and ancient Roman painting at Pompeii, admiring the calm mastery and drawing skills of the one and the enchanted mystical atmosphere of the other. In January 1882, while still in the south of Italy, Renoir had the chance to paint the German composer Richard Wagner, and made a special trip to Palermo for that purpose; he doubtless remembered that Bazille,

Pierre Auguste Renoir. *Muslim Festival at Algiers*. 1881. Also known as *The Kasbah of Algiers* (that is, the Arab quarter, shown in the upper left hand part of the picture) and *Fantasia*. Monet bought the painting in 1900: perhaps it reminded him of his period of military service in Algeria. Musée du Louvre, Paris.

Maître and other friends of his youth had been ardent Wagnerians in the days when the musical world was sharply divided between enraptured admirers and outraged detractors. There was only one short sitting for the painting, and the resulting portrait is an interesting sketch rather than a Renoir portrait at its best.

In the spring of 1882, Renoir was invited to exhibit with the Impressionists again. Like Monet and Sisley, he eventually agreed, but only after some petulant, self-justifying correspondence with Durand-Ruel; his consent was virtually a favour to the dealer (who owned all the pictures by Renoir that were shown) rather than an expression of solidarity with his old friends. Renoir now insisted that his submissions to the Salon were intended to clear him of the 'revolutionary taint' that he claimed was attached to the group – though it is doubtful whether anybody ever thought of Degas or Berthe Morisot as revolutionaries; apart from references to 'the Israelite Pissarro' Renoir failed to elaborate the charge. He also remarked, even less endearingly, 'Since I exhibit with Guillaumin [a minor Impressionist] I may as well exhibit with Carolus-Duran [a fashionable Salon painter]'. Renoir was ill when he wrote: he had caught pneumonia while staying at L'Estaque with Cézanne, who had devotedly nursed him back to health. This fact may account for Renoir's tone; he later apologised for some of his remarks. But the variety of self-justifications he put forward suggests that he suffered from a bad conscience about his original defection. Closer to his real feelings was the remark 'Delacroix used to say, quite rightly, that a painter should acquire every honour he possibly could' – which was also, of course, what Manet had been advocating all the time. Though 25 of his paintings were shown, Renoir did not put in an appearance at the 1882 show, but went on another trip to Algiers.

In the early 1880s Renoir was making ready to break with the Impressionist way of painting as well as with the Impressionists as a group, although he remained on good terms with individuals, notably Monet, Cézanne and Degas. In 1881 he told Durand-Ruel that he was having to scrape off his pictures time after time, feeling he had blotted them as badly as a schoolboy blots his exercise book. The rapid transcriptions of

186

Pierre Auguste Renoir. Two decorative panels commissioned by Paul Durand-Ruel. Above: *Dancing in the Town*. Left: *Dancing in the Country*. Both 1883. The man is Renoir's friend Paul Lhote, the woman the model Suzanne Valadon, who later became a painter in her own right; she was also the mother of Maurice Utrillo. Though close in mood to paintings such as the *Moulin de la Galette*, these pictures show Renoir's increasing interest in solidly modelled forms. Durand-Ruel et Cie, Paris.

Impressionism now seemed inadequate to him: plein-air painting emphasised light at the expense of composition – for which there was no time – and reduced everything to a multi-coloured mist in which objects had no bulk or weight. On a less theoretical level, Renoir was beginning to tire of realistic or 'modern life' subjects, and to ask himself how he could achieve the timeless quality that he found in so many of the Old Masters. In search of a new direction, he began to appreciate the virtues of Ingres, and also turned back to Corot, who had advised that open-air paintings should be worked

Above:
Pierre Auguste Renoir. *The Umbrellas*. 1884. A famous painting, though one that is not quite satisfactory. The difference in style between the little girls and the other figures – and above all the hard outlines of the umbrellas – is striking. National Gallery, London.

Above right:
Pierre Auguste Renoir. *The Large Bathers*. 1884-87. A large (115 × 170 cm) painting on which Renoir worked intermittently for three years. Immensely charming and wonderfully coloured, though the figures in action are unconvincing. This painting, with its clear-cut figures and non-realistic colour, is in sharp contrast to High Impressionist works. Philadelphia Museum of Art, Pennsylvania (Mr and Mrs Carroll S. Tyson Collection).

Below right:
Pierre Auguste Renoir. *Figures in a Garden*. Probably 1890s. Although this seems to date from Renoir's later period, he has succeeded here in recapturing the light, unpretentious atmosphere of his work in the 1870s. Ashmolean Museum, Oxford.

Above left:
Pierre Auguste Renoir. *Two Girls in a Garden.* About 1890. In 1890-91 Renoir painted a whole series of pictures with young girls in large summer hats drawing or reading, or simply idling together. Private Collection, Paris.

Below left:
Pierre August Renoir. *Children in the Afternoon at Wargemont.* 1884. Painted at the country house of Renoir's friend Paul Bérard, this is another example of the *manière aigre,* the severely outlined style that Renoir used in the early 1880s. Nationalgalerie, Berlin.

Above:
Pierre Auguste Renoir. *Young Girl Combing Her Hair.* 1894. The combination of a childlike, immature face and an opulent body evidently fascinated Renoir. Lehman Collection, New York.

Pierre Auguste Renoir. *Young Woman Dressing
Her Hair*. 1901. A characteristic figure painting
of Renoir's later years: monumental, suffused
with deep rich reds and silvery highlights. The
sense of physical immediacy is more powerful
than ever. Private Collection, Paris.

Pierre Auguste Renoir. *Portrait of Ambroise Vollard*. 1908. The great art dealer is shown examining a statuette by the sculptor Aristide Maillol, whose work Renoir greatly admired; Renoir's own sculpture was in a very similar style. This portrait of Vollard can be profitably compared with Cézanne's version of the subject. Portraitists are popularly supposed to be discerning psychologists; but the very different styles and moods of these paintings indicate that the painters are revealing themselves rather than their sitters. Courtauld Institute Galleries, London.

over in the studio; in Italy, as we have seen, Renoir found some very un-Impressionist works to admire.

The outcome of his scrapings-off, travels and meditations was what he called his 'sour style' (*manière aigre*), which it might have been better to call his 'harsh' or 'severe style'. It was certainly severe by comparison with the rich, dense and free brush-work of his Impressionist period. Now the outlines were firmly drawn, the brush-work was smoother, the light was less brilliant, the figures were more substantial, and the composition was more deliberate and insistent. The fullest expression of the style was *The Bathers* of 1884-87, in which naked girls cavort by the riverside in an enchanted pastel Never-Never Land. But even more fascinating is *The Umbrellas*, a uniquely clear example of a painter changing styles in mid-picture. The bottom right-hand side, centred on the delightful little girl with a hoop, is soft and fluffy in Renoir's Impressionist vein; the rest of the picture is more restrained and hard-edged, dominated by the firm pattern of the umbrellas.

Renoir's 'sour style' was less popular than the kind of portrait work he had been doing in the early 1880s, and he again found difficulty making ends meet. The style itself was not completely satisfactory, though Renoir assured Durand-Ruel that 'I have rediscovered, never to leave it, the old painting style, full of sweetness and light', which Renoir claimed to have derived from the 18th century he so much admired.

The fact was that such a severe style did not suit Renoir's genius, and was not commercially successful either. By the end of the 1880s he had begun to attempt a synthesis between his Impressionist and 'sour' manners – a style in which a free painterly technique was super-imposed on a ground of rigorous drawing and composition. Increasingly he also looked for models whose skin 'caught the light', enabling him to put a pearly sheen on the flesh of otherwise solidly modelled figures. This was Renoir's personal solution to the seeming contradiction between Old Master solidity and the kind of ephemeral moment-in-time feeling that Impressionist painters strove to capture.

With the exception of a few portrait subjects, Renoir retreated further and further

from reality into a kind of ideal world peopled with luscious nudes, young girls and small children, illumined with pearly reflections and, usually, a general glow of Rubens red. These characteristics are so ubiquitous that art historians often refer to Renoir's 'pearly style', indicating the most distinctive feature of his work after about 1890.

Renoir's favourite model during this period was Gabrielle, one of his wife's relations. She came to work for the Renoir family as the children's nurse, and appears as such in a number of paintings, including *The Artist's Family* (1896), a lively and, for Renoir, rather uncharacteristic group portrait. But Gabrielle was also a sturdy girl with a powerful sensual presence, and Renoir liked to paint her in opulent deshabille, with a filmy blouse or negligé framing (but certainly not concealing) her breasts. In life, Gabrielle was a tough character who proved highly effective, if tactless, in shielding her master from an ever-increasing number of importunate visitors.

By this time, international recognition had come at last, and with it financial security. But on the physical level Renoir's last years were tragic. He suffered increasingly from the damp and spent more and more time in the South of France. Eventually he settled in his wife's native village, Essoyes, only to suffer the effects of a fall from a bicycle. The fall brought on arthritis, which in combination with rheumatism eventually became so severe that Renoir's right side was paralysed. None the less he carried on painting, even when the brushes had to be thrust between the rigid fingers of his twisted hands. In 1903 he bought a house at Cagnes, on the Mediterranean coast, between Antibes and Nice, where he later acquired an attractive property with an olive grove attached to it. In this he set up his own separate studio, and even did some sculpture by directing the actions of an assistant; but by 1913 he was confined to a wheelchair by his ailments. He lived long enough to see his paintings hang in the Luxembourg, and at last in the Louvre – and also to see his son Jean threatened with the loss of a leg as a result of service in the First World War. Over all these years of personal and public suffering, Renoir continued to celebrate the joy of life – an achievement admired even by those who find the paintings of his last period somewhat overblown. Auguste Renoir died at Cagnes on 3 December 1919.

194

Pierre Auguste Renoir. *Woman Tying her Shoelace.* About 1916. Like many late Renoirs, dominated by a rich wine red. The colour fantasy and the everyday subject are combined with surprising success. Courtauld Institute Galleries, London.

Above right:
Pierre Auguste Renoir. *The Large Bathers.* 1918. Compare this with the 'sour style' *Bathers* of 1884-87. This is not to everybody's taste, but Renoir believed it was the culmination of his efforts as a painter. The nude in a landscape – traditionally an idyllic subject – was certainly one of Renoir's chief preoccupations; and in the late paintings he combines solid forms and emphatic designs with a rich vigorous painting style that records gleaming flesh and friendly, colourful landscapes with more than a touch of fantasy. Musée du Louvre, Paris.

Below right:
Pierre Auguste Renoir. *Landscape at Cagnes.* About 1902. The countryside of the South of France, where Renoir lived for the last 15 years of his life. Private Collection, Paris.

Sisley

Alfred Sisley's existence after 1871 can be summed up as one of quiet productivity, and also of quiet poverty and ill-success. The Franco-Prussian War caused this dramatic change in his way of life. His father fell ill, made some bad business decisions, and found himself ruined. He died shortly afterwards, leaving Sisley with no way of supporting his wife and two children except by his painting. The elegant gentleman-amateur of Renoir's double portrait now became a hard-working, hard-pressed professional who always had difficulty in making ends meet. In spite of this, in the 1870s Sisley's art reached maturity and he did his best work; it was only later that overproduction seems to have led to a certain unevenness of quality.

Until the war Sisley lived at the Cité des Fleurs in the Batignolles quarter, close to the Café Guerbois and many of his painter friends. He evidently spent the war in the capital too; Durand-Ruel's later claim to have been introduced to Sisley in London seems to have been a trick played by an old man's memory. But during the Commune Sisley moved out to the Louveciennes area, and he never returned to Paris for any length of time. Until 1880 he stayed on the outskirts, first at Louveciennes, later at Marly and Sèvres. Living was cheaper in these places, and Sisley was close to the kind of landscape views he wanted to paint. Indeed, the countryside and villages outside Paris, and the River Seine, virtually exhaust the subject matter of Sisley's painting; even in his direst poverty he appears never to have tried earning money by portraiture or the kind of decorative work done by Renoir.

At Louveciennes, Sisley was not isolated from his friends (as he was to become later in life): for a time Auguste and Edmond Renoir were his neighbours, and he saw both Renoir and Monet at Argenteuil. His main commercial outlet was Durand-Ruel, to whom he was introduced by Monet and Pissarro. Sisley was even more affected than they were by the business recession, Durand-Ruel's embarrassments, and the failure of the first Impressionist exhibition, where none of his five pictures was sold; and at the subsequent Hôtel Drouot sale his 21 paintings went for an average of 122 francs each. The one bright spot in these years was a trip to England (July-October 1874) at the invitation of the opera singer Faure; there Sisley, approaching the zenith of his creative powers, executed splendid atmospheric paintings of Hampton Court.

In 1876 Sisley painted the floods at Port Marly. He contributed to the second and third Impressionist shows, but remained so poverty-stricken that he made a desperate offer to the critic Théodore Duret: if Duret could find a client who would pay Sisley 500 francs a month for six months, Sisley would paint 30 pictures for him in that time. In other words, Sisley was prepared to accept 100 francs a picture for the sake of financial security. Duret did not know of such a client, but he did succeed in finding a buyer for seven pictures by Sisley. Given the desperation Sisley was evidently feeling, it is hardly surprising that he joined Renoir in writing off the group shows and submitting paintings to the Salon again. He explained in a letter to Duret: 'I'm tired of vegetating as I've done for such a long time. The moment has come for me to take a decision. Our exhibitions have served to make us known, it's true, and in that respect have been very useful; but it seems to me that we need not remain in isolation any longer. The time is still a long way off when one will be able to do without the prestige attached to the official shows ...' But the outcome of his decision was humiliating: both Sisley's paintings were rejected by the jury, whereas Renoir had a great success with his portrait of Madame Charpentier and her children. And as if this were not bad enough, Sisley was evicted from his house at Sèvres and had to appeal to Charpentier for money to rent somewhere new. Apart from Duret, Sisley's chief supports during this period were Charpentier and the pastry-shop owner Eugène Murer; his regular Wednesday lunches at Murer's place on the Boulevard Voltaire also helped to keep Sisley in touch with old friends, particularly Renoir.

But in the following year, 1880, Sisley moved much farther away, to Veneux-Nadon,

197

Alfred Sisley. *Cornfield at Argenteuil.* 1873.
Kunsthalle, Hamburg.

close to the forest of Fontainebleau where the friends from Gleyre's had set up their
easels in the open air some 18 years before. Perhaps he was still 'tired of vegetating'
and felt he had exhausted the environs of Paris: over the years he had painted at
Louveciennes, Villeneuve-la-Garenne, Marly, Argenteuil, Bougival, Sèvres, St Germain,
Versailles, St Cloud and Meudon. All the same, his move to Veneux-Nadon proved to
be the first step in the dispersal of the Impressionists that took place in the 1880s. At
the time, Sisley had no intention of isolating himself. In 1881 he was trying to persuade

Monet to join him, describing the cheapness of the rents at nearby Moret-sur-Loing, and pointing out that it was only a two-hour rail journey from Paris; he invited Monet to visit him at Veneux-Nadon, 'ten minutes from the station at Moret'. But when Monet did decide to move out of Paris, he went in the opposite direction, down instead of up the Seine, perhaps to be within easy reach of his beloved Norman-Breton coast.

Sisley moved to Moret itself in 1882, and was in fact to spend the rest of his life in or around the little town, moving several times but never going very far. Because of his

poverty he hardly travelled; and when he did manage a trip to the Isle of Wight in June 1881, he was pursued by his usual bad luck. 'I have taken several walks round the island', he wrote to Durand-Ruel, 'and as soon as my canvases arrive I shall set myself to work'. But, thanks to the incompetence of Sisley's suppliers, the canvases were lost in transit and his stay was completely unproductive.

The rest of Sisley's life is the same story of unrelieved hardship. On 17 November 1885 he wrote to Durand-Ruel, 'On the 21st I shall be penniless again. In the meantime I have to give something to the butcher and the grocer: I haven't paid one for six months and the other for a year.' In 1886 Sisley was so poor that he tried to make some money decorating fans, with advice from Pissarro, who had earlier been forced into the same line of work, and still occasionally practised the difficult craft as an artistic discipline; Sisley apparently failed to acquire the knack and gave up the work. Over the next few years his paintings appeared with increasing frequency at shows in France and abroad. Thanks to Durand-Ruel he was shown with the other Impressionists in New York and Boston, London, Berlin and Rotterdam; and in 1889 he had a one-man show of 27 paintings in Durand-Ruel's gallery in New York. But Sisley's prices remained low, even after he left Durand-Ruel for Georges Petit. Eventually he grew resigned to his lot, and realised that he would not be recognised in his own lifetime. According to one account he grew morose and suspicious in his last years, though the writer Gustave Geffroy, who later wrote a book on Sisley, described him as impressively cultivated and dignified. He seems to have lost touch with all his old friends, but when he was mortally ill he sent for Monet to take a last farewell of him. He died of throat cancer on 29 January 1899.

Sisley's art was hardly more eventful than his life. Whereas the other Impressionists went through periods of crisis or changed direction, Sisley consistently practised the open-air, small-brush-stroke style. There was a change of emphasis in the 1880s – but no more – when his quiet, lyrical manner gave way to a more strident, more highly coloured style that was not entirely suited to his temperament; he may well have adopted it in the belief that it was more likely to attract attention than his overlooked masterpieces of the 1870s. This, together with overproduction to make ends meet, brought about the unevenness already referred to. However, at every stage of his career Sisley painted scenes of subtle charm. That charm was only appreciated after his death, as he had come to expect. But it was so soon afterwards that it looks as though the gods had decided to have a last joke at poor Sisley's expense: within a year the prices of his works had rocketed, and in 1900 the collector Camondo paid 43,000 francs for *Floods at Port Marly,* painted a couple of years before Sisley's futile attempt to get as little as 3,000 francs for 30 of his pictures.

Top:
Alfred Sisley. *Snow at Veneux-Nadon*. About
1880. Snow was one of Sisley's favourite
subjects, lending itself to delicate lyrical effects;
the painter worked outdoors in winter so
persistently that he suffered intermittent attacks
of facial paralysis. Veneux-Nadon was a village
south-east of Paris to which Sisley moved in
1880; from this time he was rarely in touch with
the other Impressionists. Musée du Louvre, Paris.
Paris.

Above:
Alfred Sisley. *Small Meadows in Spring*. About
1885. An unusually bold and bright painting for
Sisley, painted by the river near his home at
Moret-sur-Loing. Tate Gallery, London.

Morisot

Berthe Morisot was one of the staunchest figures in the Impressionist movement during its central years. She exhibited at the first show of 1874, despite all Manet's attempts to dissuade her; and she sent paintings to every later show except that of 1879, which was held while she was pregnant. (She had married Eugène Manet, the painter's younger brother, in 1874.) She was not spared the ridicule heaped on the Impressionists: in his absurd 1874 *Charivari* review, Leroy remarked with ironic praise that five slashes with a brush were all she needed to depict the fingers of a hand; and two years later Albert Wolff's critical indignation exploded in simple abuse ('Five or six lunatics – one of them a woman ... There is a woman in the group, as in all notorious gangs'). Berthe Morisot shrugged it off, though Eugène Manet was so furious that he had to be talked out of challenging Wolff to a duel. It was Eugène Manet, too, who became involved in

Pierre Auguste Renoir. *Berthe Morisot and her Daughter.* 1895. A pastel done in the last year of Berthe Morisot's life. Renoir was a close friend whom she asked to watch over her daughter, Julie Manet, after her death. Musée du Petit Palais, Paris.

Right:
Berthe Moristot. *The Cradle.* 1873. Shown at the first Impressionist exhibition of 1874. The mother is based on Morisot's married sister, Edma Pontillon, who was her favourite model. Edma herself had been a painter until her marriage in 1869 abruptly ended her career. Musée du Louvre, Paris.

Below:
Berthe Morisot. *Chasing Butterflies.* 1873. A charming, sentimental – but acceptably sentimental – painting of Berthe Morisot's sister, Edma Pontillon, and her children. Musée du Louvre, Paris.

Above:
Berthe Morisot. *Madame Boursier and her Daughter.* About 1874-76. Despite her audacity in becoming involved with the anti-official art of the Impressionists, Berthe Morisot accepted many of the limitations imposed by her class and time. Her painting has a distinctly 'feminine' touch, and her subjects tend to be women and/ or children. The Brooklyn Museum, New York.

Right:
Berthe Moristo. *In the Dining Room.* 1886. A charming interior, painted with typical Morisot freedom; no other Impressionist could have produced this light, quivering, tenderly domestic scene. National Gallery of Art, Washington, DC.

hostilities with Pissarro and his new divisionist friends in 1886; Berthe Morisot seems to have remained above all the squabbles that increasingly swept through the Impressionist camp, and to have stayed friendly with them all.

Her wealth made life easy and pleasant for Berthe Morisot, with summers in the countryside around Paris or in Normandy, and even a painting trip to the Isle of Wight in England in 1875; later trips to the Côte d'Azur and Italy were less carefree, since they were partly motivated by concern for her daughter Julie's health. Manet's death in 1883 removed Berthe Morisot's long-time master and perhaps made it easier for her to come under the influence of Renoir; in retrospect it seems a natural evolution for her, since she and Renoir were the only major Impressionists who were interested in portraying humanity with both intimacy and warmth of feeling. Many of her later paintings have something of Renoir's pearly glow, superimposed on Morisot's unmistakable feminine manner. In the '80s and '90s the Manet-Morisot house in the Rue de Villejust became a meeting place for artists and writers; Renoir, Degas and Monet put in occasional appearances.

Eugène Manet died in 1891, followed by Berthe Morisot on 2 March 1895; during her last illness she turned to her old friend Renoir and asked him to look after her daughter Julie and her two nieces.

Some Minor Impressionists

Mary Cassatt An American-born painter who became affiliated to the Impressionist movement was Mary Cassatt (1845-1926), who came from a wealthy Pittsburgh banking family. She had spent part of her childhood in France, and after four years at the Pennsylvania Academy of Fine Arts she braved her father's disapproval and returned to Europe. With Paris as her headquarters, she travelled in western Europe studying the Old Masters. In the 1870s she was reasonably successful at the Salon; and since she possessed a comfortable private income, her alignment with the Impressionists – still the butt of Parisian cartoonists and revues – seems to have been a quite gratuitously courageous gesture of independence, comparable to Berthe Morisot's. There was perhaps an element of aristocratic disdain, too. Cassatt violently resented

Mary Cassatt. *The Little Sisters*. About 1885. Despite the assertively 'rough' technique, a more sentimental painting than the sharply observed *Girl Arranging her Hair*. Glasgow Art Gallery.

having to submit her works to a self-appointed jury, although hers was an attitude most painters who were French and poor – born into the system and dependent on it – must have found difficult to understand.

The suggestion that Mary Cassatt should exhibit with the Impressionists came from Degas, who was introduced to her in the late 1870s and became one of the chief influences on her life. As a result of their meeting, Cassatt contributed to the fourth Impressionist exhibition of 1879, and to the next two shows. In 1882 she was sufficiently committed to Degas to refuse to take part once he had withdrawn from the seventh show; and like him she exhibited again in 1886. She sat for many of Degas's pictures, including the *At the Milliner's* series, but though they had many tastes in common she was never his pupil, formally or informally. If they were lovers, as some contemporaries believed, they were uniquely successful in bequeathing neither documents nor anecdotes to posterity. Mary Cassatt certainly remained independent enough of Degas to break off all relations with him for some considerable time in the 1880s when he made rude remarks about her abilities.

As a painter, Cassatt's affinities were with Manet and Degas rather than the more 'feathery-touched' of the Impressionists. Like Degas, she placed a high value on composition and draughtsmanship; and if her work lacks the range and rigour of her friend's, it is by no means imitative and has a kind of solemn charm of its own. Cassatt's characteristic pictures are of women, girls and children, usually rendered with the faintest tinge of sentimentality.

Not the least of Mary Cassatt's contributions to Impressionism was the help she extended to other members of the group. She bought paintings she admired; and since, despite her choice of career, she remained socially acceptable and acceptably sociable, she was able to persuade wealthy American acquaintances to buy an occasional Degas or Pissarro. With such a respectable champion, Impressionist paintings won a certain recognition in the United States at a relatively early date.

Mary Cassatt. *The Boating Party.* 1893. National Gallery of Art, Washington, DC (Chester Dale Collection).

Armand Guillaumin Guillaumin was a talented but lesser figure whose failure to develop was probably caused by material circumstances. Born at Moulins in 1841, he came to Paris when he was 16, worked for his uncle, and then took a job with the Parisian municipal authorities. Less lucky – and less ruthlessly single-minded – than other Impressionists, he never fully succeeded in overcoming family pressures, and remained tied to a job until well into middle age. Even when he briefly tried to live as a full-time artist (1868-72) he was forced to paint blinds and do other commercial jobs to survive. Within these limits Guillaumin's devotion to painting was considerable: it seems to have absorbed almost every moment of his free time. But for too many years he was really no more than a superior amateur; and in fact there was considerable opposition to his participation in several of the Impressionist shows. His closest friends in the movement were Pissarro and Cézanne, whom he met at the Académie Suisse and often worked beside in the open air. Pissarro secured Guillaumin's admission to the first Impressionist show, just as he secured Cézanne's. Guillaumin's influence on Pissarro was accidental: he introduced him to Seurat, and the meeting led to Pissarro's adoption of the divisionist technique.

The most extraordinary event in Guillaumin's life had nothing to do with art: in 1891 he won a prize of 100,000 francs in a lottery and was able to give up his job. At 50

he thus became a full-time painter. He was the last of the 1874 Impressionists to die (in
June 1927), surviving Monet by six months. Guillaumin left a respectable body of
work, and in a few examples, such as *Sunset at Ivry*, his brilliance of colouring
achieved outstanding effects.

Gustave Caillebotte (1848-94) was a talented minor painter, but his real importance
was as an organiser and patron. He and Pissarro were chiefly responsible for organising
the group shows of 1879 and 1880. His growing hostility to Degas and his followers
caused him to drop out in 1881, and he rejoined the group only for the 1882 show,
which excluded Degas.

207

Caillebotte's private fortune was used to back the shows and, more important, to keep the artists themselves going. His buying was judicious as well as helpful, so that by the end of his life he had built up one of the greatest collections in European history. Renoir's *The Swing* and *Moulin de la Galette,* Monet's *Gare St Lazare,* Manet's *Balcony* and Pissarro's *Red Roofs* were only a few of the paintings reproduced in this book that Caillebotte acquired. Despite his early death, he had already made provision for his collection, bequeathing it to the French nation with the proviso that the pictures should not be stacked away in a basement or exiled to a provincial museum. The relatively low reputation of the Impressionists, even in 1894, is shown by the fact that 29 of Caillebotte's 67 paintings were refused; ironically, Degas – Caillebotte's bête noire – was the only artist to have all of his works accepted. The Caillebotte bequest was shown at the Luxembourg from 1896 and was admitted to the Louvre only in 1929, along with other generous donations that have given the Louvre collection a distinction the French authorities tried very hard to repudiate.

Armand Guillaumin. *The Bridge at Charenton.* 1878. Musée du Louvre, Paris.

Paul Camille Guigou. *Provençal Landscape.* 1867. Guigou, like Cézanne, was a Provençal, though his was a much quieter talent. He was introduced into the Café Guerbois circle by Dr Gachet, who collected a number of Guigou's pictures after the painter's death. Musée Fabre, Montpellier.

Paul Guigou (1834-71) was a member of the Café Guerbois group who painted in the open air with a panache that made his work acceptable at the Salon. He served through the Franco-Prussian War, only to die a few months later, possibly with greater achievements before him.

Eva Gonzalès (1849-83) was not in any important sense an Impressionist. She was Manet's pupil and follower, and like him refused to take part in any of the group exhibitions. Berthe Morisot's professional and/or personal jealousy has already been noticed; but in spite of (or because of) Manet's praise, Eva Gonzalès was never more than an imitator of her master. She was capable of watering down his style to make it acceptable to the Salon, as in a variation on his rejected *Fifer*; but her best works, such as *A Box at the Théâtre des Italiens*, are more directly inspired by Manet. Eva Gonzalès had just given birth when she heard of Manet's death; she was griefstricken and insisted on making him a wreath, but herself died of an embolism a few days later.

Édouard Manet. *Portrait of Eva Gonzalès.* 1870. Shown at the Salon of 1870. Mlle Gonzalès was the only formally accepted pupil that Manet ever took. Manet's friend Berthe Morisot was jealous of the beautiful Mlle Gonzalès, anxiously noted Manet's comments on her own and the other woman's work, and took a malicious pleasure in the difficulties Manet experienced with this painting. National Gallery, London.

Beyond Impressionism

The painters in this section are generally known as Post-Impressionists. This is a portmanteau term that means no more than it implies – that they worked in styles that were not Impressionist and were developed later than Impressionism. Cézanne, Gaugin and Van Gogh had almost nothing but genius in common: they worked in widely different styles, each of which inspired a major tradition of modern art. From the point of view of this book, however, what matters is that they were at one time or another closely linked with Impressionism; and that side of their work is given a prominence here that would be out of place in a more general history of painting. Similarly, though the later development of each painter is outlined and illustrated, it is given nothing like the emphasis it would receive in a different context. And, after all, Impressionism was a central fact in their lives: without its liberating influence, both their techniques and their styles would have been utterly unthinkable.

Cézanne

Cézanne's development was a kind of chronological anomaly. He was much the same age as the Impressionists, yet by virtue of his finest work he belongs with the 'Post-Impressionists' of the late 1880s and 1890s. Even temperamentally he was more akin to the doubt-haunted, self-obsessed men of the later generation than to 'objective' painters like Pissaro and Monet, in whose pictures private griefs find no place. However, the matter of temperament does explain why he became an Impressionist late – after working in an uncertain, prematurely expressionistic style in the 1860s – as well as why he moved away from Impressionism after a relatively brief experience with it.

Cézanne's contact with Pissarro from 1872 gave him more than a tutor in Impressionism. Pissarro believed in him, secured his admission to the first Impressionist show, and remained sympathetic when Cézanne developed away from the main Impressionist style. The closeness of the relationship is indicated by the fact that Cézanne settled with Hortense and his little son Paul at Auvers, close to Pissarro (1872-74), and again worked beside Pissarro in 1877 and 1881 – when, however, the presence of a new acolyte, Paul Gauguin, threw Cézanne into a fit of suspicion and jealousy. The kind of support Pissarro gave him was all the more important, because Cézanne was isolated – very much the 'wild man' among the Impressionists, and the special butt of journalists, who found that his defiant outbursts made excellent copy. The only other people who began to understand Cézanne's struggles were non-artists: his boyhood friend Zola, the collector Dr Gachet, whom he met at Auvers, and an old vendor of painting materials, Père Tanguy, whose picture shop was the only place where Cézanne's paintings could be seen in Paris.

Cézanne was largely responsible for his own isolation, dressing and behaving with wilful eccentricity and ensuring that his works were not seen in the capital. He exhibited with the Impressionists in 1874, and only once more after that, in 1877. Most years he preferred to send paintings to the Salon, where they were refused with monotonous regularity. He finally secured acceptance in 1882, but only because his friend Guillemet was a member of the jury and exercised the juryman's privilege of having one work by a pupil accepted without debate; so Cézanne finally made his appearance at the Salon as the 'pupil of Guillemet' – in spite of which his entry attracted little or no attention.

Paul Cézanne. *Self-Portrait*. 1880-81. Cézanne's obsession with self-portraiture is one of the characteristics that sets him apart from the Impressionists proper and makes him akin to the 'generation' of Gauguin and Van Gogh – neither of whom he liked or admired. This unfinished self-portrait is actually very small (26 × 15 cm), but typically powerful. Musée du Louvre, Paris.

The main exception to the general indifference was Victor Chocquet, whose enthusiasm for Impressionism was so strong that he haunted the group exhibitions trying to make converts by pointing out the merits of the pictures to anyone who would listen. Chocquet admired Renoir's work intensely; yet when Renoir introduced him to Cézanne in 1875 he seems to have realised at once that he had encountered a still more profound talent. He became the painter's first devoted collector, and also his close friend; he seems to have played a stabilising role in the life of Cézanne, who alternated between megalomaniac boasting and total collapses of self-confidence. Cézanne painted Victor Chocquet several times.

Although remaining almost unknown, Cézanne spent most of the 1870s in or around Paris. His secret liaison with Hortense Fiquet, and the existence of their son Paul, made

Paul Cézanne. *The House of Pére Lacroix*. 1873. In this early work of Cézanne's Impressionist period, he is already bringing his sense of structure to bear on the landscape: more important than the light playing over the forms is the solidity of the forms themselves beneath the light. National Gallery of Art, Washington, DC (Chester Dale Collection).

living in Aix difficult. Cézane's father grew increasingly suspicious and, suspecting the truth, deliberately kept his son short of money; his mother helped as much as she dared, but as Cézanne's father opened all the letters that came into the house (including those addressed to his son), communication was difficult. Zola, now a successful novelist, proved a generous friend, sending money to Hortense and frequently playing host to Cézanne in his new house at Médan.

The year 1886 was a turning point for Cézanne. In April he married Hortense and was able to lead a normal family life (though his later behaviour suggests that he may not have found this a blessing). At the same time he broke with Zola, whose novel *L'Oeuvre* ('The Work' or 'The Masterpiece') revealed his diminished enthusiasm for Impressionism. Even more to the point, the central character – who ends in madness and suicide – was partly based on Cézanne, and many incidents were drawn from Cézanne's and Zola's shared experiences. When he received his complimentary copy

Above:
Paul Cézanne. *Auvers: Village Panorama.* 1873-75. Cézanne lived at Auvers in 1873-74. In this picture, painted at the height of his Impressionist period, Cézanne employs the broken brush-work of his colleagues but makes little attempts to modify the strong local colours of the roofs to indicate atmospheric effect. Art Institute of Chicago, Illinois (Mr and Mrs Lewis L. Coburn Memorial Collection).

Right:
Paul Cézanne. *Portrait of Victor Chocquet.* About 1877–82. The customs official Victor Chocquet was one of the most discerning collectors of his time. He bought a number of works by Delacroix, and later by Renoir, who painted portraits of Chocquet and his wife. It was Renoir who introduced Cézanne to Chocquet. The Columbus Gallery of Fine Arts, Columbus, Ohio.

Above:
Paul Cézanne. *The Bridge at Maincy*. 1882-85. The cool, hard, clear architectural quality of this painting is very remote from the Impressionism of the '70s. It is interesting to compare the reflections here, apparently as durable as solid objects, with the dissolvent role of water in, for example, Monet's La Grenouillère pictures. Musée du Louvre, Paris.

Left:
Paul Cézanne. *The Card Players*. About 1890-92. Cézanne painted no less than five versions of this subject. Paintings involving relationships between human figures are otherwise rare in Cézanne's *oeuvre* except for the various *Bathers* canvases. Musée du Louvre, Paris.

Paul Cézanne. *Boy in a Red Waistcoat*. About
1894–95. The humanity of the subject is more
important here than in much of Cézanne's work.
He was usually ill at ease with living models,
but this young professional, Michelangelo di
Rossi, must have had a soothing effect on the
artist's nervous irritability. He posed for Cézanne
several times, and at least three portraits of him
are among Cézanne's finest paintings. This
version is particularly complex in design, and
the elongated right arm is a famous example of
the liberties Cézanne sometimes took with
'Nature'. Bührle Collection, Zürich.

Paul Cézanne. *Sous-Bois* (Undergrowth).
About 1895-1900. A wonderful example of
Cézanne's late style, verging on abstraction and
yet remaining in touch with reality: nature is still
present, and a feeling of depth. The whole
picture surface is mobilised by the march of the
brush-strokes, organised in dynamic groups of
parallels. Galerie Beyeler, Basel.

Cézanne wrote a polite note of thanks ('I thank the author ... and ask him to allow me
to press his hand in memory of old times. Ever yours under the impulse of years gone
by'.). The two men seem never to have communicated with each other again.

More important for Cézanne's way of life was the death of his father, aged 88, in
October 1886. Cézanne inherited a fortune and was at last free from dependence. In the
long run this encouraged his tendency to withdraw into his painting at the expense of
human contacts. He spent a good deal of time in Paris during 1888-90, but from then
on stayed in the South for longer and longer periods: first at the family house, the Jas
de Bouffan, outside Aix; then, after the house had to be sold to settle his mother's
estate, in Aix itself. In the 1890s he gradually cut himself off from his old friends. He
fell out with some through his near-insane suspiciousness, which led him to believe that
people were making fun of him or trying to steal his work. But he also seems to have
decided to break most of his old ties: when he saw Pissarro or Renoir on the street in
Paris he would signal them to cross to the other side of the road; and the morning after
a convivial evening, he is said to have sent Monet a note saying how much he had
enjoyed it – and that it would be better if it were the last meeting of their lives.
However, though he could be wildly disparaging about other painters, Cézanne
remembered his debts: in the last year of his life, at an exhibition in Aix, he had himself
entered in the catalogue as 'Paul Cézanne, pupil of Pissarro'.

Part of the explanation of Cézanne's behaviour is that he regarded himself as far
ahead of his time, and therefore more at home with younger men. (Another way of
putting it is that Cézanne wanted to be a master among pupils rather than vice versa: 'I
think the younger painters are much more intelligent than the others – the old ones see
in me only a disastrous rival.') From about 1890 he began to attract a few younger men

Above:
Paul Cézanne. *Still Life with Apples and Oranges*. 1896-1900. Cézanne was the only one of the Impressionists to paint still lifes regularly, and make them one of the main categories of his work. This fact emphasises his commitment to construction rather than light or movement as the essential feature of his art. Musée du Louvre, Paris.

Left:
Paul Cézanne. *Old Woman with a Rosary*. About 1897-98. The old woman was Cézanne's maid, who had been a nun. Cézanne himself had become a fervent Catholic by this time. But, typically, he avoids injecting a specifically religious emotion into the painting, redolent though it is of the old woman's strength and humility. National Gallery, London.

Above:
Paul Cézanne. *Portrait of Ambroise Vollard.*
1899. The dealer Vollard (1865-1939) was
Durand-Ruel's successor as the leading
commercial champion of the modern in art,
organising the first exhibitions of Cézanne, and
later of Picasso, Matisse and others. Musée du
Petit Palais, Paris.

Above right:
Paul Cézanne. *The Large Bathers.* 1898-1906.
One of a whole series of *Bathers* painted by
Cézanne in his last years. Both in subject and
method – they were painted without models –
they represent a break in Cézanne's development
from the 1870s. They may be linked in some
way with his early work, though their mood is
rather different. Philadelphia Museum of Art,
Pennsylvania (W.P. Wilstach Collection).

Below right:
Paul Cézanne. *The Large Bathers.* 1900-06.
National Gallery, London.

– critics like Huysmans and Roger Marx, painters like Émile Bernard – and in 1895 an ambitious young dealer, Ambroise Vollard, was encouraged by Pissarro to seek out Cézanne; the result was the first exhibition of Cézanne's works in Paris. Then, through the Caillebotte bequest, two of Cézanne's paintings entered the Luxembourg en route for the Louvre. Thus Cézanne received a measure of support and recognition in his old age. All the same, his art – more radical than that of the Impressionists – was still derided by most critics, and he was not widely known when he died on 22 October 1906. In *Reminiscences of the Impressionist Painters*, published in the same year, George Moore described his work as 'the anarchy of painting . . . art in delirium'.

One of the earliest of Cézanne's Impressionist paintings, *The House of the Hanged Man*, shows the sense of structure and monumental form that impelled him 'to make of Impressionism something solid and durable, like the art of museums'. Though he admired the Impressionists' liberated brush-work, and above all their direct contact with nature, Cézanne laid more emphasis on organising the sensations nature gave him. By the late 1870s his work can no longer be described as Impressionist: a painting like the wonderful *Bridge at Maincy* is as highly organised in its way as anything by Degas, even if the organisation was done on the spot. Cézanne increasingly used the brush-marks themselves as part of this organisation; instead of vivid multi-coloured dots or strokes blended by the eye, he built up the picture into a modern pattern of parallel strokes like hatching. In retrospect, a picture like *Sous-Bois*, though still a response to

Paul Cézanne. *Mont Sainte Victoire*. About 1904-06. Cézanne painted Mont Sainte Victoire many times in the last 20 years of his life, setting up his easel in the valley of the River Arc, which was redolent of his boyhood expeditions with Zola and Baille. The mountain seems also to have symbolised in Cézanne's mind the kind of strong, rock-durable art he wished to create. Kunstmuseum, Basel.

nature, is almost an abstract – a pattern of colours and brush-strokes. Though Cézanne insisted that a painter's response to nature – his 'little sensation' – ought to be the starting point of his work, he must rank as a forerunner of one of the important movements in modern art: abstraction, in which the picture is seen as something separate from reality – an autonomous surface consisting of visible marks, shapes and colours. Cézanne has also been linked with Cubism, since a painting such as the portrait of Vollard radically simplifies the planes of the figure; and Cézanne's famous advice to Émile Bernard, to 'treat nature by the cylinder, the sphere and the cone', can be interpreted as a classic statement of Cubist principles.

Despite all this emphasis on order and method, an only half-controlled emotional turmoil seems to be present in the *Bathers* that Cézanne painted intermittently over the years. These are strikingly different from the main body of his work: increasingly generalised figures in generalised landscapes, grouped in a strained-for harmony that looks like the painter's effort to *classicise away* some erotic obsession – perhaps the same obsession that produced Cézanne's early paintings of rapes and murders. Incidentally, some such aspect of Cézanne's personality, otherwise unremarked, is indicated in Claude Lantier, the central character of Zola's *L'Oeuvre*; and Zola, his closest friend from the age of 12 to 47, knew Cézanne better than anybody else.

Finally, Cézanne is important neither as a forerunner of the modern nor as an exponent of neurotic art. He is the giant creator of an art 'solid and durable, like the art of the museums'.

Paul Cézanne. *Le Château Noir*. 1904–06. A fascinating, vertiginous painting. The daring brush-work makes most of the pictures in this book look conventional: it helps to explain the very late recognition of Cézanne's genius. Private Collection

Gauguin

Paul Gauguin. *Self-Portrait in front of an Easel.* 1884-85. Painted in Copenhagen, where Gauguin was forced to work in the attic while his wife Mette gave French lessons to support the family. The vulnerable, reflective figure in this self-portrait must express the painter's mood at the time: contemporary photographs as well as later self-portraits show the familiar, powerful, saturnine Gauguin. Collection Dr Jacques Koerfer. Berne.

Everybody knows the legend of Paul Gauguin. He was a middle-aged stockbroker who abandoned his family and career to become a painter, and ended his days in an exotic South-Sea apotheosis. The legend is not exactly wrong, though it overdramatises by condensing the facts of Gauguin's life; and, as legends will, it omits the lengthy tedious apprenticeship of the hero – in this case his apprenticeship in the school of Impressionism.

Gauguin was born in Paris on 7 June 1848. His father was a journalist on the liberal organ *La Nation* who took a gloomy view of his future under the régime of Louis Napoleon, soon to turn into the Second Empire; so he emigrated to Peru, where his wife had rich and powerful relations. Clovis Gauguin died on the voyage out, but his

Right:
Paul Gauguin. *The Seine at the Pont d'Iéna*.
1875. An early painting, done while Gauguin
was still a well-off gentleman-amateur. Musée
du Louvre, Paris.

Below:
Paul Gauguin. *The Beach at Dieppe*. 1885. After
returning from Copenhagen in June 1885,
Gauguin spent a few days at Dieppe in
September. There he met Degas and quarrelled
with him, though the two men later became
friendly again. Ny Carlsberg Glyptotek,
Copenhagen.

Paul Gauguin. *Mandolin and Flowers.* 1885.
The flattened-out, highly decorative
arrangement of this still life indicates that
Gauguin is beginning to move away from
Impressionism. Musée du Louvre. Paris.

widow and her two children spent five years in Peru (1849-55) before returning to France; and it seems quite likely that Paul Gauguin's taste for the primitive and exotic was fostered by this early experience.

At 17, after an undistinguished school career, Gauguin decided to join the merchant navy. As a cadet, and later a second mate, he served on runs between France and South America. Then, in 1868, he started his military service in the French navy on the cruiser *Jérôme Napoleon*, whose name was hastily changed to *Desaix* as the Second Empire collapsed under the Prussian onslaught. In April 1871, tired of the brutalities and boredom of life at sea, Gauguin left the navy. Helped by his guardian, Gustave Arosa (his mother had died in 1867), he found a job with a stockbroking firm.

This began the period of Gauguin's great prosperity. He was actually not a

Paul Gauguin. *Martinique Landscape*. 1887. In Martinique, Gauguin and his friend Charles Laval lived in 'a negro hut' on the beach. Though illness and poverty made it impossible for him to stay on the island, Gauguin was delighted with the climate, landscape and people. But he found that tropical colours could not be captured by using the broken-brush-work Impressionist technique. National Gallery of Scotland, Edinburgh.

stockbroker but a broker's agent, employed to find clients who could be persuaded to buy or sell shares. Gauguin had a gift for the work – a surprising fact in view of his enclosed, unsociable personality – and he started out at a favourable time, when the French economy was experiencing a post-war boom. Soon the one-time sailor was doing well enough to marry. He picked for his bride Mette Sophie Gad, a Danish girl who was working as a governess in Paris. They were married in November 1873, and over the next ten years Mette gave him five children.

Meanwhile, art thrust itself into Gauguin's life. On shipboard he seems to have done a little drawing to pass the time, but without any sense of vocation. In Paris, however, he was positively haunted: the Arosas' home was full of paintings (especially paintings by Delacroix); Gauguin's firm was in the Rue Lafitte, where there were leading Parisian

225

galleries to attract his attention as he passed to and from work; and a colleague within the firm itself, Émile Schuffenecker, was an enthusiastic amateur painter. Thanks to these stimulants, Gauguin became a keen 'Sunday painter', making trips to the outskirts of Paris to work in the style of Corot and other admired masters. He and Schuffenecker attended one of the 'free' academies, the Atelier Colarossi, and in 1876 Gauguin even had a landscape accepted and shown at the Salon. He also experimented with sculpture, and seemed destined for a pleasantly insignificant career as a talented amateur of the arts.

Meeting Pissarro and becoming involved with the Impressionists was a turning point. This occurred in 1877 or '78, and almost every year until 1884 Gauguin spent his holidays painting with Pissarro at Pontoise and Osny. In later years Gauguin, who was

not always generous in his attitudes to fellow-artists, defended Pissarro's openness to a variety of influences and summed up his own debt to him: 'He was my master and I do not deny him'. Pissarro taught him to abandon the sombre Corot-like colours and style of his earlier work, using the primaries and the small brush-strokes of the Impressionists. Many of his paintings over a period of eight years or more are typically Impressionist in subject and treatment, including village, snow and beach scenes.

Gauguin exhibited with the Impressionists/Independents at the last five shows, initially thanks to Pissaro's backing; to some of the others he seemed no more than a pretentious amateur, and Monet's remarks about the Impressionist club opening its doors to any dauber may well have been a reference to Gauguin. Renoir was equally uncomplimentary; he seems to have believed that Gauguin was an anarchist like his

mentor Pissarro. But Degas appreciated Gauguin's works in the most direct way – he actually bought some – though relations between the two men were occasionally strained. Gauguin opposed Degas's faction in the rows of 1882, and his threat of resignation seems to have persuaded Pissarro that it was impossible to keep Degas with the group; and this, arguably, led to the 'reunion' eventually arranged on the initiative of Durand-Ruel. In general, Gauguin seems to have taken a very active part in the planning and intriguing that went on before the shows, perhaps because it strengthened his sense of belonging to the movement. To some extent he may have been tolerated as a wealthy amateur like Caillebotte, who was worth cultivating as a patron. Though never rich, Gauguin certainly made a good deal of money in the late 1870s and early '80s, thanks to the speculative mania, centred on the Catholic-sponsored Union Générale bank, that engulfed the Paris Bourse. Gauguin built up a fine collection of Impressionist paintings; he felt a special admiration for Degas and (a very advanced taste) for Cézanne – despite Cézanne's dislike of him. These admirations were pointers to his own future development, as yet invisible in his paintings.

In 1883 Gauguin carried out a resolution which he had confided to Pissarro more than a year before: he resigned from his job and became a full-time painter. His decision may have been precipitated by the crash of the Union Générale, which probably cost Gauguin a lot of money as well as radically diminishing his prospects on the Bourse. He carried on painting in company with Pissarro, whose feelings about him were now ambivalent: Gauguin's arrogance bothered him, and also his apparent commercialism. But if at this time Gauguin seemed desperate to sell and get good prices, this must have reflected his wish to maintain his wife and children in the manner to which they were accustomed – not any lack of determination to endure hardship if need be. And in fact, after an abortive stay in Rouen which ate up most of his money without resulting in any sales, Gauguin began to experience the poverty from which he was never to free himself.

In December 1884 Gauguin took his wife and children to Copenhagen, where he found his wife's family hostile and had no success either as a painter or working as the representative of a French tarpaulin manufacturer. After six months he returned to Paris with his second son, Clovis, leaving Mette and the other children behind. He was never to live with her again, though neither of them realised it at the time. Mette resented the loss of her comfortable bourgeois life and was understandably anxious about the future of her five children; besides, she had no sympathy with Gauguin's

painting or understanding of his aims. Significantly, it was in the next year or so, away from Mette, that Gauguin's mature personality formed – or perhaps it would be more accurate to say that he found the stance that it suited him to adopt vis-à-vis the world: a combination of utter dedication and brutal egoism that was incompatible with family ties and made it possible for him to exploit Schuffenecker and other friends quite ruthlessly without any apparent pangs of conscience. Poverty and illness did not shake his resolve, but hardened him. All that was lacking was the opportunity to assume the role of master, which he could hardly do among the equally gifted, older Impressionist painters. On his first visit to Pont-Aven, a veritable colony of young artists on the Brittany coast, Gauguin was himself able to play the old master. He discarded the respectable image of the Danish self-portrait, let his hair and moustache grow, and

228

Paul Gauguin. *Self-Portrait with a Halo.* 1889. Painted on the right-hand door of large cupboard in a room at Mlle Henry's inn at le Pouldu, Brittany. The room was decorated throughout by Gauguin, Sérusier, Meyer de Haan and other friends; de Haan appears – as the Devil – on the other door of the cupboard. National Gallery of Art, Washington, DC (Chester Dale Collection).

Paul Gauguin. *Self-Portrait with the Yellow Christ.* 1889-90. A mirror portrait of the artist in front of his painting *The Yellow Christ*, done in 1889. Musée Denis, St Germaine en Laye.

Paul Gauguin. *Soyez Amoureuses et Vous Serez Heureuses* (Love and You Will be Happy). 1889. Painted wood relief. Museum of Fine Arts, Boston, Massachusetts (Arthur Tracy Cabot Fund).

dressed bohemian-style in berets, embroidered jackets and clogs. His physical strength commanded respect, and his moodiness, fits of taciturnity and egoism were increasingly accepted as evidence of genius.

The genius itself was slow in becoming evident, since it depended on Gauguin's self-liberation. As this neared completion, Gauguin's primitivism asserted itself strongly for the first time. At the heart of this phenomenon was the belief that civilisation was corrupt, and that in warmer climes and among unspoiled peoples a man might live a more meaningful as well as a happier life. In Gauguin's case this was complicated by his painters' dream of working in a land where warmth, shelter and food cost virtually nothing; and, further, by his visionary businessman's conviction that instant fortunes were to be made in the tropics. With these mixed motives, Gauguin sailed for Panama in April 1887. There, work had begun on a canal to link the Atlantic and Pacific oceans; this was not the present canal, but Ferdinand de Lesseps' disastrous venture of 1887-89, which ended in bankruptcy and failure. Gauguin's trip was a disaster too, and he had to work on the canal as a labourer to earn enough money to leave. From Panama, Gauguin and his companion, the painter Charles Laval, went to the island of Martinique. In this paradise of dazzling colours, Laval suffered from fever, Gauguin

Left:
Paul Gauguin. *Hina Te Fatou.* 1893. The moon goddess Hina encounters Fatou, spirit of the earth. Gauguin was deeply interested in traditional Tahitian beliefs, which had virtually disappeared as a result of European colonisation, and he described them in his book *Noa-Noa.* Museum of Modern Art, New York (Lillie P. Bliss Collection).

Right:
Paul Gauguin. *Nevermore.* 1897. In 1896-97, as he grew more depressed and discouraged, Gauguin gave his paintings grater symbolic content, though the precise meanings are usually elusive. The title of this famous painting clearly refers to Edgar Allan Poe's *The Raven* ('"Nevermore," quoth the Raven'), though Gauguin rather strangely explained in a letter, 'For title, *Nevermore*: not the raven of Edgar Allan Poe, but the bird of the devil that is keeping watch'. Courtauld Institute Galleries, London.

Right:
Paul Gauguin. *Where Do We Come From? What Are We? Where Are We Going to?* 1897. According to Gauguin's own account, this large (139 × 274·5 cm) picture was painted in a burst of frenzied activity, straight on to the canvas without preparatory studies or models. It was intended as a grand summary of Gauguin's art before, depressed by debts and lack of recognition, he killed himself. He took arsenic in December 1897 but succeeded only in making himself ill. Museum of Fine Arts, Boston, Massachusetts (Arthur George Tompkins Residuary Fund 36,270).

from dysentery. In November 1887 Gauguin worked his way back to France on a ship. But the episode failed to cure him of his obsession with tropical places, though Madagascar, and later Tahiti, replaced the Caribbean as the longed-for lands of enchantment.

Gauguin's Martinique paintings mark the beginning of his break with Impressionism. The mood in his earlier work is often non-Impressionist, as in the self-probing mirror-image portrait. In *Martinique Landscape* the technique too has changed, with areas of brilliant colour hardly varying in tone. To some extent this may represent Gauguin's response to the landscape of Martinique, with colours so much harder and stronger than in the milder, mistier North. If so, Gauguin carried that version of reality back to France with him. Back at Pont-Aven in 1888 he painted *The Vision after the Sermon*, a bold departure from both academic and **Impressionist** art which **Gauguin** took with the encouragement of the young painter Émile Bernard, whom he knew slightly from his first stay at Pont-Aven. (Bernard was one of those unlucky people whose ideas inspire the achievements of greater men, and who spend most of their lives vainly claiming the credit they believe to have been stolen from them.) The flat colours, emphatic contours and imaginary subject matter announced a new master and a new style: Synthetism or *Cloisonnisme,* so called after the cloisonné enamel technique, in which the enamel colours are separated by metal ridges that keep each colour in its own compartment. Despite the name, Japanese prints and perhaps stained glass were more important influences on Gauguin and Bernard.

Gauguin now became the chief of the 'Pont-Aven school', and over the following two years frequently stayed there or at nearby Le Pouldu. In the autumn of 1888, however, Gauguin joined Van Gogh in the South at Arles, a disastrous episode described in the next chapter. The rest of Gauguin's time was spent in the capital, trying to earn some

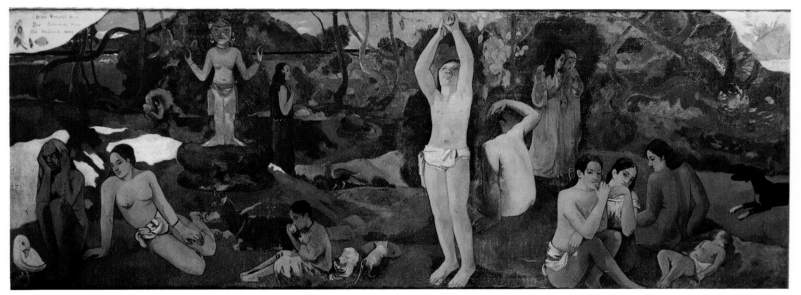

money and/or living with the Schauffeneckers. He inevitably became involved with the Parisian Symbolist movement – inevitably, since Symbolist art and literature too dealt in dreams, evocations and allusions, rejecting both the naturalism of Zola and the 'objective' approach of the Impressionists.

In a sense, therefore, Gauguin, like Van Gogh, represents an anti-naturalist mood that became predominant among the artists and intellectuals of the '90s, expressing itself in Art Nouveau, the 'Decadents' and similarly related phenomena. Gauguin made a lithograph of the poet Jean Moréas entitled *Soyez Symboliste* ('Be a Symbolist!') and became friendly with Mallarmé, who had now come into his own. By 1891 Gauguin was quite a well-known figure, at least in Symbolist circles, but at an auction at the Hôtel Drouot, 30 of his paintings raised 9,350 francs, an average of 310 francs each: far

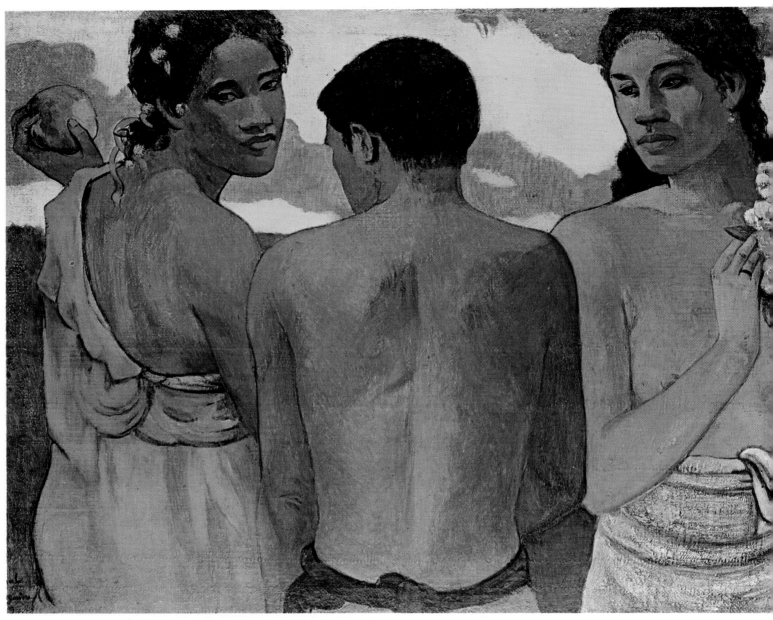

better than the Impressionists 16 years before, but little enough for an artist approaching 43 years old. The object of the sale was to finance Gauguin's journey to Tahiti. He had decided to leave civilisation altogether, and after a last visit to his family in Copenhagen and a 'Symbolist banquet' in his honour presided over by Mallarmé, he embarked in April 1891.

Gauguin's years in Tahiti are at the heart of his legend. He produced his finest work on the island, making the Tahitians the vehicle for his sense of the mystery of human existence; technically his manner is a modified Synthetism, less heavily outlined and with more modelling, but still rich in large areas of flat colour. To some extent the mystery was in Gauguin's mind rather than the Tahitians themselves. Just as his writings describe a primitive form of Tahitian society that had vanished before he arrived, his paintings show men and women untrivialised by contact with Europeans. Yet in reality Europeans were everywhere; Gauguin suffered agonies from one of Europe's gifts to primitive peoples – syphilis; and most of the time he was desperately in debt. Still, a two-year interval (June 1893 – June 1895) in his old haunts failed to convince him that life in Europe was preferable, even with a legacy and Anna the Javanese to bear him up. In June 1895 he left France for the last time. Yet his second stay in Tahiti was no more successful: as well as his old troubles he had a bad foot (resulting from a broken leg incurred during a brawl with some sailors in France) and a running fight with the colonial administration, of whose behaviour towards the Tahitians Gauguin was violently critical. Friends and buyers in France proved so unreliable that in December 1897 Gauguin even tried to poison himself. After this, though better off for a time thanks to a regular allowance from Vollard – who in return got Gauguin's pictures for 200 francs a piece – the pattern continued with little change. The amazing.thing is that this way of life – in some respects more tortured and turbulent than Gauguin's life in France – appears only occasionally in his art, with its cool, timeless, enigmatic quality.

In September 1901 Gauguin settled in the Marquesas, where living was cheaper, only to fall foul of the colonial administration again. Suffering from eczema and in the process of appealing against a three-month gaol sentence for libel, he suddenly died of a heart attack on 8 May 1903.

Paul Gauguin. *Three Tahitians*. 1897 or 1899. The enclosed, intimate mood – characteristic of Gauguin even in his Tahitian paintings with wide, lush landscape backgrounds – is reinforced here by the bold device of placing the central figure with his back to the spectator. National Gallery of Scotland, Edinburgh.

Van Gogh

Vincent Van Gogh is an even more extreme example than Gauguin of the artist who puts his life, beliefs and sufferings on to the canvas. Through his Breton women and dark-skinned Tahitians, Gauguin painted his dreams and ideas; Van Gogh may be said to have painted the state of his soul. In his late works, the stars grow larger and brighter, cornfields gleam with unnatural brilliance, buildings tremble and warp with the upheavals of the painter's reason. From time to time in the past, artists had used non-natural colours and shapes to convey emotion, but it was Van Gogh's example that inspired the whole modern movement of Expressionism, still very much alive today in both figurative and abstract form.

Van Gogh was born on 30 March 1853 at Groot Zundert, in the Dutch province of North Brabant, where his father was a Protestant clergyman. The household was not a particularly affluent one, but Vincent's uncles were prosperous art dealers; one of them – also named Vincent Van Gogh – was the proprietor of Goupil's, which was at that time the largest firm of its sort in Europe. At 16 Vincent went to work for Goupil's, and as his uncle was childless he might well have inherited the business. His seven years with the firm included a long stay in London (1873-74) during which he fell in love with his landlady's daughter, who turned out to be engaged to somebody else. This rejection set off a religious crisis that destroyed his interest in the art business, and in 1876 he lost his job at Goupil's.

Having started in life with the closest possible links with the world of art (he even worked in Paris, the art capital, for a time), Van Gogh abandoned it without any idea that it might ever be part of his own destiny. He returned to England, where he took teaching jobs at Ramsgate and Isleworth. Then he worked in a Dordrecht bookshop, studied Latin and Greek with the idea of going to university, and finally trained for three months at an evangelical school in Brussels. He was sent to the Borinage, a mining district in the south of Belgium, where his attempts to live a Christlike life and share the miners' poverty outraged superiors and brought about his dismissal.

In 1880 Van Gogh at last found his vocation for art. He had practised drawing since his boyhood, using it to record places and people, and also to express his emotions. Now he settled in Brussels for a time, taking lessons in anatomy and perspective and

Vincent Van Gogh. *The Potato Eaters.* 1885. Inspired by Millet, Van Gogh saw himself at this time as a socially conscious painter of work and workers. He executed three versions of this subject, in which the toil-worn peasants are shown as almost grotesque. It constitutes a painted sermon on manual labour and honestly earned food. Rijksmuseum Vincent Van Gogh, Amsterdam.

learning from fellow-students. Apart from a turbulent month at Antwerp Academy in 1885, this was Van Gogh's only formal training; for the rest he was self-taught, often working his way conscientiously through standard texts.

Over the next five years Van Gogh pursued his vocation relentlessly, though his eccentric and unconventional behaviour made life particularly difficult in the quiet, rather stuffy atmosphere of the 19th-century Netherlands. In 1881, staying with his family at Etten, he fell violently in love with his cousin Kee Vos, a widow with a young son, and pursued her with a frightening, self-defeating intensity that was to doom most of his relationships. Leaving his disapproving family, he settled at the Hague, where he was helped by his cousin Anton Mauve, a successful academic painter, and became acquainted with many of the local artists. But he quarrelled with Mauve and lost most of his friends by living with a prostitute, Sien, who had one child and was expecting

another. In September 1883, after 18 months during which it had become increasingly difficult to paint and cope with Sien and her two children, Van Gogh fled. Later he lived with his parents in his father's new parish at Nuenen, but here too his unconventional behaviour made him unpopular and isolated. After the death of his father he soon found life at Nuenen impossible. He moved to Antwerp, quarrelled with the academy professors who, like his cousin Mauve, wanted him to copy plaster casts for day after day, and at last left to join his brother Theo, who was working for Goupil's in Paris.

It is easy to sympathise with the Van Gogh who alarmed his respectable neighbours at Nuenen because he cared nothing for money, dressed like a peasant in order to paint the peasants at work in the fields, and always said what he meant bluntly and sincerely. (He was steeped in the works of writers such as Dickens and Hugo, so what he said about hypocrisy and the social order was likely to have a sharp cutting edge.) But he

Above:
Vincent Van Gogh. *Girl in White in the Woods.* 1882. Painted during Van Gogh's period of study at The Hague. Although this is a careful exercise in the manner of the dominant Dutch school, Van Gogh's artistic personality is already apparent in the freedom with which the paint is handled and in the bright notes of colour. Rijksmuseum Kröller-Müller, Otterlo.

Left:
Vincent Van Gogh. *Self-Portrait.* 1887. A small (32 × 23 cm) self-portrait done in oils on paper. Impressionist in technique but definitely not so in mood. Rijksmuseum Kröller-Müller, Otterlo.

also showed a hyper-excitement and instability that made it hard for him to form relationships and impossible to maintain them. The loneliness he experienced only intensified his frightening ardour and emotional expectations when he found a potential friend or lover. The relationship became impossible, and Van Gogh was thrust back into loneliness. In this downward spiral, love and religion failed him; only in art was he able to advance, working furiously, though art was to prove inadequate for his personal salvation.

During his years in the Netherlands, Van Gogh painfully mastered drawing, lithography and painting, and experimented with several styles. In his graphic work he sometimes gave a direct, semi-literary expression to his feelings and beliefs, as in the *Sorrow* series. Many of his nature studies are objective in approach, but others are austerely mysterious (*The Vicarage Garden at Nuenen in Winter*). And in his numerous studies of peasants working in the fields, weaving, or eating, Van Gogh was trying to capture gestures, postures and other effects of toil, as well as the dignity he believed it to possess. He always regarded Millet as one of the 19th-century masters, on the strength of peasant paintings that now seem to us very sentimental. Van Gogh in fact got much closer to the reality of work and the soil. In his drawings, for example, he worked to capture the massy quality of the women, with their thickened figures shrouded in heavy shawls and voluminous skirts; his omission of academic details that would have weakened its impact is already complete. And in *The Potato Eaters*, his best-known painting from this period, he creates an atmosphere at once stifling, brutalised and oddly dignified.

Despite the sombre colour demanded by this particular subject, Van Gogh was already experimenting with a much lighter palette than that favoured by the Hague school. He had studied Delacroix's colour theories, and was therefore ready to appreciate the advances made by the Impressionists. In Paris he saw the final Impressionist exhibition, met Pissarro (then an ardent divisionist), and had Impressionist techniques explained to him by Guillaumin. Later he met Paul Gauguin, whom he admired enormously, and with whom he shared a love for the linear strength and flat strong colours of Japanese prints. Until 1888 elements of all three influences – Impressionism, divisionism, *Japonaiserie* – appear with more or less emphasis in his work. *Le Moulin de la Galette* is Van Gogh at his most Impressionist; *Road with a Peasant Shouldering a Spade* is an advanced divisionist work; while *Le Père Tanguy* has elements of both techniques combined with an entirely 'Japanese' background. The landscapes are the most 'objective' of Van Gogh's works in this period; whatever his technique, objects and especially people retain an obstinate force of their own which is alien to both Impressionism and Neo-Impressionism. Then, at Arles, he discovered the hard light and blazing colours of the South; and they inspired him to use colour with the intense emotive force that characterises his most famous work.

Van Gogh moved to Arles in February 1888 in search of warmth and peace. In Paris he had lived with his brother Theo. Though Vincent was four years older, the two had an almost symbiotic relationship in which Theo played the steady sensible brother, making Vincent an allowance that enabled him to go on painting – despite which, Vincent made periodic attempts to persuade Theo that he should give up his bourgeois life and become an artist. Close as they were, Theo cannot have found Vincent easy to live with, and Theo's letters hint that Vincent had alienated almost everybody they knew in Paris. Arles, then, represented a new start, and Van Gogh was soon dreaming of founding an artist's colony there. At its head he wanted to see Paul Gauguin, for whom he had developed an intense, boyish hero-worship; and he pressed Theo to persuade Gauguin to join him at Arles.

Left:
Vincent Van Gogh. *Le Moulin de la Galette*. About 1886. Not, apparently, the windmill from which Renoir's pleasure-garden took its name: each of the several windmill studies done by Van Gogh in Paris is conventionally known as 'Moulin de la Galette'. Glasgow Art Gallery.

Right:
Vincent Van Gogh. *Le Père Tanguy*. 1887. Julien Tanguy made his living hawking painting materials at the popular painting spots around Paris. He also had a little shop in the Rue Clauzel where he sold materials and – when anyone would buy – Impressionist paintings; for years his shop was the only place in Paris where Cézanne's work could be seen. The background celebrates Van Gogh's admiration for Japanese colour prints. Musée Rodin, Paris (A. Rodin Collection).

Gauguin came in October 1888, encouraged by a financial arrangement he had made with Theo. For a few weeks the two artists got on well; then they began to quarrel. Soon afterwards, on 23 December 1888, Van Gogh attacked Gauguin and later the same evening cut off a piece of his own ear. He had had his first breakdown and never fully recovered. The exact causes of this disaster have been impossible to identify. Van Gogh and Gauguin certainly argued over paintings; but painters usually do. Under Gauguin's influence Van Gogh tried to work from memory, but found the results banal: he needed the stimulus of contact with nature, however much he then distorted what he saw in the interests of emotional expression. None of this is in itself material for disaster. That must have been caused by Van Gogh's increasing instability, brought to its head by sharing a house with a man whose personality was as incompatible with

Van Gogh's as it is possible to imagine. The one was wildly, naively, enthusiastic, thin-skinned and demanding; the other had developed a self-protective egoism that could make him appear invulnerable, cynical and brutal – a pose that he probably exaggerated for Van Gogh's benefit. Coming on top of Van Gogh's nine months of feverish work and isolation at Arles, there could hardly have been an unluckier mis-mating. Incidentally, Van Gogh was later full of remorse for his behaviour, and resumed friendly relations with Gauguin.

He remained on his own at Arles until April 1889 in spite of several new breakdowns and the growing hostility of the townspeople, who understandably looked on him as a dangerous lunatic. He then voluntarily entered a mental hospital at Saint Rémy, about 24 kilometres from Arles, where his attacks recurred intermittently. Eventually, in May

Vincent Van Gogh. *Souvenir de Mauve.* 1888. a pink peach tree in blossom, painted at Arles for the widow of Anton Mauve – Van Gogh's successful painter cousin, with whom he had worked and quarrelled seven years before. Rijksmuseum Kröller-Müller, Otterlo.

Vincent Van Gogh. *La Mousmé* 1888. Painted at Arles in July 1888. The title is another of Van Gogh's tributes to the Japanese: a *mousmé* is a teahouse attendant. As in many of his paintings, the chair is at least as important as anything else in the picture. National Gallery of Art, Washington, DC (Chester Dale Collection).

1890, Theo had him brought to Paris; he himself had now married, and though Vincent had loyally welcomed the event, it can hardly have made him feel more secure. He was settled in a café at Auvers, where Dr Gachet (whom we have previously met as a friend and patron of Cézanne and others) could watch over him; Van Gogh had hoped to board with the Pissarros, but Julie refused to have a 'madman' in the house. At Auvers Van Gogh worked as intensely as ever. In these last years of his life his colours were rather less brilliant than in the early months at Arles. Now wild, swirling lines dominate many of his canvases; rocks seem to be pouring over a landscape in great waves, cornfields ripple and swell, houses buckle, and trees writhe upwards into a sky of whirling, enlarged suns, moons and stars ... On 27 July 1890 Van Gogh shot himself in the chest while working at his easel in the fields. Two days later, attended by Theo and Dr Gachet, he died. Less than three months later Theo Van Gogh too went insane; he was taken back to Holland by his wife, and died there in January 1891.

During his lifetime Vincent Van Gogh, one of the most revered of all modern masters, sold exactly one painting.

Vincent Van Gogh. *Sunflowers*. 1888. One of a
series painted in August 1888 at Arles. Yellow
was Van Gogh's favourite colour, and
sunflowers obsessed him. National Gallery,
London.

Right:
Vincent Van Gogh. *Café Terrace on the Place du Forum, Arles, at Night.* 1888. Painted in September, shortly before Gauguin's arrival. The cold, lonely atmosphere of the scene reflects Van Gogh's personal situation at Arles. Rijksmuseum Kröller-Müller, Otterlo.

Below:
Vincent Van Gogh. *Vincent's Chair with his Pipe.* December 1888-January 1889. The famous yellow chair is the companion piece to *Gauguin's Armchair.* Imposing armchair and humble chair express the master-disciple relationship between Gauguin and Van Gogh at Arles. Tate Gallery, London.

Below right:
Vincent Van Gogh. *Self-Portrait with Bandaged Ear.* 1889. Painted in January, while Van Gogh was still at Arles after cutting off a piece of his ear. Jeering crowds outside the house where he lived added to his torment. Courtauld Institute Galleries, London.

Vincent Van Gogh. *The Garden of St Paul's Hospital*. 1889. One of Van Gogh's calmer works from the period of his stay at the Saint Rémy asylum. Rijksmuseum Kröller-Müller, Otterlo.

Vincent Van Gogh. *The Starry Night.* 1889.
Painted at the Saint Rémy asylum in June 1889.
In Van Gogh's private symbolic world, the sun
appears to be a beneficent force whereas the
moon and stars are malign. Here, the peaceful
life of the village is threatened by the turbulent
forces of night; the stars are growing larger and
seem destined to crash into the earth. Museum
of Modern Art, New York (Acquired through the
Lille P. Bliss Bequest).

Right:
Vincent Van Gogh. *Vestibule of St Paul's
hospital at Saint Rémy.* 1889. A study in black
chalk and gouache that conveys Van Gogh's
sense of mental and physical confinement: light
and freedom lie across a threshold the painter
cannot cross. Rijksmuseum Vincent Van Gogh,
Amsterdam.

Vincent Van Gogh. *Road with Cypresses and Star*. 1890. Painted at Saint Rémy in May 1890, shortly before Van Gogh left for Paris. The heaving, sinister quality of the painting needs no commentary. Cypresses figure in a number of Van Gogh's late paintings; they are of course associated with graveyards. Rijksmuseum Kröller-Müller, Otterlo.

Right:
Vincent Van Gogh. *Portrait of Dr Gachet.* 1890.
Paul Gachet was an amateur painter and an
early collector of Impressionist paintings. Living
at Auvers, he came to know Pissarro and
Cézanne well from 1872. When Van Gogh
returned from Arles, Pissarro suggested that he
should be put under Gachet's care. The portrait
reflects the painter's rather than the sitter's
desolation. The books are novels by the de
Goncourts. S. Kramarsky Trust Fund, New York.

Below:
Vincent Van Gogh. *Street and Stair with Five
Figures.* 1890. Painted in Auvers in July, shortly
before Van Gogh's suicide. St Louis Art
Museum, St Louis, Missouri.

Impressionism
After 1886

Signs indicating a gradual acceptance of Impressionism have already been mentioned in the biographical sketches of Monet and others. Two important signs were the subscription raised to buy Manet's *Olympia* for the nation and the Caillebotte bequest of 1894. Even at that date there were hostile voices, and the refusal of part of the bequest was motivated by an unwillingness to swamp the Luxembourg with Impressionist paintings; most authorities now recognised that they had some merit, but thought of them as a minor genre. However, time faded the glories of the academic paintings that had once seemed more serious and weighty than the art of the Impressionists; and the advent of new and still more radical art movements gradually made Impressionism seem respectable, tame, and eventually quite 'classical'.

However, Impressionism remained a sufficiently vital tradition to influence a number of later French artists down to the First World War. As a young man, Henri Matisse (1869-1954), one of the most famous modern painters in various decorative and conventionalised modes, was capable of painting an Impressionist-inspired picture such as *The Dinner Table*. Pierre Bonnard (1867-1947) painted in styles combining

Right:
Pierre Bonnard. *Nude at the Window*. Born in 1867. Bonnard drew on both Impressionism and the decorative trends that followed it. The two impulses, varying in strength, dominated his work right down to his death in 1947. Galery Beyeler, Basle.

Below:
Henri Matisse. *The Dinner Table*. 1897. Shown at the Salon de la Nationale in 1897. This painting by the 27-year-old Matisse shows the Impressionist influence on his early work. A few years later he was to become chief of the Fauves – the 'wild beasts' whose raw, strong colours created as great a scandal as Impressionism had done in its own day. Stavros S. Niarchos Collection.

Impressionist and decorative elements in several ways. And in Henri de Toulouse-Lautrec (1864-1901) even the cantankerous Degas found a disciple and successor. Like his master, Toulouse-Lautrec was a superb draughtsman and a lover of women, theatres and racecourses, though his style is more caricatural than Degas's, and imbued with slightly sinister emotion.

A European avant-garde began to emerge in the 1890s, long after the heyday of Impressionism. One result of this was that 'modern' French movements such as Impressionism and Art Nouveau, separate in time and so different in character as to be antagonistic, were taken up simultaneously by breakaway groups like the 'Secessions' of Munich, Vienna and Berlin. Thanks to this kind of confusion, a powerful Expressionist such as the Norwegian Edvard Munch (1863-1944) also practised Impressionism as a young man.

Germany produced a vigorous, specifically Impressionist school from the 1890s. It leader was Max Liebermann (1847-1935), who despite his age developed into an Impressionist from being the enormously successful painter of *Jesus in the Temple* (1879), which was the sensation of its day. Of equal importance were two younger men, Lovis Corinth (1858-1925) and Max Slevogt (1868-1932), both of whom eventually abandoned Impressionism for a form of Expressionism.

In 1886, the year of the final group exhibition in Paris, Durand-Ruel took up an invitation to hold a show in the United States. Though he sweetened the pill with works by some well-known academic artists, he gave the American public its first look at a representative selection of Impressionist paintings. The reaction, though mixed, was surprisingly favourable; later on, Durand-Ruel opened a gallery in New York, and American patrons provided much-needed support for the Impressionists. However, there were no really outstanding American Impressionists apart from the French-resident Mary Cassatt. Another American, John Singer Sargent (1856-1925), was a friend of Monet and an Impressionist for a time, but after 1884 he settled in England and developed a distinctive line in portraits.

Despite Durand-Ruel's gallery in Bond Street, British taste remained too conservative to absorb Impressionism until the 20th century. The leading British Impressionist was Walter Sickert (1860-1942), notable for atmospheric theatrical interiors and open-air views of Dieppe and other places. The landscapist Philip Wilson Steer (1860-1942) was influenced by both Impressionism and Neo-Impressionism. Sickert's admired teacher was another American who settled in Britain, James McNeill Whistler (1843-1903), who had studied in France, where his *White Girl* was as vehemently and unjustly abused as the *Déjeuner sur l'Herbe* in the same show. In Britain, Whistler developed a subtle tonal style, seen for example in *Old Battersea Bridge*, which has some affinities with Impressionism despite technical differences and an evocative rather than naturalistic way of describing the world.

Above:
Toulouse-Lautrec. *Jane Avril at the Entrance to the Moulin Rouge.* 1892. Courtauld Institute Galleries, London.

Right:
Henri de Toulouse-Lautrec. *Marcelle Lender Dancing the Bolero in 'Chilpéric'.* 1895. Museum of Modern Art, New York (Collection John Hay Whitney).

Right:
Max Liebermann. *A Country Inn in Bavaria.*
Musée du Louvre, Paris.

Below:
Max Slevogt. *Landscape.* 1930. A bright,
pleasing landscape by one of the leaders of
German Impressionism. Like so many 'Northern'
(German, Dutch, Scandinavian) artists, Slevogt
introduced a certain turbulent emotional quality
into his work that was alien to the cooler French
spirit. Kunstmuseum, Bern.

Left:
James McNeill Whistler. *Nocturne in Blue and Gold: Old Battersea Bridge.* 1872-75. Like the Impressionists, Whistler regarded the subject of a painting as relatively unimportant, but his aestheticism, concentration on tonal harmonies and near-abstraction place him apart from them. A painting in similar style to the one here, the *Nocture in Black and Gold,* was described by the critic Ruskin as 'a pot of paint flung in the face of the public'. Whistler sued, and was awarded damages – of a farthing. Tate Gallery, London.

Below:
Philip Wilson Steer. *Girls Running, Walberswick Pier.* 1894. Tate Gallery. London.

Conclusion

In the introduction the question was asked why the most widely popular of all paintings should once have been treated as daubs or practical jokes. The rest of this book has been an extended answer, outlining conventional 19th-century theory and taste, detailing the Impressionist innovations, and following the whole movement of revolt against academic art. More narrowly technical definitions of Impressionism have been indicated (broken brushwork, spontaneous open-air working, etc.), but seemed unhelpful as an exclusive mode of approach in a general work of this sort. Instead we have surveyed the whole group of interrelated artists and the series of shows that landmark their individual and collective development. Finally, consideration of the latecomers – the Post -Impressionists – has shown the extent to which the Impressionists, rejecting conventional rules about colour and subject matter, liberated later artists and encouraged them to explore still further. Impressionism made possible the works of Cézanne, Gauguin and Van Gogh, just as they made possible the works of Matisse, Picasso and a host of others. For that reason, Impressionism can be said to stand at the beginning of the whole adventure of modern art.

Index

Figures in italics refer to the captions and the illustrations.

Absinthe (Degas) *150*
Absinthe Drinker, The (Manet) 24, 30, 36
abstract painting 36, 57, *216*, 221
academic art 6, 8–17 passim, 20, 30, 39, 45, 91, 98, 227, 231, 235, 246, 247
Académie Suisse 54, 55, 56, 91, 97, 206
Academy of Fine Arts 8, 10, 17, 108
Aix-en-Provence 91, 95, 138, 212, 216
Alexis, Paul 116
Alfred Sisley and his Wife (Renoir) 76, 78
Algiers 63–4, 182, 186, *186*
Ambulance Improvisée, L' (Bazille) *81*
American Civil War 36, *36*
anarchism 168, 169
Andrée, Ellen *150*
Angelus, The (Millet) *21*
Angler, The (Renoir) *132*
Anonymous Society of Painter, Sculptors, Engravers etc. 117, 130, 168
Antwerp Academy 235
Après-midi d'un Faune (Mallarmé) 144
Argenteuil 15, 68, 116, *116–7*, 120, 129, *129*–32, 142, 170, 178, 180, 196, 198, *198*
Argenteuil (Manet) 142, *143*
Arles 231, 237, 238, *238*, 239, *239–41*
Arosa, Gustave 224, 225
Art Nouveau 231, 247
Artist's Family, The (Bazille) 83, *83*
Artist's Father, The (Renoir) *76*
Artist's Father Listening to Pagans, The (Degas) *51*
Artist's Studio, Rue de la Condamine, The (Bazille) 83, 99, *99*
Arts Quarterly Review 34
Astruc, Zacharie *31*, 98, 99, 119
At La Grenouillère (Renoir) *101*
At the Milliner's (Degas) *153*, 206
At the Seaside (Degas) *150*
Atelier Colarossi 226
Auvers *115*, 126, 210, *213*, 239, 245
Auvers: Village Panorama (Cézanne) *213*
Avenue of Chestnut Trees near La Celle-St Cloud (Sisley) *85*

Baille, Baptistin 91, 220
Balcony, The (Manet) 41, *41*, 89, 90, *143*, 208
Banks of the Cousin, The (Corot) *18*
Bar at the Folies-Bergère, The (Manet) 142, *147*
Barbizon 17, 18
Barbizon School of painters 10, 13, 18, *18*, 20, 56, 60, 66, 77, 110, 116
Barge during Floods at Port Marly (Sisley) *200*
Barrias, Félix Joseph 44
Barricade, The (Manet) *109*
Bather Diving into the Water (Cézanne) *95*
Bathers, Asnières (Seurat) *139*
Bather of Valpinçon, The (Ingres) 10, 44
Batignolles Quarter 86, 99, 116, 196
Baudelaire, Charles 21, 24, 30, 41, 49, 142
Bazille, Frédéric 12, 13, *31*, 41, 56, 59, 63, 64, 66, 68, 69, 70, 77, 78, 79–84, 85, 97, 98, 99, 99, 105, 108, 112, 185
Bazille and Camille (Monet) *59*
Beach at Dieppe, The (Gauguin) *223*
Beach at Trouville (Monet) *103*, 103
Beer Waitress, The (Manet) 142
Before the Performance (Degas) *159*
Belgium 26, 233
Béliard, Édouard 114
Bellelli, Countess 42
Bellelli Family, The (Degas) 44, 45
Bérard, Paul *191*
Bernard, Émile 221, 231
Berthe Morisot and her Daughter (Renoir) *202*
Bibesco, Prince George 110
Birth of Venus, The (Cabanel) 9, 32
'Bloody Week', May 1871 9
Boating Party, The (Cassatt) *206*
Boating Party, The (Renoir) *101*

Bon Bock, Le (Manet) 120, 142
Bonaparte, Louis. See Napoleon III
Bonaparte, Mathilde *10*
Bonjour, Monsieur Courbet (Courbet) 10, *15*
Bonnard, Pierre 246
Boucher, François 76, 180
Boudin, Eugène 19, 20, 21, 23, 58, 60, 64, 65, 66, 69, 98, 104, 109, 119
Bougival 69, 78, 103, 178, 198
Boulevard Montmartre in the Spring (Pissarro) *169*
Bourbon, Louis Philippe 6
Boy in a Red Waistcoat (Cézanne) *215*
Bracquemond, Félix 99, 119
Brasserie des Martyrs 60
Bridge at Argenteuil, The (Monet) 129, *129*, 130
Bridge at Charenton, The (Guillaumin) *208*
Bridge at Courbevoie (Seurat) *169*
Bridge at Hampton Court (Sisley) *196*
Bridge at Maincy, The (Cézanne) *214*, 220
Bridge of Louis Philippe, Paris, The (Guillaumin) *207*
Bridge over the Thames (Monet) *177*
Britain 8, 175
Brittany 56, 90, 108, *161*, 174, 227
broken brush-work 15, 23, 104, *213*
Bruyas, Alfred *15*

Cabanel, Alexandre 32
Café Les Ambassadeurs *150*
Café de Bade 99
Café Guerbois 13, 41, 42, 51, 95, 98, 99, 112, 145, 153, 196, 208
Café Nouvelle-Athènes 99, 145, 153
Café Tortoni 99
Café-Concert at the 'Ambassadeurs' (Degas) 51, 153, *153*
Café Terrace on the Place du Forum, Arles at Night (Van Gogh) *241*
Cagnes-sur-Mer 194
Caillebotte, Gustave 35, 129, *131*, 132, 135, 140, 165, 207, 220, 227, 246
Canal St Martin, Paris, The (Sisley) 86, *86*
Card Players, The (Cézanne) *214*
caricature 57, 58, 74, *150*
Carnot, Sadi 168
Carolus-Duran 90, *186*
Carriage at the Races (Degas) *52*
Cassatt, Mary 132, 134, *138*, 165, 205–6, 247
Castagnary, Jules 35, 122
Cézanne, Louis-Auguste 91
Cézanne, Marie 93
Cézanne, Paul 13, 16, 41, 53, 56, 64, 84, 91–6, 97, 98, 99, 104, 108, 114, *115*, 116, 119, 126, 128, 128, 129, 132, 135, 138, 142, 160, 165, 167, 170, 176, 177, 182, 186, *193*, 206, 210–21, 227, 237, 245
Chabrier, Emmanuel 51
Chailly 18, 58, 66, 77, 82, 83
Champs Elysées during the Paris International Exhibition of 1867, The (Renoir) 78
Charigot, Aline 140, 185, *187*
Charivari 122, 234
Charmeuse, La (Gleyre) 12
Charpentier, Georges and Madame 130, 132, 132, 170, 172, 182, *183*, 186, 196
Chasing Butterflies (Morisot) *203*
Chavannes, Puvis de 46, 90
Cherbourg 36
Chevreul, Eugène 104
Chez le Pere Lathuile (Manet) 142, *145*
Children in the Afternoon at Wargemont (Renoir) *191*
Chocquet, Victor 129, 182, 211, *213*
chromatic harmony 15, 23, 104, *213*
cityscapes 65, 69
Classe de Dance (Degas) *125*
Classicism 9, 10
Claude Monet Painting at the Edge of a Wood (Sargent) *251*
Claude Monet Reading a Newspaper (Renoir) *179*
Claus, Jenny 41
Clemenceau, Georges 147, 148, *177*
Cloisonnisme 231
Clouet, François 45, 48
Colardet 24
Commune, The 6, 8, 9, 51, 53, 96, 108, 109, 110, 149, 160, 169, 178–9, 196
Constable, John 19, 23, 85, 111
Concert Champêtre (Giorgione) 28, 32
Concert in the Tuileries Gardens

(Manet) 24, 30, 114, 142
Copenhagen 222, 227, 232
Corinth, Louis 247
Cornfield at Argenteuil (Sisley) *198*
Corot, Camille 10, 13, 15, *18*, 20, 21, 54, 56, 60, 66, 78, 86, 90, 97, 98, 104, 111, 114, 116, 119, 160, 187, 226, 227
Côte d'Azur 175, 204
Cotman, John Sell 19, 111
Cotton Market, New Orleans (Degas) 49, *150*, 151
Count Emilien de Nieuwerkerke (Ingres) *10*
Country Inn in Bavaria, A (Liebermann) *249*
Courbet, Gustave 10, *15*, 17, 18, 21, 24, 35, 49, 53, 59, *54*, 56, 60, 66, 78, 94, 98, 104, 108, 110, 111, 165
Couture, Thomas 6, 15, 26, 60
Cradle, The (Morisot) *203*
Crystal Palace, The (Pissarro) *113*
Cubism 16, 221

Dancer, The (Renoir) 122, *126*
Dancing in the Country (Renoir) 185, *187*
Dancing in the Town (Renoir) *187*
Danube School, The *18*
Daubigny, Charles François 17–18, *18*, 56, 60, 78, 90, 97, 104, 109, 110, 111, 116, 118, 122
Daudet, Madame Alphonse 184
Daumier, Honoré 8, 90
Dead Christ with Angels (Manet) 32, *34*
Death of Sardanapalus (Delacroix) 10, *12*
Deauville 21, 23
Decadents, The 231
Degas, Achille *150*
Degas, Auguste 42, *51*
Degas, Edgar 13, 24, 35, *35*, 41, 42–52, 54, 81, 97, 98, 99, 104, 108, 110, 114–138 passim, 125–6, 135–6, *138*, *138*, 144, 145, 149–159, 165, 167, 185, 186, 204, 206, 207, 220, 223, 227, 247
Degas, René Hilaire 149, *150*
Déjeuner, Le (Monet) 66, *122*
Déjeuner à l'Atelier, Le (Manet) 38, *129*
Déjeuner sur l'Herbe, Le (Manet) 12, 28, 31, 35, 36, 45, *61*, 81, 97, 128, 247
Déjeuner sur l'Herbe, Le (Monet) *61*, 66, 68, 76, 82, 97
Delacroix, Eugène 10, *12*, 16, 18, 23, 30, 54, 60, 64, 89, 95, 104, *119*, 129, 185, 186, *213*, 225, 236
Desboutin, Marcellin *150*
Diana (Renoir) 75, *78*
Diaz, Narcisse Virgile 17, 66, 77, 109
Dieppe 169, 174, 184, 223, 247, *251*
Dihau, Désiré 47, *51*
Dihau, Marie *51*
Diligence at Louveciennes, The (Pissarro) 54, 97, 111
Dinner Table, The (Matisse) 246, *246*
divisionism 167, 169, 185, 206, 236
Doncieux, Camille 66, 68, 69, 103, *103*, 108, *113*, 170, 176
Dr Gachet's House at Auvers (Cézanne) *115*
Dreyfus, Alfred 148
Dreyfus Affair, The 6, 156, 169
Dupré, Jules 18
Durand-Ruel, Paul 68, 110, 111, 114, 116, 117, 130, 131, 134, 142, 160, 168, 170–1, 186, *186*, 193, 196, 200, 218, 227, 247
Duranty, Edmond 99, 153
Duret, Théodore 36, 99, 111, 196
Dutch Masters of the 17th century 10, 18, 116, 117

East Anglian school 19
École des Beaux-Arts 8, 20, 26, 44, 45, 54, 75, 110, 147
Edge of the Village, The (Pissarro) *114*
Engagement of the Kearsage and the Alabama (Manet) 36, *36*, 114
English landscapists 18
Engraving after Raphael's Judgement of Paris (Raimondi) 28, *36*
Entrance to the Village of Voisins (Pissarro) *114*
Eragny 165, 168, 169
Esmeralda (Renoir) 77
Espagnolisme 39
Estaque, L' 96, 108, 186
Événement, L' *91*, 97
Evening on the Boulevard Montmartre (Pissarro) *169*
Execution of the Emperor Maximilian, The (Manet) 36, 38,

40, 100
Exhibition of Impressionists, First (1874) 119–22, 125–8, *128*, 165, 178, 196, 203, 207, 210
Exhibition of Impressionists, Second (1876) 130, *134*, 178, 196
Exhibition of Impressionists, Third (1877) 117, 131, 178, *181*, *182*, 196, 210
Exhibition of Impressionists, Fourth (1879) 132, *167*, 167, 170, 206, 207
Exhibition of Impressionists, Fifth (1880) 47, 132, *136*, 206, 207
Exhibition of Impressionists, Sixth (1881) 132, 136
Exhibition of Impressionists, Seventh (1882) 165, 170, 207
Exhibition of Impressionists, Eighth (1886) *138*, 138, 172, 207, 236
Expressionism 93, 144, 210, 233, 247, 248

Fantasia (Renoir) *186*
Fantin-Latour, Henri 30, *31*, 41, 77, 89, 90, 98, *98*–9, 99
Fauré, Jean Baptiste 116, 142, 146, 196
Fauves, The 246
Fécamp 69
fêtes champêtres 34, 76
fêtes galantes 180
Fifer, The (Manet) 36, *36*, 40, *129*, *143*, 209
Figaro, Le 98
Figures in a Garden (Renoir) *188*
Fiquet, Hortense 210, 211, 212
First Empire 6, 32
First Outing, The (Renoir) *183*
First World War 86, 148, 156, 177, 194, 246
Fishing Nets, Pourville (Monet) *174*
Flament, Alexandre 68
Fleurs du Mal, Les (Baudelaire) 30, 41
Floating Ice on the Seine (Monet) 170, *172*, 174
Floods at Port Marly (Sisley) 200, *200*
Fontainebleau, the forest of 18, *18*, 58, 66, 77, 86, 110, 178, 198
Fragonard, Jean Honoré 76, 180, *181*
Franco-Prussian War 6, 18, 21, 51, 56, 84, 86, 96, 106–10, 129, 178, 196, 209
French Revolution 6, 24, 109, 180
French Romantic painting *12*
French School in Rome 45
Funeral at Ornans, The (Courbet) 10, *15*

Gachet, Dr Paul *115*, 116, 131, 208, 210, 239, 245
Gad, Mette Sophie 222, 225, 227
Gambetta, Léon 7, 108, 146
Garden of St Paul's Hospital, The (Van Gogh) *242*
Gare St Lazare (Monet) 23, 97, 131, *171*, *177*, 208
Garibaldi, Giuseppe 45
Gas, de. See Degas
Gauguin, Paul 9, 16, 53, 132, 135, 137, 160, 165, 177, 210, 211, 222–32, 237, *238*, 241
Gauguin's Armchair (Van Gogh) *241*
Gautier, Théophile 30, 35
Geffroy, Gustave 200
Germany 7, 26, 175
Gérôme, J. L. 110
Giorgione 28, 32, 33, 36, 76
Girl Arranging her Hair (Cassatt) *138*, 205
Girl in White in the Woods (Van Gogh) 235
Girls Running, Walberswick Pier (Steer) *252*
Giverny 61, 138, 172, *176*, 177, *177*
Gleyre, Marc-Gabriel Charles 9, 12, 13, 65, 66, 75, 77, 81, 82, 85, 97, 178, 196
Goethe, Johann Wolfgang von 151
Gogh, Vincent Van. See under Van Gogh
Goncourt Brothers 49, 153, 245
Gonzalès, Eva 90, 209
Gounod, Charles 72
Goupil 233, 235
Goya, Francisco de 38, 41, *41*
Grand Canal, Venice, The (Manet) *143*
Great Exhibition, Crystal Palace, 1851 *147*
Great Vale of Optevoz, The (Daubigny) *18*
Greece 9
Greek Slave, The 9
Grenouillère, La 69, 84, 103, *103*, 104, 170, 178, 214
Grenouillère, La (Monet) *103*
Grenouillère, La (Renoir) *103*

Grey Day on the Banks of the Cise (Pissarro) 167
Grosz, Georg 156
Guerbois, Café 13, 36, 41, 42, 51, 96, 99, 113, 145, 153, 196, 208
Guigo, Paul Camille 208, 209
Guillaumin, Armand 56, 97, 114, 117, 132, 135, 165, 186, 206, 207–8, 236
Guillemet, Antoine 41, 99, 119
Gust of Wind, The (Corot) 20

Haan, Mayer de 228
Hague, The 235, *235*
Hague School, The 236
Halévy, Ludovic 153, 156
Hamerton, P. G. 34
Hampton Court 196
Harbour at Lorient, The (Morisot) 89, *90*
Harvest at Montfoucalt (Pissarro) *161*
Havre, Le 20, 57, 58, 60, 62, 64, 66, 69, 108
Hay Wain, The (Constable) 18, 23
Head of an Old Man (Cézanne) 93
Head of Victorine Meurent (Manet) 24
Hina Te Fatou (Gauguin) 230
Holland 26, 113, 116, 175
Honfleur 20, 57, 66, 82, 83, 86
Hoschedé, Ernest 116, 131, 146, 161, 170
Hoschedé, Madame 170, 172, 176
Houssaye, Arsène 63
Hôtel Drouot Auction 129, 170, 182, 196, 231
House of the Hanged Man, The (Cézanne) 126, 128, 220
Hugo, Victor 10, 30, 91, 235
Huysman, Joris-Karl 220
Hyde Park 111

Imperial Superintendent of Arts 51
Impression: Sunrise (Monet) 122, *125*
Impressionism 9, 10, *10*, 16–21 *passim*, 54, 56, 66, 69, 70–1, 78, 79, 84, 98, 103, 104, 115, 122, 125, 138, 139, 145, 150, 156, 169, 170, 171, 177, 178, 187, 188, 210, 211, 212, 222, 224–5, 227, *227*, 230, 235, 246, 247
In the Dining Room (Morisot) 204
Independent Artists Exhibition, 1879 132, 167, 170, 206, 207
Ingres, Jean Auguste Dominique 10, *10*, 42, 44, 49, 54, 187
Institut de France 7
International Exhibition, Paris, 1855 10, 44, 54
International Exhibition, Paris, 1867 31, 40, 97
International Exhibition, Paris, 1878 146
International Exhibition, Paris, 1888 147
International Exhibition, Paris, 1889 176
International Maritime Exhibition 69
Intransigents, The 130

Jane Avril at the Entrance to the Moulin Rouge (Toulouse-Lautrec) 247
Japanese prints 39, 231, 236, 237
japonaiserie 236
Jean on his Wooden Horse (Monet) 171
Jetty at Deauville, The (Boudin) 23
Jetty at Le Havre, The (Monet) 104
Jockeys in the Rain (Degas) 155
Jongkind, Johan Barthold 20, 21, 23, 30, 65, 66, 98, 104
Joyce, James 37
Juárez, Benito 41

Kasbah of Algiers, The (Renoir) 186

Lady with a Parasol (Monet) 172
Lamothe, Louis 44
Landscape (Slevogt) 249
Landscape at Cagnes (Renoir) 194
Landscape at Eragny (Pissarro) 169
Landscape painting 13, 17, 60, 66, 97
Lantier, Claude 221
Large Bathers, The (Cézanne) 218, 221
Large Bathers, The (Renoir) 188, 193, 194, *194*
Last Meeting of the Ex-Ministers, The (Daumier) 8
Lavacourt in Winter (Monet) 172
Le Coeur, Jules 72, 74, 78
Le Havre 20, 57, 58, 60, 62, 64, 66, 69, 108

Lecadre, Madame 58, 62, 65, 69
Leenhoff, Ferdinand 28
Leenhoff, Léon 38, 41
Leenhoff, Suzanne 34
Légion d'Honneur 32, 45, 146
Lejosne, Commandant 70
Lépine, Stanislas 119
Leroy, Louis 122, 128, 131, 202
Lesseps, Ferdinand de 229
Lévy Brothers factory 72–4
Lhote, Paul 187
Liebermann, Max 35, 247, 248–9
Lise: Summer (Renoir) 78
Lise with a Parasol (Renoir) 75, 78
Little Dancer, Aged Fourteen (Degas) 136, 156
Little Sisters, The (Cassatt) 205
Loge, La (Renoir) 127, *183*
London 18, 19, 56, 85, 109, 111, 138, 168, 176, 233
Lost Illusions (Gleyre) 12
Louveciennes 54, 56, 74, 108, 110, 113, 114, 160, 161, 196, 198
Louvre, 28, 32, 44, 66, 70, 72, 74, 76, 77, 89, 147, 194, 208, 220
Lower Norwood under Snow (Pissarro) 110, 113
Luncheon of the Boating Party, The (Renoir) 140, *185*
Luncheon on the Grass, see *Déjeuner sur l'Herbe*
Luxembourg, Musée du 147, 176, 194, 208, 220, 246

Madame Boursier and her Daughter (Morisot) 204
Madame Camus at the Piano (Degas) *51*
Madame Charpentier (Renoir) 184
Madame Monet on a Sofa (Monet) 113
Mlle Fiocre in the Ballet 'La Source' (Degas) 47, 48
Mlle. Marie Dihau (Degas) 51
Maillol, Aristide 193
Maître, Edmond 98–9, *186*
Malheurs de la Ville d'Orléans (Degas) 45, 46
Mallarmé, Stéphane 144, 231
Man in the Blue Cap, The (Cézanne) 93
Mandolin and Flowers (Gauguin) 224
Manet, Édouard 12, 13, *15*, 17, 24–41, 44–53 *passim*, *52*, 63, 66, 70, 75, 78, 80, 81, *81*, 84, 86, 89, 90, 90, 97–104 *passim*, 109, 116–7, *120*, 126, 128, *128*, 129, 131, 132, 134, 135, 142–8, 170, 176, 186, 204, 208, 209, *209*
Manet, Eugène, 28, 167, 202, 204
Manet, Julie 202, 204
Manette Solomon (de Goncourt brothers) 49
manière aigre 191
Marcelle Lender Dancing the Bolero in 'Chilpéric' (Toulouse-Lautrec) 247
Marlotte 74, 78, 86, 97
Marly 196, 198
Marquesas, The 232
Martin, Père 161, 165
Martinet, Louis 30, 31
Martinique 225, 229, 230
Martinique Landscape (Gauguin) 225 230
Marx, Roger 220
Massacre at Chios, The (Delacroix) 12, 23
Maternity (Renoir) *185*
Matisse, Henri 218, 246, *246*
Maupassant, Guy de 101, 153
Mauve, Anton 235, 238
Maximilian, Emperor of Mexico 38, 40–41
May, Ernest *135*
Meadow, The (Renoir) 122, *180*
Meadow in Giverny (Monet) 175
Meet, The (Degas) 48
Meissonier, Ernest 108
Melbye, Antoine 56
Melbye, Fritz 56
Memorial Service for Kaiser Friedrich at Kosen (Liebermann) 248
Mériméec, Prosper 30
Meurent, Victorine 24, 28, 33
Millet, Jean François 20, 21, 56, 66, 233, 235
Miss Lala at the Cirque Fernando (Degas) 51, 154, 155
Misty Morning (Sisley) 196
Modern Olympia, A (Cézanne) 128, 128
Monet, Claude 8–9, 12, 13, *15*, 16, 18, 20, 21, 23, 23, 31, 36, 41, 56, 57–69, 75–86 *passim*, 91, 95, 97, 98, 99, 99, 101, 103, 103, 104, 104,

108–42 *passim*, 113, 116, 117–8, 120, 122–3, 125, 129–31, 147, 148, 160, 165, 167, 170–7, 179, *179*, 180, 180, 184, 186, 196, 199, 200, 200, 204, 207, 210, 214, 216, 227, 246, 247, 251
Monet and his Wife in his Floating Studio (Manet) *15*
Monet working in his Garden at Argenteuil (Renoir) 116, *120*
monotype 153, *156*
Monk, Sainte Victoire (Cézanne) 220
Montfoucault 161, 165
Montijo, Eugénie de 30
Montmartre 86, 130, 156, 169, 182
Montpellier 81
Moore, George 220
Moréas, Jean 231
Moreau, Gustave, 45
Morisot, Berthe 17, 41, 41, 88–90, 97, 99, 110, 116, 117, 128, 129, 132, 135, 136, 138, 142, 144, *144*, 186, 202–4, 209, *209*
Morisot, Edma 89, 89, 90, 203
Mother Anthony's Inn (Renoir) 74, 78
Moulin de la Galette (Renoir) 103, 130, 134, 140, 180, *181*–2, 185, 187, 208
Moulin de la Galette (Van Gogh) 235, 237
Mousmé, La (Van Gogh) 239
Murder (Cézanne) 95
Murer, Eugène 165, 184, 196
Musicians in the Orchestra (Degas) 47, 49, 51, 153
Muslim Festival at Algiers (Renoir) 186
Musset, Alfred, de 91
Musson, Célestine 44
Musson, Michel 150

Nadar, A. 117, 132
Nana (Manet) 144, *145*
Napoleon III (Louis Bonaparte) 6, 7, 10, 30, 31, 32, 106, 110, 116, 117, 222
Nation, La 222
Naturalism 10, 97, 98, 231, 247
Neo-Impressionism 165–9 *passim*, 237, 247
Nevermore (Gauguin) 230
New Orleans 116, 150, 151–2
New Painting, The (pamphlet by Duranty) 153
Nieuwerkerke, Count Emilien de *10*, 97
Nittis, Guiseppe de 119
Noa-Noa (Gauguin) 230
Nocturne in Black and Gold (Whistler) 252
Nocturne in Blue and Gold: Old Battersea Bridge (Whistler) 247, 252
Normandy 20, 51, 57, 60, 66, 90, 105, 161, 165, 172, 204
Notre Dame from the Quai des Tournelles, Paris (Jongkind) 23
Nude at the Window (Bonnard) 246
Nude in the Sunlight (Renoir) 134
Nuenen 235

Oeuvre, L' (Zola) 138, 212, 221
Old Battersea Bridge (Whistler) 247
Old Bedford, The (Sickert) 251
Old Masters 17, 26, 39, 57, 70, 78, 104, 180, 187, 205
Old Musician, The (Manet) 24
Old Woman with a Rosary (Cézanne) 217
Olympia (Manet) 28, 33, 34, 35, 36, 39, 39, 41, 45, 66, 78, 97, 99, 128, 145, 147, 176, 246
Orangerie, Musée de l' 177
Orchard in Pontoise, Quai de Pothuis (Pissarro) 165, 167
Oudinot, Achille François 90
Outskirts of Paris: Road with Peasant shouldering a Spade (Van Gogh) 139

Painter of Modern Life (Baudelaire) 49
Painter's Studio, The (Courbet) 10
Palais d'Industrie 10, 98
Paris 6, 9, 21, 26, 54, 56, 57, 60, 65, 65, 66, 69, 71, 78, 85, 91, 95, 98, 107, 108, 108, 109, 110, 116, 145, 149, 151, 165, 168, 169, 172, 179, 204, 205, 216, 220, 225, 235, 237, 247
Parisian Pleasures: Boating at Joinville le Pont (Sahib) 101
Parisian Women Dressed as Algerians (Renoir) 119

Panama Canal 229
Path across the Fields, The (Pissarro) 167
Path Climbing through Long Grass (Renoir) 180
Pedicure, The (Degas) 149, 151
Penge Station, Upper Norwood (Pissarro) 110, 111
Pennsylvania Academy of Fine Arts 205
Père Tanguy, Le (Van Gogh) 236, 237
Perroneau, Jean Baptiste 182
Peru 222, 224
Petit, Georges 165, 171, 175, 200
Picasso, Pablo 37, 154, 218
Piette, Ludovic 161, 165
Pink Dress, The (Bazille) 79, 83
Pissarro, Camille 13, 15, 17, 19, 21, 41, 53–6, 60, 70, 91–9 *passim*, 108–38 *passim*, 110, 113–5, 126, 137, 153, 156, 160–9, 170, 186, 196, 200, 200, 204, 206, 210, 216, 220, 226, 227, 236, 245, 247
Pissarro, Lucien 56, 165, 167, 169
plein-air painting (open-air) 17, 18, 21, 35, 42, 51, 56, 57, 58, 63, 68, 69, 77, 83, 84, 90, 97, 99, 103, 104, 116, 134, 142, 160, 178, 187, 200
Poe, Edgar Allan 144, 230
Pointe de la Hève, Honfleur (Monet) 57
pointilliste technique, See divisionism
Pont-Aven 228, 230, 231
Pont Neuf, The (Renoir) 118
Pontillon, Edma 203
Pontoise 54, 56, 96, 114, 160, 163, 165, 226
Poplars on the Epte (Monet) 177
Portrait of a Young Woman (Degas) 48
Portrait of Achille Empéraire (Cézanne) 95
Portrait of Ambroise Vollard (Renoir) 193, 217
Portrait of Artist's Father Reading L'Événement (Cézanne) 91
Portrait of Auguste Renoir (Bazille) 70
Portrait of Berthe Morisot (Manet) 90
Portrait of Claude Monet (Renoir) 179
Portrait of Clemenceau (Manet) 148
Portrait of Dr Gachet (Van Gogh) 245
Portrait of Émile Zola (Manet) 39
Portrait of Eva Gonzalès (Manet) 209
Portrait of Frédéric Bazille at his Easel (Renoir) 80, 98
Portrait of Jules Le Coeur at Fontainebleau (Renoir) 72
Portrait of Madame Gaudibert (Monet) 69
Portrait of Mlle Romaine Lacaux (Renoir) 70
Portrait of Mlle Sicot (Renoir) 72
Portrait of Marie Cézanne (Cézanne) 93
Portrait of Mrs Charles Clifford Dyer (Sargent) 251
Portrait of Paul Cézanne (Pissarro) 115
Portrait of Paul Cézanne (Renoir) 91
Portrait of René Hilaire de Gas (Degas) 42
Portrait of Stéphane Mallarmé (Manet) 144
Portrait of Théodore Durer (Manet) 36
Portrait of Victor Chocquet (Cézanne) 213
Portrait of Zacharie Astruc (Manet) 31
Portraits at the Bourse (Degas) 135
Potato Eaters, The (Van Gogh) 233, 236
Proust, Antonin 34, 146
Provençal Landscape (Guigou) 208

Quai du Louvre, Paris, The (Monet) 65

Racecourse Scene, with Jockeys in front of the Stands (Degas) 49, 52
Races at Longchamp (Manet) 35, 52
radicalism 63
Raffaëlli, Jean François 132
Raimondi, Marcantonio 28, 36
Rain, Steam and Speed, Great Western Railway (Turner) 23
Raphael 185
Raven, The (Poe) 144, 230
realism 10, *15*, 34, 42, 49, 56, 63, 78, 97, 104, 117
Red Roofs, Edge of a Village (Pissarro) 160, 164, 208

Redon, Odilon 122, 138
Regatta at Argenteuil (Renoir) *131*
Renoir Auguste 9, 12, 13, 16, 18, 23, 42, 56, 63, 64, 66, 69, 69, 70–8, 79, 80, 81–99 *passim*, 84, 91, 98–9, 101, 103–10 *passim*, 114–45 *passim*, 116–20, 122, 126, 127, 131–2, 134, 144, 153–72 *passim*, 178–95, 196, 200, 202, 204, 208, 213, 216, 227, 237
Renoir, Edmond 71, *118*, 119, 122, 127, 183, 196
Renoir, Jean 81, 103
Rigault, Raoul 110
River, The (Monet) 69
Road in Louveciennes, A (Pissarro) *54*
Road to Chailly at Fontainebleau, The (Monet) *58*
Road with a Peasant Shouldering a Spade (Van Gogh) 236
Road with Cypresses and Star (Van Gogh), *244*
Roche-Guyon, La (Pissarro) *53*
Rocks at Belle Ile (Monet) *174*
Rodin, Auguste 175
Romans of the Decadence, The (Couture) 6, 26
Romantic Impressionists 138
Romanticism 30, 64, 95, 104
Rome 9
Rome Prize 85
Roualt, Georges *154*
Rouart, Henri 128
Rouen 168, *169*, 227
Rouen Cathedral in Bright Sunshine (Monet) *176*, 177
Rousseau, Jean 13, 56
Rousseau, Théodore 17, 19, 116
Royal Academy 111
Rubens, Peter Paul 194
Rue Montorgeuil Decked out with Flags, The (Monet) 172
Rue Mosnier Decorated with Flags (Manet) 65
Ruskin, John 252
Ruy Blas (Hugo) 30

Sahib, M 101
Salon, The 8, 10–12, 15–20 *passim*, 18, 24, 24, 26, 26, 30, 31, 34, 36, 38–9, 40, 41, 42, 45, 46, 47, 48, 56, 60, 63, 66–70 *passim*, 75, 75, 76, 78, 80, 83, 83–4, 86, 90, 91, 95, 97, 98, 116, 117, 118, *119*, 129–32 *passim*, 142, 143–4, 145, *145*, 147, 170, 178, 182–6 *passim*, 205, 209, 210, 226
Salon des Indépendents 15
Salon des Refusés 10–13, 21, 28, 31, 34, 56, 86, 97, 98, 116, 128
St. Germaine l'Auxerrois, Paris (Monet) 65
St. Jacques, Dieppe (Sickert) *251*
Saint Siméon Farm 66
Saint Rémy 242, 243, 244
St. Thomas 54, 56
Sainte Adresse 82

Samary, Jeanne 184
Sargent, John Singer 247
Scenes of War in the Middle Ages (Degas) 45, 46
Scholderer, Otto 98
Schuffenecker, Emile 226, 228, 231
Scientific Impressionism 138
Scream, The (Munch) 248
Secessions, The 247
Second Empire 6, 7, 66, 222, 224
Second Republic 6
Seine at Argenteuil, The (Manet) *132*
Seine at Argenteuil, The (Renoir) *132*
Seine at the Pont d'Iéna (Gauguin) 223
Self Portrait (Cézanne) *211*
Self Portrait (Monet) *170*
Self Portrait (Van Gogh) 235
Self Portrait in front of an Easel (Gauguin) 222
Self Portrait with Bandaged Ear (Van Gogh) 241
Self Portrait with Charcoal Holder (Degas) 42
Self Portrait with Halo (Gauguin) 228
Self Portrait with Yellow Christ (Gauguin) 229
Semiramus Building a City (Degas) 45, 46, 49
Sentimental Realism 10
Sérusier, Paul 228
Servante de Bocks, La (Manet) 142, 147
Seurat, Georges 138, 139, 154, 167, 168, 172, 184, 206
Sick Child, The (Munch) 248
Sickert, Walter 247, 251
Siege of Paris 106–8, 251
Signac, Paul 138, 139, 167, 172
Sisley, Alfred 12, 13, 41, 66, 74, 76, 77, 78, 82, 83–87, 97, 98, 99, 103, 108, 114, 116, *116*, 117, *117*, 128–38 *passim*, 137, 160, 170, 186, 196–201
Sisley, William 86
Skaters in the Bois de Boulogne (Renoir) 76
Sleeping Venus, The (Giorgione) 33
Slevogt, Max 249
Small Meadows in Spring (Sisley) 103, 201
Snow at Veneux-Nadon (Sisley) 201
Snow, Rue Carcel (Gauguin) 137
Society of Independent Artists 138
Sorrow (Van Gogh) 235
Sous-Bois (Cézanne) 216, 220
Souvenir de Mauve (Van Gogh) 238
Soyez Amoureuses et Vous Serez Heureuses (Gauguin) 229
Soyez Symboliste (Gauguin) 231
Spanish Guitarist, The (Manet) 24, 30, 114
Spanish Masters of the 17th century 10, 30, 34
Spring Landscape (Renoir) *185*
Square in Argenteuil (Sisley) 116
Starry Night, The (Van Gogh) 243
Steer, Philip Wilson 252

Still Life with Apples and Oranges (Cézanne) 96, 217
Still Life with Jar and Coffee Pot (Cézanne) 96
Still Life with Salmon (Manet) 41
Street and Stair with Five Figures (Van Gogh) 245
Street in Upper Norwood, London (Pissarro) 110
Studio in the Batignolles Quarter (Fantin-Latour) 31, 98–9
Summer Scene, Bathers (Bazille) 80, 84, *84*
Summertime (Monet) 125
Sunday Afternoon on the Grande Jatte (Seurat) 139, 167
Sunflowers (Van Gogh) 240
Sunset at Ivry (Guillaumin) 206, 207
Sunshine and Snow, Vétheuil (Monet) 172
Superintendent of Fine Arts 97
Swing, The (Fragonard) *181*
Swing, The (Renoir) 97, 130, 134, 180, *181*, 208
Sylvester, Armand 99
Symbolism 90, 138, 156, 231, 232
Synthetism 231, 232

Tahiti 230, 230, 232
Tallyrand, Charles-Maurice de 180
Tanguy, Pére Julien 210, 237
Temptation of St. Anthony (Cézanne) 96
Thames, The 176
Thames below Westminster, The (Monet) *113*
Thiers, Louis Adolphe 6, 8
3rd of May 1808, The (Goya) 38
Third Republic 6, 7, 106
Three Tahitians (Gauguin) 232
Tipperary (Sickett) 247, 251
Tissot, James 119
Titian 18, 33, 36, 39, 76
Toilette, La (Bazille) 80
Toulmouche, Auguste 65
Toulouse-Lautrec, Henri de 86, 86, 150, 153–4, 156, 247, 247
Tréhot, Clémence 78
Tréhot, Lise 16, 78, 103
Troyon, Constant 21, 60
Tub, The (Degas) 156
Turner, Joseph Mallord William 18, 19, 23, 85, 111
Two Girls in a Garden (Renoir) *188*

Ulysses (Joyce) 37
Umbrellas, The (Renoir) *188*, 193
Uncle Dominique (Cézanne) 93
Upper Norwood *110*, 111
Utrillo, Maurice 86, 187

Valadon, Suzanne *187*
Valpinçon family 44, 45, 51
Van Gogh, Theo 211, 235, 237, 239
Van Gogh, Vincent 9, 16, 21, 93, 139, 210, 231, 233–245
Velázquez, Diego 30, 37, 70
Vellay, Julie 56, 110, 113, 160, *161*,
165, 167
Venice 143, 172, 176
Veronese, Paolo 76
Venus of Urbino (Titian) 33, 36, 39
Vestibule of St Paul's Hospital at Saint Rémy (Van Gogh) 243
Vétheuil 170, 172, *172*
Victorian art 9
vie de bohème 60
Vie Moderne, La 134, 146, 170, 172, 183
View of Montmartre, Painted from the Cité des Fleurs (Sisley) 86
View of Pontoise, Quai de Pothuis (Pissarro) 54
Village of Pontoise, The (Pissarro) 163
Ville d'Avray 69, 77, 78, 89, 103
Vincent's Chair with his Pipe (Van Gogh) 241
Vision after the Sermon, The (Gauguin) 227, 230
Vollard, Ambroise 193, 218, 221, 232

Wagner, Richard 41, 185
Water Lilies (Monet) 177
Watteau, Jean Antoine 76, 180
Where Do We Come From? What Are We? Where Are We Going To? (Gauguin) 232
Whistler, James McNeill 12, 32, 247, 251
White Girl (Whistler) 12, 31, 247
Wild Poppies (Monet) 123, 180, *180*
Wildenstein, George 61
Wolff, Albert 130, 131, 134, 147, 153, 202
Woman at her Toilet (Morisot) 136
Woman Drying Herself (Degas) 156
Woman in a Green Dress (Monet) 63, 68, 69
Woman of Algiers (Renoir) 16
Woman Tying her Shoelace (Renoir) 194
Woman with a Jug (Gauguin) 227
Women at the Races (Manet) 35
Women in a Café at Night (Degas) 153
Women in the Garden (Monet) 63, 69, 82
Women Ironing (Degas) 156
Women of Algiers (Delacroix) 12, 16
Wooden Bridge at Argenteuil (Sisley) 117

Yellow Christ, The (Gauguin) 229
Young Girl Combing her Hair (Renoir) 191
Young Spartans Exercising (Degas) 45, 46
Young Woman Dressing Her Hair (Renoir) 192

Zola, Émile 36, 38, 41, 56, 84, 91, 91, 97, 98, 99, 99, 110, 116, 130–47 *passim*, 165, 210, 212, 220, 221, 231

Picture Acknowledgements

Acquavella Galleries, New York 91 top; Agraci/Ziolo, Paris 41 bottom, 63; Alinari-Giraudon 33 top; Art Institute of Chicago, Illinois 34, 68, 112 bottom, 136 top, 213 top, 250 top left; Bayerische Staatsgemäldesammlungen, Munich 111, 130; B.B.C. Hulton Picture Library 54 bottom; Bibliothèque Nationale, Paris 13 bottom; Birmingham Museum of Art 251 top; Bridgeman Art Library, London 28 top, 33 centre, 36 top, 38 bottom, 76, 113 top, 209, 247 bottom right, 248 bottom; Brooklyn Museum of Art, New York 49, 204 left; J. E. Bulloz, Paris 14 bottom, 81 bottom, 172 right, 187 left, 202, 203 bottom; Franco Cianetti, Clohars-Carnoet 221; Cincinnati Art Museum, Ohio 35; Cleveland Museum of Art, Ohio 71; Cooper-Bridgeman – Christies 57 top, 104–105; Courtauld Institute of Art, London 110, 231 top, 241 bottom right, 241 bottom left; Fogg Art Museum, Harvard University, Cambridge, Massachusetts 10, 84; Fundação Calouste Gulbenkian Museu, Lisbon 173 top; Photographie Giraudon, Paris 8, 20, 23 top, 37, 48 bottom, 80, 86, 124 top, 155 top, 164–165, 170, 172 left, 176 bottom, 181, 182, 184, 185, 190 top, 191, 192, 193, 195 bottom, 214 bottom, 216, 218, 249 top; Glasgow Art Gallery 205; Haags Gemeentemuseum, The Hague 65, 174 top; Hamlyn Group Picture Library 2–3, 13 top, 15, 19, 26, 29 top, 29 bottom, 30–31, 32, 33 bottom, 36 bottom, 38 top, 40, 42, 44, 47, 50 top, 50 bottom, 50 bottom right, 51, 74 bottom, 90, 95, 96 top, 100 top, 103, 112 top, 120 left, 133 top, 134, 136 bottom, 139 top, 139 bottom, 143 top, 144 top, 144 bottom, 145, 146, 147, 149 left, 150 bottom, 151, 152, 153, 154, 155 bottom, 156, 158–159, 166 top, 169 top, 171 top, 176 top, 189 bottom, 190 bottom, 194, 200, 201 bottom, 213 bottom, 215, 217 bottom, 219 top, 219 bottom, 222, 223 top, 225, 226, 227, 232, 236, 241 bottom left, 246, 248 top, 252 top; Hamlyn Group – John Webb 1, 22 bottom, 46 top, 155 top, 169 bottom, 177 bottom, 250 bottom, 252 bottom; Colorphoto Hans Hinz 12, 77 right, 162–163, 177 bottom, 247 top; Kunsthalle, Bremen 62; Kunsthalle, Hamburg 198–199; Kunstmuseum, Basel 220; Kunstmuseum, Bern 249 bottom; Lauros-Giraudon 23, 52 top, 58, 61 right, 69, 70, 98, 115 bottom, 229 top; Mansell Collection, London 7 top right, 107 top, 107 bottom; Mr and Mrs Paul Mellon 55 bottom; Metropolitan Museum of Art, New York 28 bottom, 92, 102 bottom; John Mitchell and Son, London 133 bottom; Musée Rodin, Paris 237; Musées Nationaux, Paris 7 bottom, 11, 14 top, 18, 21, 43, 48 top, 55 top, 79, 81 top, 82–83, 87 top, 87 bottom, 93 bottom, 94, 96 bottom, 99, 113 bottom, 114, 116, 117, 125, 128, 129, 135, 148, 157 top, 161 bottom, 166 top, 166 bottom, 167, 168 bottom, 171 bottom, 174 bottom, 180 top, 195 top, 197 top, 201 bottom, 203 bottom, 207 top, 208 top, 217 top, 224, 245 top; Museum of Fine Arts, Boston, Massachusetts 27 bottom, 52 bottom, 109 bottom, 204 bottom; Museum of Modern Art, New York 230, 243 top; Museu de Arte de São Paulo 73; Nationalgalerie, West Berlin 53, 124 bottom; National Gallery, London 22 top, 27 top, 173 bottom, 183, 188, 240; National Gallery of Art, Washington, D.C. 16 top, 59, 72, 75, 88–89, 91 bottom, 118–119, 126 top, 131, 138, 204 right, 206, 207 bottom, 214 top, 239; National Gallery of Scotland, Edinburgh 157 bottom; Nationalmuseum, Stockholm 74 top, 101; National Museum of Wales, Cardiff 95 bottom; National Museum of Western Art, Tokyo 119 right, 186; Novosti Press Agency, London 60, 175; Ny Carlsberg Glyptotek, Copenhagen 25, 137, 223 bottom; Philadelphia Museum of Art, Pennsylvania 85, 189 top; Phillip's Collection, Washington, D.C. 140–141; Portland Art Museum, Oregon 132; Radio Times Hulton Picture Library, London 6, 9, 106 top, 109 top; Rijksmuseum Kröller-Müller, Otterlo 234, 235, 238, 241 top, 242, 244; St Louis Art Museum, Missouri 77 left, 93 top, 245 bottom; Sammlung Oscar Reinhart, Winterthur 102 top; Scala, Antella 211, 214 top; Shelburne Museum, Vermont 41, 143 bottom; Sotheby Parke Bernet, London 115 top; Staatliche Museen Preussischer Kulturbesitz, Berlin 64; Städelsches Kunstinstitut, Frankfurt am Main 67; Städtische Kunsthalle, Mannheim 54 top; Stedelijk Museum, Amsterdam 233, 243 bottom; H. Roger-Viollet, Paris 7 top left, 24, 57 bottom, 61 left, 100 bottom, 108 bottom, 149 right, 161 top, 178; Walker Art Gallery, Liverpool 250 top right; Wadsworth Atheneum, Hartford, Connecticut 120 right–121; Wallace Collection, London 180 bottom; Wallraf-Richartz Museum, Cologne 197 bottom; John Webb, London 251 bottom; J. Ziolo, Paris 39, 126 bottom, 127, 179.
©S.P.A.D.E.M., Paris 58, 61 right, 69.
Front and back jacket subjects © Hamlyn Group Picture Library